The Great Western Railway
GAS TURBINES
A Myth Exposed

The powerful Metropolitan Vickers-built gas turbine, No. 18100 at speed near Hay Lane west of Swindon, on the 'Merchant Venturer' express in April 1952

A.C. Sterndale

The Great Western Railway
GAS TURBINES
A Myth Exposed

KEVIN ROBERTSON

SUTTON PUBLISHING

First published in the United Kingdom in 1989
Alan Sutton Publishing Limited
an imprint of Sutton Publishing Limited
Phoenix Mill · Thrupp · Stroud · Gloucestershire

British Library Cataloguing in Publication Data

Robertson, Kevin
The Great Western Railway gas turbines: A myth exposed
1. England railway services Great Western Railway
turbine locomotive. gas
I. Title
625.2'62'0942

ISBN 0-86299-541-8

Library of Congress Cataloging in Publication applied for

*Front cover: 'Box Tunnel and the two Great Western Railway Gas Turbines.' From a painting by
Mike Turner*
*Front endpaper: The Swiss-built gas turbine, No. 18000 on an up train from Cheltenham to
Paddington at Ruscombe in 1950 – Maurice Earley/National Railway Museum*
*Back endpaper: Metropolitan Vickers gas turbine, No. 18100 at the head of the down 'Merchant
Venturer' express near Reading – Maurice Earley/National Railway Museum*

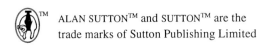
ALAN SUTTON™ and SUTTON™ are the
trade marks of Sutton Publishing Limited

Typesetting and origination by
Alan Sutton Publishing Limited
Printed in Great Britain by
Dotesios Printers Limited

For Tony, Jack and Stan;
three former Great Western men

CONTENTS

ACKNOWLEDGEMENTS

In writing the gas turbine story I feel that once again I put myself in the position of dealing with railway politics. Indeed, the GWR gas turbine story is very much a political drama and, although I cannot recall having seen one of the engines in person, my studies have led me to feel as if I was actually there at the time. To achieve this familiarity as a result of *individual* study and research would be impossible. As a consequence I must initially thank three persons without whose help and assistance none of this could have been written: Tony Tyler, Stan French and Jack Gardner. Tony has been a veritable mine of information and besides several enjoyable talks on the subject has guided me through the text where my own efforts tended perhaps to the extreme. Stan I had the privilege to meet when he was still working for BR and had the pleasure of a number of enjoyable footplate rides in his company. Despite failing health he has provided a most valuable contribution without which much would be missing from the text. I have had the privilege of knowing Jack for some years; his encouragement has kept me going when I was prepared to give up.

I would also like to thank the following persons for their contributions:

David Abbott, for valued guidance and finding time to read the manuscript in among his busy schedule of professional life; Asea Brown-Boveri for the loan of valuable photographs and permission to quote from its own magazines; British Rail (Western Region), in particular John Barrett and Chris Watts; Derek Clayton; Ron Cover; Stanley Creer; David Cross; Jim Davenport; Maurice Dart; Maurice Deane; Mike Esau; Les Elsey; John Fairman; Courtney Haydon; Barry Hayward – many thanks indeed; Fred Healey; George Heiron; Ray Hinton; Geoffrey Jefferson; Brian Jeffery; Philip Kelley; Kenneth Leech – his foresight in recording the railway scene was so valuable; Lens of Sutton – what would we do without him?; Vince Liddicoat – a chance, but very valuable, meeting; R.A. Lissenden; Colin Maggs; Colin Marsden; S.G. Morrison for facilities provided by The Institution of Mechanical Engineers; Tom Middlemas; the National Railway Museum, especially Phil Atkins and John Edgington; Jeremy Page; David Postle; Norman Preedy; The Keeper and Staff of the Public Record Office at Kew; Ruston Gas Turbines, in particular Mr J.C. McMillan; the Science Museum Library; Ian Shawyer – what would I do without him?; Shell UK Oil; Brian Stephenson; A.C. Sterndale; Richard Stumpf; Peter Swift – for coming to my aid at a time when I was almost in despair, with information on No. 18000 in Switzerland; the Swiss Embassy; Mr R.R. Webber and Mrs B. Webber; Ron White; Bernard Williams. Also to all those photographers whose work has been used.

I must also thank Lyn, Jennie, Carole and Sharon – the supply of coffee and biscuits at frequent intervals has allowed the text to be completed.

Finally, to Peter, Ian, Joyce and Tessa at Alan Sutton. Their support is more welcome than they can ever realize.

The Great Western Railway
GAS TURBINES
A Myth Exposed

INTRODUCTION

Britain in 1945 presented an austere face; the result of six years of war. Such austerity was apparent in almost every aspect of life, from the ration queues on street corners to the dilapidated buildings and bomb-sites in so many towns; public transport, too, reflected this sombre mood.

It is important to set the scene before going on to explain the gas turbine episode. The railways of the country, including the Great Western, were attempting to redress the effects of the war years but were hampered by shortages of the necessary raw materials. It is easy to understand, in a land tired of conflict, how the chance for a change of government was seen as a breath of fresh air, even though this would bring about a radical change to public transport, with the nationalization of the railways promised in the socialist election manifesto.

Before the Great Western ceased its independent existence it had embarked upon an experiment unique to the railways of Britain. This was an order for two gas turbine-driven railway engines, at a time when only one other engine of this type was running anywhere else in the world.

During the last months of the Great Western, Swindon and Paddington still attempted to lead the way, though hindsight may reveal a slightly misguided approach.

In attempting to record the strengths and weaknesses of the project I make no excuses in that some of the text may 'disturb' the Swindon purist. I have tried to tell the gas turbine story in the context of the railway arena of the period – a story in many ways more controversial and topical than that told in my previous book on 'Leader'.

Had the Great Western not been persuaded to experiment with the gas turbine someone else assuredly would have done. How it all came about is fortunately well recorded although, as with any research, it is only when attempting to piece together the final text that the gaps become ever visible.

Kevin Robertson
Eastleigh, 1989

THE SWINDON TRADITION

Post-war Swindon was a vastly different place from Churchward's times. Although some would beg to differ, for years the GWR Locomotive Department had seemed content to rest on its laurels, lacking the influence it had once had over almost every other railway in the land.

Such a bold statement demands clarification, although can it not be truly said that the last major development was in the form of the 'King' class back in 1927, which was really nothing more than an enlarged 'Star'? A similar definition could be applied to the 'Castle' of four years earlier, while the *prototype* 'Hall' was one of Churchward's 'Saint' class with smaller wheels. This is not just the opinion of the present writer for others have previously echoed similar sentiments.[1]

However, we should not condemn out of hand all the locomotives working on the Great Western in the 1940s, for in many respects Churchward was years ahead of his contemporaries. Indeed, the very designs produced by Churchward and modified by Collett and Hawksworth were to see out steam on the Western Region in the 1960s. The family of Standard steam engines produced by Riddles for British Railways also owed much in ancestry to Churchward, even though they had been much modified in the course of development.

It could perhaps even be argued that there was no need to advance the cause of steam at Swindon, compared with the work of Stanier at Derby and Crewe. Churchward's engines were adequate for what was expected of them, although it was the advent of high-degree superheat and improved draughting that really put the polish on their last years – ironically a change brought about well into the BR era.

It is clear then, that in the 1940s Swindon and the office of the Chief Mechanical Engineer formed a conservative group. As far as the railway historian is concerned much of the Hawksworth era is shrouded in mystery. Certainly Hawksworth would appear to have been a very secretive man and, although a highly competent engineer, he lacked the apparent charisma of Churchward. Bulleid, Hawksworth's contemporary on the Southern, was cast in a different mould and with considerable guile was able to progress with his 'Leader' design. Hawksworth's shortcomings though, could hardly be described as being all his fault. Promoted to the position of CME in 1941 at a time of national austerity, he was prevented from fulfilling his potential first by the requirements of war and then by the post-war depression and eventually nationalization of the railways.

It would be very easy then, to subscribe to the view that the development of the gas turbine came about as a result of a failure to succeed in the building of a proposed Hawksworth 'Pacific' which has been described by O.S. Nock[2] who states:

> . . . war or no war there was a feeling that the Great Western Railway ought to be making some preparations towards post-war traffic, and the resumption

---

1. *Great Western Locomotive Design – A Critical Appreciation.* Revd John C. Gibson, David & Charles.
2. *The GWR Stars, Castles and Kings (Part 2), 1930–1965.* O.S. Nock, David & Charles.

1

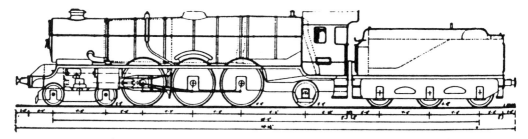

Weight diagram for Hawksworth's proposed four-cylinder Pacific of 1946. An excellent artist's impression of the engine by Victor Welch appears in O.S. Nock's book, *The GWR Stars, Castles and Kings, Part 2*

of high-speed running with heavy trains. The more progressive of the younger men in the Chief Mechanical Engineer's department felt that in any new work the principles of André Chapelon should be carefully heeded. During the war, with the accent on munitions production and a policy of 'make do and mend' prevailing in locomotive affairs, the drawing office, once Churchward's right hand throughout his brilliant development, had rather lost caste, but when the suggestion of a new 'Pacific' engine was made the opportunity was welcomed.

At the same time it seems to have been something of a 'cloak-and-dagger' business. Those concerned have told me they had only the sketchiest of directives from F.C. Mattingly (the Chief Draughtsman). They were asked to put forward their ideas for a 'Pacific', and the only positive instruction issued in those early stages was that the boiler pressure was to be 280 lb per sq in. In response to requests for more information the reply was that standard practice was to be followed. A good deal of design work was done on the boiler. While bearing in mind all the basic features of Churchward's classic development the restriction in steam flow that to some extent handicapped the 'Kings' was eliminated, and a very high degree of superheat provided for. Two different schemes were worked out, using five-row and six-row super-heaters respectively. In these preliminaries standard practice was certainly not followed, because provision was made for accommodating the regulator in a steam dome on top of the boiler. While preliminary work was thus being done on the boiler another draughtsman had taken the 'King' front-end, and completely streamlined the ports and steam-passages in the Chapelon style.

Then, alas, those concerned had another visit from Mattingly, only the second he had paid while the project was live, and then it was to tell them to stop work. From that moment nothing more was done, and all that remained was a preliminary line drawing of what might have been Swindon's *chef d'oeuvre*. How the project originated in the first place and how it was stopped one can only guess. Two points only may be put forward; it was essentially an express passenger engine (unlike Bulleid's 'Merchant Navy' class, officially designated 'mixed traffic'), and Authority probably frowned upon work expended on a super-express passenger engine in wartime. The second point is this; it would seem that hope was not entirely dead in the hearts of those who had initiated the project, when the 'County' class 4–6–0s appeared in 1945. These engines included two features quite out of normal context; the

2

Sir James Milne, KCVO, CSI, General Manager of the GWR from 1929 to 1947. It was under the leadership of Sir James Milne that the Great Western gas turbine project was pushed through, although he would no longer be in charge at Paddington when the first of the engines entered service – preferring to resign rather than accept the position of Chairman to the newly formed nationalized Railway Executive

GWR Magazine

use of a boiler pressure of 280 lb per sq in, and the otherwise inexplicable introduction of an entirely non-standard coupled wheel diameter of 6 ft 3 in. Both these features were included in the stillborn 'Pacific'. Is it not a logical thing to guess that the 'County' was a guinea pig for the 'Pacific' which it was still hoped sometime to build?

New research though tends to cast some doubt on Mr Nock's comments and in order to clarify them it is first necessary to describe the arrangements which existed in the Swindon drawing office during this time.

As Nock correctly states, in charge of the department at the time was F.C. Mattingly, although in practice his assistant Mr Scholes ran it. The drawing office at the time would act in one of two ways, either at the suggestion of the CME or of its own volition. In the latter category ideas would be submitted to the CME which, if he liked them, would then be developed further.

Viscount Portal, Chairman of the GWR, and F.W. Hawksworth, Chief Mechanical Engineer, depicted at Paddington alongside No. 5955 *Garth Hall*, newly converted to burn heavy oil fuel. (An account of the GWR venture into oil firing at this time can be found in Appendix B)
GWR Magazine

The proposed 'Pacific' is thought to have emanated in the form of an idea from Scholes who, it is recalled, worked on this for some time, taking care to cover up his board at lunch and other times when he was away from his desk. When completed the proposal was taken in to Hawksworth who immediately brushed it aside. Perhaps this explains the CME's reluctance to later talk about a proposal for which he saw no future.

Even so, the design showed a number of interesting departures from Swindon practice. The firebox was pure Bulleid and copied from the 'Merchant Navy' class while a number of LMS features were also present, giving the whole the appearance of the early 'Princess Royal' class. Here it would seem that at last there was an attempt to break away from the strangle hold of standardization of Great Western locomotive design which, although having served the company well for some decades, was now becoming its Achilles' heel. In addition, it was known that Hawksworth was a close admirer of Stanier's work on the LMS, so what better way of seeking approval for a project than by including ideas which it was hoped would be well thought of?

Nock's comment that the 'County' class was a prelude to the 'Pacific' design may therefore be taken as slightly inaccurate. Indeed the reasons for the adoption of a 6 ft 3 in driving wheel on the 'County' were no more than when the class was in the process of design, during the period 1943/4, no express passenger class being permitted. A 6 ft 3 in driving wheel could almost be classified as mixed traffic whereas the larger 6 ft 6 in of the 'Kings' and 6 ft 8½ in for the 'Castles' most certainly was an express design. Thus, with the smaller wheel diameter, approval for construction was given. (Bulleid had used the same argument in the production of his 'Pacific' design which utilized a 6 ft 2 in wheel size.)

4

But with a surfeit of large engines the next question to be asked is: Was there really any need for the 'County' class at all? In truth probably not, but what CME does not wish to be remembered for an express locomotive design? So, when built, the 'Countys' not only ran in Cornwall and on the North and West line as intended, but also through Swindon, so, as the Motive Power Department put it, '. . . the Chief could see one of his designs running past his office window'.

Hawksworth's 'Pacific' then, was doomed to be stillborn. The 'County', for all its political beginnings, was perhaps not really needed. With this in mind it is perhaps easier to see how Swindon looked elsewhere and it was towards the diesel and gas turbine designs that enquiries now turned.

Before referring to this development though, it should be pointed out that besides the 'Pacific', Swindon had produced a number of other steam designs during the same period that were not proceeded with for a variety of reasons. These included in 1944 an outside cylinder 4–4–0 and the following year a 2–6–0 pannier tank. Instead the new locomotives followed conventional thinking and were of the various well-tried types. The need for express designs for example, was fulfilled by increasing the 'Castle' class with a number built in 1946, 1948, 1949 and, finally, No. 7037 *Swindon* in August 1950.

Hawksworth did of course produce some steam designs and, besides the thirty members of the 'County' class referred to above, there were also some 200 94xx pannier tanks and the ten 15xx engines. In addition, there were seventy-one new 'Hall' class engines modified from the original Collett design, the latter being excellent engines.

At some stage then, investigations were instigated into alternative types of motive power, including the possibility of diesel-electric traction. How far these enquiries into the diesel progressed is unclear, although it is known they were soon abandoned. Today this may appear strange, though it must be remembered that the use of the diesel engine itself was by no means standard at the time, while there was still considerable debate as to the varying merits of the types of transmission then available, e.g. electric, mechanical, hydraulic, etc. Unfortunately, no papers pertaining to these early investigations on the GWR appear to have survived. However, it may be said with certainty that a decision against the diesel-electric was reached at a very early stage, as on 2 January 1946 the CME's report into this type of traction was presented at the Locomotive Committee meeting while, less than six weeks later, a decision had been taken to investigate the possibilities of the gas turbine.

Indeed, when taken collectively, the various developments at Swindon, as well as those of the other main-line companies, begin to piece together a pattern in which the gas turbine project fits neatly.

So what were the other companies doing with regard to their future requirements for post-war express motive power? On the Southern the Bulleid 'Pacific' designs, both heavy and lightweight, were being increased in number at a quickening rate, while the proposed 'Leader' was also beginning to emerge as a potentially feasible proposition. But the Southern was shrewd enough not to place all of its trust in the future of steam development and already had two straight electric locomotives working in 1946 with design work well advanced on a 1,600 hp main-line diesel-electric.

The LMS meanwhile, was well equipped with steam in the form of the superb 'Duchess' class, though thoughts were being directed towards the future with an order for two 1,600 hp diesel-electric engines. The LNER too, had recognized a need to design for the future, with the A2 class almost ready to emerge, while still to come was the A.H. Peppercorn-designed A1 Pacific. More importantly perhaps, the LNER had planned for future electrification and already had a Bo-Bo electric engine built to a design later extended to the EM1 class.

No. 4078 *Pembroke Castle* at Old Oak Common, 29 August 1954. Despite dating back to as early as 1923 the 'Castle' class engines remained on top link passenger duties right up to the end of Western Region steam. No. 4078, built at Swindon in February 1924, was withdrawn thirty-eight years later in July 1962 after having run a recorded 1,917,380 miles, the third highest mileage from the 171 members of the class. It was for duties similar to those taken by the 'Castles', and to some extent by the 'King' class, that the gas turbines were intended

W. Gilburt, author's collection

For shunting work it was recognized by both the LMS and SR that the diesel displayed untold advantages and both companies were actively developing this type of motive power.

Where then was the Great Western? The answer is not just very close behind, but poised as an athlete ready to exert a final push to finish ahead of the other runners. For shunting purposes the company had purchased a 350 hp diesel engine from Hawthorn, Leslie & Co. in 1936. This was followed by an order in 1946 to English Electric for the power units for seven more similar shunters, the mechanical parts of which were to be built at Swindon.

Behind the scenes at Swindon and Paddington then, moves were already afoot, with the first reference to these developments in a letter of 11 February 1946 from Hawksworth to the company Metropolitan Vickers. Unfortunately the full text does not appear to have survived although a précis reveals a fascinating development:

> . . . confirmed verbal agreement between Sir James Milne and Sir George Bailey, viz; each Company to bear 50% of total cost of providing the locomotive and carrying out necessary trials.

This is the first clear reference to what was to emerge as No. 18100, the British-built gas turbine, and pre-dates the well-recorded visit of Hawksworth to Switzerland in June 1946, during which it has been generally thought the GWR gas turbine project was first mooted. The questions as to how and why matters had already got to this stage cannot, regretfully, be answered at this time.

A full account of the précied correspondence pertaining to the politics behind the constuction of No. 18100 between Metropolitan Vickers and the GWR from February 1946 to April 1947 can be found in Appendix A.

Less than three weeks after the February letter came the shareholders' Annual General Meeting of the GWR for 1946, held as usual at the GWR Royal Hotel adjacent to Paddington station. The date was 2 March 1946. Here it was publicly announced by the Chairman of the Company, Lord Portal, that the GWR was investigating the application of the gas turbine to rail traction.

Surprisingly little public attention outside the GWR appears to have been given to the idea at the time, the only located newspaper reference appearing in an article on an inside page of the *Swindon Evening Advertiser* under the headline 'Swindon to build Jet Propelled Locos'. A certain amount of information was then given, although even allowing for journalistic licence and perhaps the intention to provide for the non-technical reader, much of what was said was hopelessly inaccurate. Later in the article there appear some interesting asides, including the suggestion that the engine would be ready for traffic in eighteen months and that '. . . the locomotives will eventually be produced at the Swindon Works. . .' An interview with a works employee reputedly questioned over the matter, extracted the comment that '. . . this was a well kept secret . . . the first I knew about it'.

Only after this does the national press seem to have become interested and the story was followed up in a number of dailies. One, the *Daily Mail*, took locomotive development a stage further and followed up the theme with an idea for an 'Atom Loco' in which mercury would be used as the fuel. This was of course before much publicity had been given to the hazards of radiation associated with atomic fusion, although even back in 1946 the newspaper article sounded a word of caution in relation to the potential dangers in the event of an accident. Not surprisingly, little in the way of serious development was undertaken on this particular form of motive power.

The centre of interest now moves abroad, with an invitation extended to the GWR to send two visitors to the June 1946 meeting of the International Railway Congress in Switzerland. Hawksworth accompanied Milne on the trip.

The two men spent over a fortnight in Switzerland, returning on 17 June. Such was the impression gained that a report of the visit was prepared at Swindon just three days later and submitted to the Locomotive Committee and then the GWR Board a week later.[3]

VISIT TO SWITZERLAND BY CHIEF MECHANICAL ENGINEER[4]

In the course of which various Engineering Works were visited and opportunity taken to inspect the rolling stock on the Swiss Federal Railways. The following are the salient features which were observed in respect to the places noted:

---

3. It was the practice for the various departmental committees to meet the day prior to the full Board meeting. Recommendations could then be passed to the latter for consideration.
4. In researching the history and development of the GWR gas turbines, the 1946 report of the visit made by Hawksworth and Milne to Switzerland is referred to in a number of documents. Perhaps surprisingly this turned out to be one of the most difficult documents to uncover. It was eventually located at the Public Record Office (RAIL 258/414) amid a pile of miscellaneous notes entitled 'Swindon Papers'. In view of its importance to the whole story it is surprisingly brief and it may well have been that the original 1946 document contained further information.

Hawksworth 'County', No. 1008 *County of Cardigan* at Oxford, 13 November 1954, complete with telegraph pole attached to the smokebox! This was one of four steam classes built during Hawksworth's tenure at Swindon, the others being the modified 'Hall', 94xx and 15xx classes. A number of additions to earlier classes were also built. The family resemblance between the 'County' and 'Castle' is clearly visible, with both very much still in the Churchward tradition. Indeed, apart from the 15xx pannier tank, which was the first class to be built at Swindon with outside Walschaerts valve gear since the days of the steam railmotors, all of Hawksworth's designs and modifications showed little in the way of progressive development. The 'County' class featured a boiler pressed to 280 psi, which was a totally new departure for Swindon. It was used purely because Bulleid had utilized the same pressure for his new designs at Eastleigh. Worth mentioning is that before final approval for the design was given, no less than fourteen different ideas for the 'County' class were submitted, including a version with outside Walschaerts valve gear. Rumour has it that a three-cylinder version was also suggested!

W. Gilburt, author's collection

Brown-Boveri Works, Baden

Considerable insight was thrown by Dr Faber of Brown-Boveri on the extensive experience with gas turbines which his Company has had. The 2,400 hp [official Swiss reports of the period suggest 2,200 hp was the true figure] gas turbine locomotive of which details have appeared in the technical press is now running on loan from the Swiss Federal Railways to the French National Railways, as between Basle and Chaumont. This locomotive was inspected at Basle and a trip made on the footplate as far as Mulhouse. In addition to this locomotive Brown-Boveri have completed the gas turbine generator portion of a 4,000 hp unit, which is mounted on an underframe in a manner suitable for its being put on a rail vehicle and it is claimed that this unit could be run within the Great Western Railway loading gauge.

In regard to gas turbines, the opinion was formed that not only have the individual problems concerned with each component in a gas turbine electric

The first GWR diesel-electric shunting engine, seen here as BR No. 15100 at Old Oak (?) in 1949.
Built in 1935 by Hawthorn Leslie & Co., the engine was purchased by the Great Western in 1936
and worked at Acton for some years, carrying the number 2. During the 1940s it spent a time
shunting the oil wharves at Swansea before returning to Acton again. Six similar shunters,
Nos. 15101–6 were built in 1948 while an additional engine, No. 15107, this time with a two-stroke
engine, was added in 1949. No. 15107 also had the shortest life, being withdrawn in June 1958.
No. 15100 was the only GWR engine re-numbered as a result of nationalization and, with
Nos. 15100–7, was withdrawn between April 1965 and August 1967

Photomatic

locomotive been closely studied, but also the relative proportions of these
components in respect of each other have been the subject of close investigation, with the result that the complete unit is much more than a collection of
separate components mounted together on a main frame.

It was stated on behalf of Brown-Boveri that a thermal efficiency (fuel to
rail) of between 18 and 22 per cent was being obtained with the 2,400 hp
engine, which is single stage, but a higher figure than this was expected on
the 4,000 hp unit, as this is a two-stage machine.

In addition to the gas turbine, velox boilers,[5] super charged gas producer
and electrically driven heat pump were inspected, as well as the new wind
tunnel recently installed for testing the aerofoil sections for turbine blades.

5. The 'velox boiler' was a pressure combustion vessel – coincidentally developed by Brown-Boveri – in
which the amount of water circulated was approximately ten times that which evaporated. It was claimed
to have a very high evaporation rate and was capable of being ready for work as quickly as a diesel engine.
Boiler efficiency was reported to be as high as 90 per cent although firing was limited to oil or gas fuel. At
least one 4–6–0 steam engine was built in France using this type of boiler in the 1930s and reputedly
performed well, oil fuel being used. There were, however, constructional problems because of the large
pressurized combustion chambers, though the design was certainly used in a number of European power
stations. It appears to have attracted little interest among railway engineers in Great Britain.

The Swiss gas turbine locomotive is referred to in detail in Appendix D.

The report continued with details of a visit to a wagon works in which aluminium was used as a prime building material. It then continued:

Swiss Locomotive and Machine Works, Winterthur

This firm, working in conjunction with other Swiss engineering firms, exhibited examples of diesel electric locomotives, electric locomotives, rail cars, etc. incorporating the use of aluminium as referred to above, and various types of spring suspension for bogie stock. The problem of reducing the unsprung weight of the traction motors on the bogie has been closely studied, and various types of flexible drive between the motor armature and the axle have been developed.

Swiss Federal Railways and other Swiss Railways, notably the Berne Loetschberg–Simplon Railway

During the course of journeys from point to point in Switzerland, note was taken of the riding qualities of vehicles, incorporating the features studied at the works visited . . .

The tour was of considerable value in showing the progress which has been made by Swiss Engineers, not only in the development of the gas turbine but in the use of light alloys for rolling stock construction as the result of continuous research in Switzerland during the war years while development in this country was restricted by war conditions.

Hawksworth made a second visit to Switzerland in September 1948, this time accompanied by A.W.J. Dymond. A further trip was made on the footplate of the Swiss engine from Basle to Lucerne.

The forerunner of today's diesel units, a GWR diesel railcar of 1934 is depicted in a wonderfully atmospheric photograph at Birmingham Snow Hill. Units of this and similar types were used extensively throughout the GWR system, with the result that re-fuelling facilities for diesel fuel were provided at a number of steam depots. Later, No. 18100 would also burn the same type of fuel

R.A. Collection

At the Locomotive Committee meeting of 27 June 1946 at Paddington the following item appeared under minute 8:

> The Chief Mechanical Engineer submitted a report on his recent visit to Switzerland. The Committee discussed its main features including the Brown-Boveri gas-turbine electric locomotive unit which he inspected, and it was agreed to raise the matter at the meeting of the Board to-morrow.

The following day the Great Western Board met under the chairmanship of Viscount Portal accompanied by thirteen of his fellow directors. The relevant minute to the meeting reads:

> The Board were informed of the conclusions arrived at by the Locomotive Committee in regard to this Unit and of the General Manager's recommendation therewith. This was approved.

Here then, lies the anomaly, for there is no record in official documents of the 'General Manager's recommendation'. Certainly the Board would have been unlikely to approve expenditure on such an item without hearing considerably more of its potential, especially as this was for a machine of untried type as far as the GWR was concerned. It remains then a matter for speculation and will probably continue as such, unless perhaps, the personal papers of Sir James Milne are found to have survived.

But this was just the first step towards what would be the arrival of No. 18000 at Harwich in 1950 and there were still many hurdles to overcome. Interestingly, as yet there was no official reference to costs although this was evidently clarified in the ensuing weeks, for on 19 September 1946 the following entry appears in the minutes for submission at the next Locomotive Committee meeting:

> On June 27th the Board approved negotiations being entered into with British Brown-Boveri Limited, regarding the provision of a Gas Turbine locomotive.
>
> The matter has been pursued with the firm who have now submitted a tender for the supply of a complete locomotive developing an output of 2,500 hp and capable of a maximum speed of 90 mph at a cost of £99,000 f.o.r. [?] Calais.
>
> The tender provides for delivery in 24 months from receipt of order and is open until September 30th. Subject to agreement on the final technical specification, it is recommended the tender be accepted.
>
> The Minister of Transport has approved the project, and has arranged with the Treasury for the necessary foreign exchange to be made available.

There were three signatories to the item, including Hawksworth.

Forty-odd years on it is interesting to speculate on the political implications of the last paragraph, so necessary at a time when the British economy was hardly in a position of strength. The reference to a delivery time is also of interest for this would imply mid-1948, though the engine was not to arrive in the country until early 1950.

As before, the whole item was passed to the Board for approval and the recommendations of the Locomotive Committee accepted. The Great Western Railway had entered the modern age, yet upon nationalization on 1 January 1948 it would cease its existence as an independent company well tuned towards the future.

It would be tempting to skip the ensuing years between 1946 and 1950 and deal directly with Nos. 18000 and 18100 when running on the Western Region. In those ensuing years however, an awful lot was to occur, having a direct bearing on the engines. The next stage must therefore be to refer to the Annual Report of the Chief

Mechanical Engineer for the year 1946, which dealt with the Locomotive Section at Swindon.

The first paragraph concerns the building programme of steam engines constructed in 1946 and it is not until the second paragraph that reference is made to the new form of traction, including some revealing comments:

Gas Turbine Locomotives

Enquiries into the possibility of using gas turbine locomotives on this Company's system have been pursued both in this country and abroad during the current year. Visits were paid to the Works of the Metropolitan Vickers Electrical Company at Manchester and Brown-Boveri, Baden, Switzerland, as a result of which an order has been placed for each firm to deliver to us a 2,500 hp gas turbine electric locomotive. Both these engines are essentially similar in principle but the whole of the detailed design is being undertaken by the firms who are respectively sub-letting contracts for the design and manufacture of the running gear, remaining themselves responsible for the development of the gas turbine and the necessary controlling gear for this unit. Both vehicles will be of the double bogie design, the Metropolitan Vickers having three driven axles on each bogie, whereas the Brown-Boveri design will have two driven axles and a third carrying axle mid-way between them on each bogie.

Concurrent with the development of the GWR gas turbines was the SR's decision to proceed with the 'Leader' project. The first 'Leader' – later numbered 36001 – is seen outside Brighton Works when brand new on 21 June 1949. Unlike the SR, which ordered five of these straight off the drawing board, the Great Western was more prudent and was careful to order just a single prototype of each gas turbine type until the design was proven

D. Broughton collection

The estimated performance in each case is a maximum speed of 90 mph on the level with a train approximately 275 tons weight. The Metropolitan Vickers machine will run on paraffin or gas oil and it is the intention for the Brown-Boveri machine to run on Heavy Fuel Oil. The maximum starting tractive efforts are in the region of 33,000 lbs. Compared with our modern steam locomotives it is anticipated that the fuel consumption of these gas turbine electric locomotives will be less than half for equal work done. [Note: In practice, the Brown-Boveri machine would use light fuel to start the turbine, with a change to heavy fuel once the required temperature and turbine speed were reached.]

Reference is then made to the oil-burning locomotives running on the GWR and, while not directly related to the gas turbine story, No. 18000, the Brown-Boveri machine, and the converted steam engines would use the same fuel. Little in the way of factual information has been recorded into this aspect of the history of the locomotives of the GWR, an area in which the company had pioneered many of the developments later used by the other main-line groups. Now may be an appropriate time to redress the balance and quote again from the CME's 1946 report.

During the current year further locomotives of the 2–8–0 28xx class heavy freight have been converted to burn oil, making a total of ten in this class. In addition, one engine of the 4–6–0 mixed passenger type, No. 5955 *Garth Hall*, and one engine of the 'Castle' class, 5091 *Cleeve Abbey*, have also been converted.

Early in the year a decision was taken to extend the use of oil burning, and plans were well advanced to increase the total number of engines and to bring into use certain additional storage installations. Before these plans could be implemented, the Ministry of Fuel and Power, with the intention of diverting 1,000,000 tons of coal annually from use by locomotives, requested all Railways to embark on a large scale conversion scheme. This involved the whole of the country in the eventual conversion of 1,229 locomotives and the installation of 58 storage depots. The Great Western Railway share in this scheme amounted to a total of 184 engines which will be running on oil, and sixteen storage depots to meet a daily consumption of 125,000 gallons and an aggregate storage capacity of about 2,000,000 gallons.

Twenty-five 'Castle' class, seventy-three 28xx class (being re-numbered on conversion to 48xx), eighty-five 49xx class (being re-numbered on conversion to 39xx) and one 43xx class locomotive will be converted and sixteen fuelling points will be situated at:

Old Oak Common	Laira
Reading	Newport Ebbw Junction
Didcot	Cardiff Canton
Swindon	Severn Tunnel Junction *
Bristol Bath Road	Landore
Bristol St Philips Marsh	Llanelly *
Westbury	Gloucester
Newton Abbot	Banbury

[* According to Christian Barman in *Next Station*, published by the GWR in 1947, neither Severn Tunnel Junction nor Llanelly featured in the original proposals.]

The conversion schemes on other lines were materially influenced by our original experiments and, at the outset of the Ministry of Fuel and Power scheme, the initiative was taken by our technical staff by giving designs and forwarding information for the benefit of the other Companies. Approximately 10,000 prints of various Great Western drawings have been produced for circulation in connection with the Ministry of Fuel and Power scheme and in a very large number of cases, this Company's standard fittings have been adopted as an all-Company standard applicable to all locomotives and storage plants in the country.

It is estimated that, with the completion of the conversion of 184 engines enumerated above, some 173,000 tons of coal will be saved annually by this Company and made available for industrial needs.

Unfortunately fate, in the form of the failure of the government to recognize it possessed sufficient foreign exchange to purchase the necessary oil, was to spell a premature end to a bold enterprise. Sufficient heavy fuel oil of the 'Bunker C' type was however available for No. 18000 from 1950 onwards. In view of what was obviously a serious government mistake, there is no reference to pressure having been exerted on the GWR to cancel the order for No. 18000 on the basis of available foreign currency. More information on the oil-burning engines of the GWR at this time can be found in Appendix B.

As an aside it is worth mentioning that during the late 1940s the public's image of the gas turbine as a method of propulsion was that of a jet engine. The jet was seen as a symbol of the latest technology. Not surprisingly then, a number of what today would be seen as fringe uses, were attempted with what is more correctly described as Sir Frank Whittle's ram air jet engine. One of these was a gas turbine power unit for use in a private motor car.

More directly related to railway operation was a GWR experiment during the severe winter of 1947/8 which involved the fitting of two Rolls Royce Derwent Mark I jet

Built by Brown-Boveri and entering service in 1941, this was the Swiss gas turbine engine which possessed the unusual 1A-Bo-A1 wheel arrangement. A description of the engine and its subsequent history is given in Appendix D

Asea Brown-Boveri

14

The first artist's impression of the proposed gas turbine design, dating from 1947. This was the illustration that appeared in Christian Barman's book *The Great Western's Last Look Forward*

engines to a flat truck, with the blast directed at impacted snow and ice. The intention was to achieve an alternative method of snow clearance compared with the traditional propelled snowplough. The results were interesting to say the least and, although of little direct consequence to the main theme, are worthy enough to warrant inclusion in Appendix C.

Around the same time as the experiments were being carried out with jet engines to clear snow, is found the first official reference to the Metropolitan Vickers gas turbine engine, this time in the form of a memorandum signed by Hawksworth and submitted to the Locomotive Committee. The date is also interesting for it is reported as Saturday 22 March 1947:

> On June 26th, 1946, the Board approved a contract with British Brown-Boveri Ltd for the provision of a gas turbine electric locomotive developing an output of 2,500 hp and capable of a maximum speed of 90 mph at a cost of £99,000. Arrangements have been made with the Metropolitan Vickers Electrical Company Ltd for the provision of a similar locomotive, the total certified cost of construction and of trials and any modifications to be borne equally by the Company and the firm. Should the locomotive prove to be a success and be taken over by the Company, an additional payment will be made to the firm representing a further 25% of their costs of construction, trials and modifications, subject to consideration later of the possibility of liquidating the cost

of certain items, such as drawing office work, patterns and jigs, on any locomotives that may be commercially produced.

The question then must be: Why was such an important subject dealt with on a Saturday? Perhaps the answer lies simply in the fact that it was already known that the days of the GWR as an independent company were rapidly drawing to a close. The Labour party's success at the 1945 general election would mean a swift end to the private railway companies in favour of a state owned and operated transport network. What is surprising is the length of time it took to bring the necessary Bill before the House of Commons, as it was not until 28 November 1946 that the papers were introduced to the House by the then Minister of Transport, Mr Alfred Barnes. In reality the outcome was a foregone conclusion for, with the large majority enjoyed by the socialists, they could afford to ease the Bill's passage. Royal Assent was obtained on 6 August 1947.

The Great Western had to work fast, and in the opinion of the author it would seem that the intention was to present as much as possible of a completed project by the time British Railways took control. Notwithstanding the fact that it would be some time after nationalization before either engine was completed, cancellation of the contracts would have been excessively expensive to contemplate. Paddington and Swindon were to present the new nationalized railways with the most powerful single-unit locomotives ever to run in this country. Swindon may have been forced to capitulate its independence, but it would not totally surrender.

Meanwhile, additional information on the gas turbines began to filter through from the various specialist publications. One of these, *The Brown-Boveri Review* for June/July 1947 reported that, 'The locomotive is required to haul express trains, and will operate chiefly on the Plymouth, Birmingham, Bristol and Swansea routes from London. Non-stop runs of five hours are included in the schedules.'

Then, in *Next Station*, Christian Barman contrived to put the whole concept into perspective:

A remarkably accurate 1949 artist's impression of the Brown-Boveri design. The original was reproduced in full colour in the periodical *The Oil Engine and Gas Turbine* and depicted No. 18000 in it striking black and silver livery attached to a train of carmine and cream stock

16

The two gas turbine locomotives which are now being built will develop a power output equal to 2,500 hp and will travel at a maximum speed of ninety miles an hour. The Great Western is determined to press forward the completion of these locomotives because it sees the possibility of a brilliant future for the new method of propulsion. One reason for this belief is that the output of power, both in relation to the weight of the engine and in relation to the fuel consumed, compares very favourably with that of the traditional piston engine. Another reason is that when sufficient experience has been gathered it should be possible to build turbine locomotives requiring only a small fraction of the maintenance work inevitably associated with steam locomotives of the traditional type.

Yet a further reason for the Railway's preoccupation is a more interesting one. The Great Western intends to maintain its position of leadership in the application of new forms of energy to railway traction. In a long view, it is possible that the gas turbine locomotives may prove to have been chiefly significant as the forerunner of even greater and more exciting Great Western locomotives to come.

Bearing in mind this publication was undertaken with the consent and assistance of the GWR, this may then be taken to be the official viewpoint, or at least the one Paddington would have the public believe. The propaganda department of the railway was defiant to the end.

Quite what Barman was referring to in his last comment on more exciting things to come is unclear although it may have been an oblique reference to the known Swindon intention of eventually using coal as the fuel for the gas turbines. Interestingly, coal as a fuel for gas turbine use will crop up again later in this book.

Taken as a whole, with just a few word changes, the statement could almost apply to what Bulleid was attempting to do with his 'Leader' class. Maintenance too, is an interesting point, for the only experience so far gained with the new type of traction was with the Swiss engine. Details of its failings are difficult to find, with the only references to them being within the in-house journal, the *Brown-Boveri Review*. Certainly it would appear strange that the Swiss engine reportedly ran trouble-free, yet No. 18000 was destined to suffer countless teething troubles.

But in 1947 all this was still some way in the future, and while the Great Western diehards eagerly awaited the first of the engines, the *Railway Gazette* made an interesting comment. Speaking of the gas turbine principle for railway traction, the GWR was praised for its '. . . courageous policy in initiating trials on an experimental basis of gas turbine traction in Great Britain. The determination with which this difficult engineering problem was pursued is the more marked when one considers how many and how futile are the arguments why such an investigation should *not* be carried out.'(The italics are as in the original article.)

Clearly then, someone was still on the side of enterprise at Swindon. But was this enough? With nationalization on 1 January 1948 and neither engine anywhere near ready to commence trials, it would be Marylebone and the Railway Executive which would now call the tune. Time would tell whether Swindon and Marylebone were really in harmony.

No. 18000

Switzerland and England to the end of 1951

With the order for the engine confirmed, work began on the building of the power unit during the latter part of 1947. Despite being credited as the builders, Messrs Brown-Boveri only built the actual gas turbine power unit and the traction motor spring drive. Construction of all the other components, although possibly to a Brown-Boveri design, together with the assembly of the components into a locomotive, was undertaken by the Swiss Locomotive Works at Arlesheim. Presumably this was a link-up between the two works although the full connection between the two is not clear.

Obviously then, the engine would not be completed in time for nationalization, both Swindon and Paddington preferring to obtain a well thought out machine rather than a rush job.

Despite the unique appeal of the engine, details of the early stages of construction are scarce and little is reported either by BR or Brown-Boveri until 25 June 1948, when it was reported that GWR 'ATC' equipment had been sent over to Switzerland. This was followed two weeks later by a number of other minor parts including buffers, couplings and fire extinguishers. These items were shipped across by one of the train ferry services. Later, a complete set of tyres was despatched by similar means, with one of the tyres being reported from Switzerland as having a crack in it, although this disappeared during machining.

It appears that construction of the locomotive complete with its power unit was planned for the early part of January 1949 and certainly the shipment of components would appear to confirm this. Delays did occur, although it would be unwise to speculate on the causes or reponsibilities involved.

Back in England much of the 1948 correspondence pertaining to the machine appears to relate to the livery that would eventually be carried. Had the engine been delivered to the GWR no doubt this would have been Brunswick Green, probably similar in style to that applied by BR in 1985 to 50.007 *Sir Edward Elgar* and 47.500 *Great Western*. In the end the matter was settled by the CME of the new British Railways, Robin Riddles, who, in a letter dated 31 December 1948, stated:

> I have decided that the above locomotive [the Brown-Boveri machine] should be painted in black and aluminium, similar to the LMS diesels, i.e. the roof and bogies to be in aluminium with an aluminium band running round the waist of the locomotive.

Swindon's comments are not recorded. It would have to wait until regional autonomy had returned some years later before its beloved green could be applied in place of this alien LNWR style of colouring. Similarly there is no reference to correspondence relating to the number later carried or any suggestions as to a name. Somewhat unkindly

'Kerosene Castle' has been suggested as perhaps being suitable but a resurrection of one of the names carried in broad gauge days would surely have been more fitting. The aluminium livery for the bogies was against that suggested by the Swiss Locomotive Works which had advised on black for durability.

On the same day that Riddles decided on the livery question a letter was received from Brown-Boveri suggesting that a member of BR staff, who would later be responsible for operating the engine, should make a prolonged visit to Switzerland where he could become familiar with the engine then in the course of building. Evidently this was considered by BR to be advisable and in due course Sidney C. Lewis, a fitter/erector, was sent from Swindon to Switzerland. In view of the complicated nature of the engine it is perhaps surprising that a more senior member of staff was not despatched.

Hawksworth himself visited Switzerland in May 1949 to witness bench testing of the completed power unit. These tests were evidently successful although a number of letters followed between Swindon and the London office of Brown-Boveri as to certain technical aspects of the turbine.

Probably shortly afterwards, Lewis travelled from Swindon to Arlesheim, where he was able to obtain lodgings close to the Swiss Locomotive Works. Besides his wages he was paid an £8 a week living allowance as well as being provided with a free second class Swiss Railways pass.

Lewis occupied himself in observing work during the day as well as providing

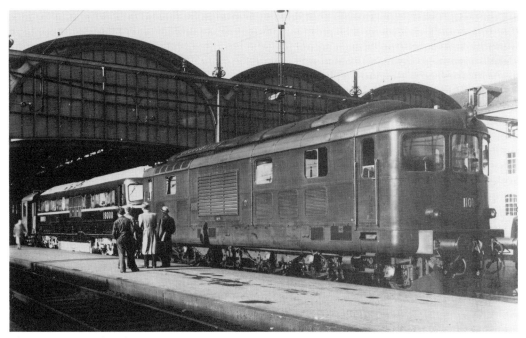

The power unit for the new engine was completed and successfully tested in February 1949, following which work began on the erection of the rest of the unit at the Swiss Locomotive Works at Arlesheim. Regretfully the final completion date is not recorded although it is thought to have been in the autumn of 1949. Following completion the engine was subjected to a number of trials on the Swiss railway system, one of these being depicted here with No. 18000 coupled inside the Swiss gas turbine, No. 1101 at Basle on 23 November 1949. A number of additional pipes were temporarily attached to the engine at this time to facilitate operation with the Swiss air-braked stock. They were removed before operation in England

Asea Brown-Boveri

En route from Harwich to Swindon the cavalcade which included No. 18000 is seen passing South Tottenham on 5 February 1950, the gas turbine being towed dead. BR was charged the full import duty on the engine by HM Customs & Excise which amounted to £24,400. The total cost of the engine including tax is reported as £138,700

J. McCarthy

handwritten weekly reports to Hawksworth at Swindon. A number of these letters have survived in the records at the National Railway Museum and make interesting reading. Overall the impression gained is that at first Lewis was acutely embarrassed by the evident lack of progress and as a result his notes contain various observations as to his own experiences of Switzerland and his lodgings. At the same time he appears proud to be able to report that he had been able to achieve a saving on his weekly allowance although the time would come when the reverse would apply. This was because as a result of a devaluation of sterling the finances available for lodgings and messing would become severely strained.

Hawksworth's response to Lewis' letters was in a polite yet clearly distanced manner; a unique insight into the relationship between a Chief Mechanical Engineer and a relatively lowly employee.

Eventually though, patience was rewarded, and on 22 August 1949 Lewis was able to report that he hoped the engine would be finished by the end of September, after which trials on the Swiss Railways system would be undertaken. He also added the comment that no two people appeared to provide the same answer to his questions! Although not referred to in any correspondence, could it have been simply a question of language incompatibility?

Official view of No. 18000 taken at Swindon shortly after its arrival. Lot No. 372 was issued to the engine regardless of the fact it had not been built at the Wiltshire town. Livery at this time was black and silver with a builder's plate half-way up the body side at No. 1 end. Because of its symmetrical external design it was extremely difficult to tell one end from the other and indeed staff recall that the works plate was often the only way of knowing! Prior to its arrival BR had requested that the engine be fitted with a toilet for use by the crew, but Brown-Boveri responded by stating there was insufficient room

British Railways

With completion pending, serious enquiries were made as to the most suitable port available at which the engine might be unloaded. A number of options were considered, which included the Dunkirk to Dover train ferry, the Zeebrugge to Harwich ferry and also the use of one of the South Wales ports. Evidently Cardiff was for some time a firm favourite but then somebody realized the overall weight of the engine was in excess of the 100-ton maximum crane capacity available, thus prompting an enquiry from the manager of the docks as to whether the engine could be dismantled for unloading. Disembarking at Dover was later rejected due to the restricted loading gauge of the SR eastern section lines.

Lewis, despite having written in good faith, was then forced to retract his original statements, for on 1 October 1949 he reported an '. . . all out effort being made to finish loco, ready for a trial on 10th October. Labour has been increased from 4 to 15 men, the problem being to keep out of each others way.'

It is interesting to pause for a moment to reflect on Lewis' statement, the conclusion being that it would appear little urgency was given to the job by the Swiss Locomotive Works. This is somewhat strange while the lack of any obvious correspondence from BR over the matter is another distinct anomaly. Was it that BR had already lost interest in the project? Perhaps so, for interestingly there is little of what would surely have normally been expected; namely, pressure to ensure completion. After this time references to Lewis in Switzerland abruptly cease and it may be concluded that he returned to Swindon. In view of his unique part in the history of the engine it is perhaps

Front end view of the engine which, because of the droop to the side windows, tended to present a slightly forlorn appearance. Above the side headlights are the sandbox fillers while the front vertical handrail afforded access together with the steps to the top lamp bracket. A red lamp was provided at each end. Besides the gas turbine power plant the locomotive was also fitted with an auxiliary diesel engine. This had two roles: to start the turbine operation which used light fuel to begin with before changing over to heavy fuel, and also for light engine moves over short distances

British Railways

also surprising that his name fails to appear in any other references to the engine throughout the time it was working.

Anticipating the pending completion of the engine, Hawksworth made a further trip to Switzerland in November 1949 accompanied by A.W.J. Dymond and W.A.L. Creighton, the latter being the electrical assistant to the Western Region. By this time the locomotive was actually completed and the three observers were able to see at first hand the performance of their new acquisition. Generally the results were as had been promised, although here again there appears to have been an overall lack of commitment by the Swiss. This is borne out from the full text of Hawksworth's report on the visit which is reproduced as Appendix E.

The first runs in Switzerland involved a number of duties working both freight and passenger trains as well as running light engine. It was anticipated that the engine would be released for shipping to Britain on 28 December 1949.

The trip to Switzerland in November 1949 was one of the last duties dealt with by the former Great Western CME before his retirement at the end of that year. With Hawksworth no longer at the helm the whole project could well have been expected to drift into insignificance, an additional hiccup for the nationalized network still trying to identify a corporate locomotive policy. In his official role as the head of Swindon, Hawksworth would never see his gas turbine arrive at the Wiltshire town; whether in his retirement he paid heed to its later workings is unknown. The answer to this, as well as to countless other questions concerning this perhaps under-estimated engineer, have yet to be revealed.

Meanwhile, Paddington and Swindon had reached a decision on the entry port for the new engine which, for clearance purposes, was to be Harwich. In addition it was decided to use the ferry *Suffolk*, this particular vessel being able to afford covered deck accommodation. BR had also been advised that No. 18000 – as it was then identified – would probably arrive at Zeebrugge under its own power although it is not certain if this actually did take place.

At Paddington meanwhile, the various departments were trying to agree as to the likely sphere of usage for the engine, with provisional approval given to Paddington–Plymouth running either via Westbury or Bristol and also Paddington–Wolverhampton.

For reasons not recorded No. 18000's arrival at Harwich was not until 3 February 1950. The *Suffolk* under Captain Davies, tied up alongside a welter of waiting newsmen, including representatives of British Paramount News, Central Press, the Swiss Broadcasting Co., Associated Press, Sport & General Press, Pathe Pictures and Metro News. In a country still stifled with austerity and limited rationing, here was a promise that development was still continuing apace. The public was hungry for items such as this and accordingly the arrival was devoured by the media. (Regretfully, none of the photograph press agencies appear to have retained prints of views taken at the time.)

A cavalcade of No. 18000 together with barrier wagons containing spares and hauled by B1 No. 61003 *Gazelle*, finally left Harwich on 5 February, and travelled by Ely, Cambridge, Bishop's Stortford, Tottenham and Cricklewood to Acton. There, the B1 came off and was replaced by No. 7901 *Dodington Hall* for the journey along the main line to Swindon. An amount of discussion had taken place earlier as to the possibility of even taking the engine straight to Old Oak Common but understandably this was not proceeded with.

At Swindon No. 18000 was the subject of familiarization and a detailed inspection for some days, although this itself was not without difficulty as there is some doubt about whether the various instruction and technical manuals were available from the manufacturers at the time. The engine was also weighed and, with the scales registering

115 tons, the route availability was confirmed as that pertaining to the 'King' class. A number of official photographs were also taken around this time.

Following light engine trials within the confines of the works sidings, No. 18000 first took to the main line under its own power on 13 February 1950, although still light engine and on one of the favourite Swindon test routes, west on the South Wales direct line as far as Badminton. A return to Swindon was made later in the day with both runs reported as successful.

Following this run, additional light engine trials took place, the purpose being to familiarize as many staff as possible with the workings of the engine. Then on 22 February No. 18000 hauled a four-coach special to Plymouth and back, the purpose this time being to gauge platform clearances *en route*. Testing continued through February and into March and involved both light engine as well as load haulage runs.

With the tests proceeding well it was decided to arrange a Press trip from Paddington to Plymouth and return for 14 March. But here fate played a part for, while working a test train of empty stock from Swindon to Bristol on 9 March, just five days before the planned Press trip, a failure of the compressor blading occurred and No. 18000 had to be returned to Swindon for repair.

Examination showed the first three rows of blades had actually been shed which, after examination, was at first thought to be due to blade 'flutter', caused by differences, compared with the Swiss engine, in the nature of the ingoing air. This itself was because a re-design of the air intake compared with the Swiss engine had taken place, No. 18000 incorporating a number of water-jet nozzles for the purpose of blade cleaning. Later though, it was realized the damage had occurred simply because of the ingress of a

Test train on 28 February 1950 photographed passing Chippenham westbound at 12.50 p.m. and making 74 mph. At the controls was Locomotive Inspector 'Charlie' Pullen, while among the VIPs in the saloon were Sir James Milne and F.W. Hawksworth, under whose jurisdiction in the days of the independent GWR the locomotive had been ordered. Accompanying them was the then Western Region General Manager, Mr K.W.C. Grand

Kenneth Leech

24

No. 18000 reversing light to Laira out of Plymouth North Road on 22 February 1950, after working a four-coach special from Swindon. This was its first visit to Devon. At this stage the engine was accompanied on all its runs by an engineer from the Brown-Boveri Works at Baden who remained in England until September 1950. The intended assistance from these visitors was not always understood due to the language difficulties

Maurice E.J. Dart

foreign body through the filter louvres. As a result a finer mesh gauze was placed over the compressor entry ducts.

It was at first feared that as a result of the damage a complete new compressor would have to be obtained from Switzerland, although in the event the Swiss engineers were able to repair the old unit at Swindon. Even so this took time and No. 18000 spent some four weeks inside the Swindon 'factory', part of the time alongside an equally strange visitor, B1 No. 61185, the latter having sustained a hot box.

Re-entry to traffic was on 14 April 1950 on a light engine working, with another return trip to Badminton three days later. The next day's movements are not clear although it is known the engine was back in A shop on 19 April. No. 18000 probably remained within the works the following day as well, for the purpose of installing various test equipment. This was because the first dynamometer car trials were planned for Friday 21 April, with a remit initiated by the Mechanical and Electrical Engineer at Swindon to establish the principal characteristics of the locomotive.

A circular route was used for these first dynamometer car trials, running from Swindon via Bath to Bristol and back via Badminton, a total of $72\frac{2}{3}$ miles. The time schedule was calculated for a trailing load of 440 tons, comprising fourteen vehicles. The opportunity was also taken to halt the train at Westerleigh Junction on the rising 1 in 300 gradient, where a temporary restriction was in force. This would allow a start on the actual gradient and an acceleration to high speeds at high rates of working.

No. 18000 leaving Swindon with fourteen coaches weighing 436 tons and including the dynamometer car – seen coupled directly behind the engine – 21 April 1950. A circular route, Swindon–Bath–Bristol–Badminton–Swindon, was used

In practice the actual load taken, including the dynamometer car, was 436 tons and, while a performance log in the form most familiar to students of locomotive performance was not adhered to, the summary of results makes for interesting reading:

Trailing load including dynamometer car	436 tons
Train miles	78.66
Ton miles exc. loco.	34,300
Time – actual running	109.4 mins
– overall inc. running of unit	
before and after trial run	133.5 mins
No. of unbooked stops	3
Special stops	1
Signal speed checks	1
Average speed on running time	43.14 mph
Work done on trailing load at draw-bar	1,233.0 db hp hr
Work done at generator	1,648.0 ghp hr

$$\frac{\text{Work done at draw-bar}}{\text{Work done at generator}} = \frac{1,233}{1,648} = 0.748$$

Heavy fuel oil	
total weight used	2,441.6 lb
lb/mile	31.05
lb/ton mile	0.071
Light fuel oil (exc. oil used by heating boiler)	
total weight used	143.1 lb
lb/mile	1.82
lb/ton mile	0.0042

Total fuel (exc. oil used by heating boiler)
lb/draw bar hp hr	2.096
lb/generator hp hr	1.568

Gross calorific value of heavy fuel oil	18,760 B th U/lb
Gross calorific value of light fuel oil	19,870 B th U/lb

Train miles under power	67.35
Time under power at draw-bar	90.2 mins
Average db hp (time under power at draw-bar)	820.0
Average db pull (time under power at draw-bar)	3.07 tons
Average generator hp (generator time under power)	1,063
Heavy fuel oil lb/hr (running time)	1,340
Light fuel oil lb/hr (running time)	78.5

Overall average thermal efficiencies on gross calorific values of fuel and inclusive of auxiliaries:

On work done at draw-bar on trailing load	6.45%
On work done by generator	8.62%
Ambient temperature	62.5°F
Wind velocity	4.4 mph
Wind direction	Westerly
Weather	Fine and dry
Barometric pressure	29.8 Hg

Although the maximum speed reached is not reported in the tables, this is referred to elsewhere in the bulletin as having been 84 mph, which was maintained for a distance of two miles near Hullavington. A maximum 4,400 amps loading was reported at the main generator.

No problems thermal, mechanical or electrical were reported, the engine seemingly impressing its observers to a considerable degree, who were clearly versed in the standards of Swindon!

The prediction of locomotive performance has never been the practice with most designers and makers of steam locomotives in this country though, on the Western Region, the estimation and prediction of locomotive performance has been a developed practice for many years. The very close agreement of estimated and actual performance in the case of Locomotive No. 18000 therefore reflects considerable credit on its builders.

The reservations expressed by Hawksworth just a few months earlier had proved to be unfounded.

Following on from the trials the test equipment was removed and on 24 April new ground was again broken with No. 18000 working to Oxford on a six-coach train. This was primarily for clearance trials, arrival being at 1.06 p.m. and departure at 1.45 p.m.

Testing then continued up to 9 May, when No. 18000 worked from Swindon to Denham via Hanwell, Drayton Green and Greenford, again for clearance purposes. At Denham there was a reversal, returning along the joint line to Old Oak where the engine was stabled overnight for the first time. Here the opportunity was taken to spruce up the

On 24 April 1950, No. 18000 worked from Swindon to Oxford and returned with a six-coach test train, believed to be the only time it traversed this route. The engine is seen running round its train at Oxford. The engine is fitted with a steam-type whistle which was the result of some experiments previously carried out at Swindon works in which a steam whistle was supplied with compressed air at 80 psi – half the pressure normally exerted by steam. The whistle performed adequately on test although in practice the sound was found to be insufficient and so in August 1951 two air horns of the type provided on GWR diesel railcars were substituted. These emitted notes of E flat and 'F flat' respectively

R.H.G. Simpson

overall appearance of the machine as the Press inspection and trip had been re-arranged for the following day.

At Paddington on 10 May, the Press was out in force, although No. 18000 apparently disgraced itself slightly by dislodging soot from the station roof as a result of the exhaust blast! The engine returned to Swindon at the head of the 2.15 p.m. passenger service at which time it had completed a total of 583 miles' running.

No. 18000 then entered regular service with runs between Swindon and Paddington, heading up with the 9.00 a.m. service and returning with the 1.18 p.m. train. This continued without difficulty up to the 21 May. Presumably the engine was retained on local workings to ensure that it was finally a reliable proposition. Cumulative mileage was now 3,272 miles.

The following day, 22 May, No. 18000 took up its intended duties between Paddington and Plymouth, working down with the 3.30 p.m. service and returning the following day with the 7.15 a.m. up train. Both these trains ran via the Berks and Hants route, with the down service including a Weymouth portion which was slipped at Heywood Road Junction. (Both of these were 'double-home' turns worked by Old Oak men. The crew of the 10.30 a.m. 'Cornish Riviera' down would return from Plymouth with the 7.15 a.m. up train, while the men from the 3.30 p.m. down returned with the 8.15 a.m. ex-Plymouth (Millbay). The tutor driver would follow the turbine diagram.)

Already though the engine was at something of a disadvantage, for unlike its steam counterparts, it did not require lengthy periods of shed maintenance between duties and as such was certainly not being utilized to the full. This was hardly the fault of the gas turbine, more likely the leisurely schedules necessarily allowed for motive power in steam days and into which any modern form of traction hardly fitted. Initial availability

No. 18000 running light from Old Oak to Paddington ready for inspection by the Press, 10 May 1950. The previous night the engine had worked a roundabout route from Swindon to the London depot where it was cleaned in anticipation of the following day's event. After the day's work was finished and before the turbine was shut down, it was allowed to idle without load for several minutes. Following shutdown an automatic barring gear would turn over the turbine unit at regular intervals in order to equalize the cooling forces and so prevent distortion. The power for this was taken either from the batteries or from an external source. This would sometimes surprise men who might be passing the otherwise quiet engine which then appeared to start up of its own accord

British Railways

figures for No. 18000 were poor compared with those achieved by modern motive power in other countries. It would be a number of years before maximum usage was made of locomotive resources, by which time diesel and electric traction was firmly established.

The Plymouth duties continued without difficulty until 5 June when a routine examination revealed the lining of the combustion chamber had become badly distorted and accordingly, No. 18000 was worked to Swindon for repairs. This was destined to be the first of numerous occasions when this particular item had to be replaced. Combustion chamber linings were later replaced with a new item or repaired according to condition. On 9 June No. 18000 re-appeared on the Plymouth turn, working back the following day before returning on the 3.30 p.m. down on the 11 June, this time remaining at Laira depot in preparation for a series of dynamometer car trials on the South Devon banks.

Compared with the earlier test of 21 April no detailed log of these trials appears to have survived, although it is known that the purpose of the runs was to ascertain the maximum trailing load that could be safely hauled up the formidable gradient from Plymouth to Hemerdon. This was to be fixed at the maximum that could be restarted on

'On the blocks' – facing the lawn at Paddington, 10 May 1950. The view was probably posed by the Topical Press cameraman with a work-stained 61xx tank alongside

Hulton Picture Library

the steepest part of the bank (i.e. 1 in 42) and hauled to the top without overheating in the electrical equipment. (Bearing in mind that No. 18000 had already operated passenger trains over this route, does this mean she had a steam pilot?)

The tests of 12 June were rather disappointing in some ways and the locomotive failed to restart on the gradient with a 350 tons gross trailing load. A successful run was made without stopping with a load of 400 tons but the speed fell to 10 mph at the summit after having commenced the gradient at about 50 mph. The generator and traction motors were examined on reaching Hemerdon and there was no evidence of excessive heating.

From the generalizations in the official records it was clear that on this occasion the dynamometer car was not being used. The failure then of the engine to haul greater loads than 350 tons on the South Devon banks effectively placed the gas turbine in the same haulage bracket as a 'Star' class engine, although with 'King' class route availability restrictions. This was itself an anomaly, for the few remaining 40xx class were already approaching fifty years of age, yet here was a comparison with the most modern form of traction running on BR. Even so, it was recognized that No. 18000 was capable of '. . . sustained efforts at speeds far beyond the capacity of a "Star"'. The comparison however would remain and later costings compared running costs of No. 18000 with the 'Star' class.

Regular passenger duties were scheduled to resume the day after the trials on 13 June

Leaving Paddington on 10 May 1950 at the head of its first revenue-earning train, the 2.15 p.m. departure, which No. 18000 hauled without incident as far as Swindon

British Railways

and accordingly the engine took over a London-bound passenger train at Plymouth. It is not clear what train this was but it may well have been part of the previous turn in the form of the 7.15 a.m. service.

Unfortunately though, No. 18000 got no further than Newton Abbot, where a failure occurred due to the cut-out switch of No. 2 traction motor operating. No. 18000 was therefore taken off its train and later worked light to Swindon. The cut-out switch had operated to protect the traction motor which, upon examination, was quickly discovered to have developed a major defect, serious damage having occurred to the windings of both stator and armature, which would require re-wiring of both. Cumulative mileage at this time was 6,919. It was realized repairs would take some while and accordingly the engine was temporarily modified to operate with just three traction motors, with a corresponding reduction of 25 per cent in available power. Officially the cause of the failure was reported as a failure of the binding wire on the armature itself, which had become detached. This whirled around inside the motor casing causing the damage. No reference was made to the full power trials of the previous day. Later diagnosis of the oil content from the crankcase of the failed traction motor revealed a 25 per cent water content, although there is no indication as to how this occurred. (A report in an official document contained at the National Railway Museum suggests No. 18000 failed with an

31

Damage to No. 2 traction motor following the failure at Newton Abbot on 13 June 1950. At this stage the various components have been dismantled, with the amount of damage caused by flailing pieces of armature obvious. No. 1008 *County of Cardigan* forms a backdrop within the works. Following this failure No. 18000 resumed working but with only three traction motors, in which form it operated until 12 July 1950 when a replacement unit was refitted unknown traction motor problem at Pewsey on 13 June 1950. It is assumed though that this was a clerical error.)

After this it is known that the engine worked a previously arranged demonstration run for leading scientists and gas turbine technologists on a circular route from Paddington via Reading, Newbury, Westbury and Swindon, then returning through Reading to the capital. Fortunately, luck was with the engine on this occasion and no problems were encountered despite running the train on just three traction motors.

Not surprisingly there was considerable media attention surrounding the introduction of No. 18000 and a number of observers from various journals were afforded the privilege of a cab pass. The general impression gained from these contemporary reports was that the footplate facilities were roomy even with four occupants and conversation was possible at normal voice levels. Apart from the initial six drivers trained to operate the engine (this number was increased later) few railwaymen other than those directly involved with the project were afforded access to the cab, even briefly when the engine was waiting at a station; it was necessary to hold a pass before boarding the engine. A later comment from Paddington asked Swindon as to why so few drivers had been trained, which provoked the reply that there was insufficient time to do so as Paddington seemingly arranged for a visitor to travel on the engine on most of its runs!

Normal passenger services were resumed on 30 June 1950 and included working the 6.04 p.m. Didcot to Swindon train. Unfortunately the engine was declared a failure before the train even left Didcot, due to problems with a bearing on the end of the control oil pump motor. The control log reported that the service train eventually departed behind a substitute steam locomotive at 6.29 p.m.

Repairs were effected at Swindon on 10 and 11 July, after which No. 18000 was reported as working local services between Didcot and Bristol. The following day, the engine was stopped for the repaired traction motor to be re-instated. Possibly the reason for a Bristol duty was that three traction motors were considered insufficient for a normal train over the South Devon banks at this time, although later the former route would also be used due to the inadequacies of the train heating boiler.

Re-entry into service was on 15 August with a Swindon–Paddington duty. This continued until 26 August, by which time 10,506 miles had been run. Paddington–

Believed to have been photographed near Westbury, this is thought to be the demonstration train of 27 June 1950, at which time the engine was working on just three traction motors following the failure at Newton Abbot

British Railways

Resting between duties in Old Oak Common depot. It was the practice to stable the engine over at the 'factory' side of the depot rather than the steam shed and so avoid as much as possible the dirt associated with the steam engine. Generally the engine was not scheduled for working on Sundays and the electrical fitters could therefore earn overtime for servicing the engine
John H. Meredith

Plymouth duties recommenced on 28 August with two return trips per week between Monday and Thursday. Friday and Saturday were spent working a London–Bristol diagram. Sunday was scheduled for maintenance. This working continued until 30 September by which date the mileage had reached 17,719. A correspondent in *Trains Illustrated* for the period reported that between 11 and 14 September No. 18000 was involved in tests to compare its performance with those of a 'King' and 'Castle', both the steam types being modified with high superheat. The timings were set at $4\frac{1}{2}$ hours for the down train and 5 hours for the up working. Loadings were 400 tons from Paddington as far as Westbury, 370 tons thence to Exeter and 240–270 tons for the final section to Plymouth. Unfortunately no official report of the trials appears to have survived although it was stated that the gas turbine had put up some very creditable perform-ances, including a speed of 89 mph on the descent of Lavington bank. The same correspondent refers to the fact that the ex-LMS diesels, Nos. 10000 and 10001 were also to take part in the trials though it is not thought that this actually occurred. Neither is it clear if the dynamometer car or possibly an alternative means of recording was used. Certainly, even at this stage in the engine's career, thoughts were being given to utilizing it on a specially devised high-speed schedule where better efficiency could probably be obtained from the power unit. Unfortunately the practicalities of fitting such a service into a congested timetable proved insurmountable and the idea was shelved indefinitely.

No 18000 draws an admiring crowd of onlookers at Paddington on 27 June 1950 after returning from a demonstration/test run. The train is drawn up into Platform 4, facing 'The Lawn'. The engine was permitted in all platforms except No. 11 at the terminus. This was because of clearance from low smoke shutes

B.Y. Williams

Not unnaturally, the performance of the engine attracted the attention of a number of outside observers. Cecil J. Allen for example, writing in a contemporary journal, stated, '. . . it is clear that the engine's capabilities are of an exceptional order,' and continued to comment favourably on 'unprecedented acceleration' from Paddington with a load of 380 tons, when 60 mph was attained in 5½ miles. Mr Allen referred also to other aspects of No. 18000 working to Plymouth, including a time of 13 minutes 10 seconds from a dead start at Taunton to passing Whiteball Summit signal-box with 345 tons. A fair comparison was also given as to the capabilities of steam under the same conditions, a 'King' with 360 tons managing 14 minutes 5 seconds and a 'Star' with 260 tons 13 minutes 23 seconds. An interesting comment appeared at the foot of the article: 'On the extreme South Devon banks the locomotive appears to have a definite advantage over anything previously achieved with steam power,' which tends to imply its loads were definitely restricted on the South Devon banks at this time.

On 2 and 3 October No. 18000 was out of service so that the lining of the combustion chamber could again be changed. Train haulage resumed shortly afterwards and continued until 15 October when a further two days were spent out of service, this time for washing out the compressor. Normal running then continued until 27 October, by which time the cumulative mileage had reached 22,031. Repairs to the train

35

heating boiler then necessitated withdrawal of the engine from service for about one month.

It may seem ironic that such an item as a train heating boiler was sufficient a problem to necessitate a prolonged period of non-working. Records on this point however are perfectly clear and there has survived a considerable amount of correspondence as to the behaviour of the train heating boiler. Neither was this problem unique to No. 18000, for oil-fired steam heat boilers carried on railway engines would continue to give trouble for many years to come. A temporary solution to the train heating difficulty was the use of a steam engine 'coupled inside', which was used officially only for supplying the steam heat. In addition the engine which brought the carriages into the platform would also heat the train to a higher degree than was usual.

Not unexpectedly, the records of the boiler trouble applicable to No. 18000 make interesting reading, although it must be said that in some ways the original GWR specification was hopelessly inadequate. Consequently the manufacturers were faced with an everlasting series of correspondence which came to a head in a letter from the Managing Director of Laidlaw-Drew in October in which, in total exasperation, he exclaims:

Powering through Maidenhead and bound for Paddington on the up fast line, No. 18000 is attached to a mixed rake of Hawksworth and Collett coaching stock. When working a train the turbine would normally be set to run at 3,500 rpm. The lower setting of 2,700 was insufficient to maintain schedules while the highest range of 5,200 rpm provided terrific acceleration although at an excessive rate of fuel consumption. A disadvantage of the power unit was also that it burnt the same amount of fuel stationary as when running

Times Newspapers

. . . you will realise that the cost is very high for a mistake which was not initially ours . . . I somewhat naturally asked myself why we should pay for;

A new fan runner because it was damaged.

A new brick quarl because the original one had not turned up at our works [referring to when the boiler was returned for repair].

A new thermostat which was damaged by you or Messrs Brown-Boveri.

More than we could have expected to make in profit in railway fares.

You can easily imagine therefore that when one of your people at Swindon suggested that we should also pay for the transport of the boiler to Swindon I immediately rang up the Railway Executive and complained about it.

I do not want to enter into any further detailed discussions and if, having read this letter you prefer to put it in the waste paper basket please do so.

Besides the difficulties with the train heating boiler another more serious problem had been identified which affected the brake release time. It had been found that on suffering a signal check the time taken to release the brakes throughout the length of the

Alongside the tranquil Kennet and Avon Canal, somewhere between Bedwyn and Hungerford, No. 18000 heads east towards Reading and London on a return passenger working from Plymouth. Despite the drivers receiving training to operate the engine, no such instruction was given to the firemen whose main duties were attending to the train heating boiler. On one occasion an inspector who was attempting to demonstrate the correct method of lighting the boiler tried a little too hard and received some singed eyebrows for his trouble. It was unkindly suggested that when the engine was working well it would be taken to Swindon and stripped down just to see why!

Times Newspapers

A wet day finds No. 18000 westbound for Plymouth passing Little Bedwyn at the head of what may well be the 'Cornish Riviera'. The performance of the engine was affected slightly by climatic conditions, with a cold frosty day being the best – although there were then additional demands placed on the train heating boiler! Sanding facilities were provided to both bogies although in practice they were not often needed

Asea Brown-Boveri

train was excessive. The problem was quickly traced to the compressor-exhauster set which, although working exactly as per its specification, was directly related speed-wise to the revolutions of the actual gas turbine. Accordingly, at a low turbine speed, as would normally occur during a temporary stop, there was insufficient vacuum being produced in the required time. As a temporary solution each of the drivers attempted to alter his driving technique either by not reducing the turbine speed or by applying just the engine air brake.

Moving forward in time, static tests in connection with the vacuum system were undertaken at Swindon on 17 August 1951 under the auspices of the Experimental Section. For the purpose of the test No. 18000 was attached to a single flat truck on which were mounted a number of tanks intended to form a reservoir of equal capacity to a thirteen-coach train. The results proved the difficulties experienced in actual running and a number of modifications to the braking system, together with the provision of an additional exhauster set, were made immediately afterwards.

Returning to 1950, around the end of November/beginning of December an additional weeks' duties on the Paddington to Plymouth route were undertaken but again difficulties with the train heating boiler caused a cessation of the turn and No. 18000 was soon out of service, this time for over six weeks. Unfortunately the total mileage for 1950 is not fully reported although it is known that on 1 December it had reached 23,272

Awaiting departure from the old Platform 9 at Bristol Temple Meads and bound for London. Despite the lavish programme originally intended at the time steam engines were being converted to burn heavy fuel, re-fuelling points capable of dispensing the similar fuel for No. 18000 were only completed at Old Oak, Swindon and Laira, the latter a tank wagon from which heavy fuel oil was pumped as required. This naturally restricted the sphere of activity of the engine
M. Deane

miles. A figure for up to 31 December 1950 would probably be around 24,500. Records of the four-week periods between 20 May 1950 and 28 November 1953 give details of the number of days spent working, spare or under repair, together with fuel consumed, in Appendix H.

The periods out of work were spent at Swindon, sometimes inside the shops and at other times outside and visible from the main line. Certainly, on 15 November it is known that No. 18000 was parked outside the works while inside a VIP reception was held to mark the completion of the last 'Castle', No. 7037, which was appropriately named *Swindon*. Why the gas turbine should not feature in the event as an example of the latest developments at the works is unclear. This fact did not go unnoticed by a number of observers.

Swindon may have been preoccupied with its heritage but meanwhile the gas turbine, and in particular its performance ability, was receiving much acclaim in the technical press. The *Railway Gazette* for example, in its issue of 2 March 1951, referred to the first few months' operation of the engine and in particular its haulage capacity. No. 18000 is stated as ' . . . equal to a Castle and probably a King', while lavish praise was heaped on its exceptional ability for hill-climbing:

> In starting from rest or in climbing exceptionally steep gradients, No. 18000 has put up performances which appear to have established new records. Among these is an acceleration to 60 mph . . . up a 1 in 90 and the completion of the climb from the east to Dainton Summit . . . at 41 mph and in the

Taken from the leading coach behind No. 18000, this rare view is of the engine leaving Bristol for London and passing underneath the GWR colour light signals. A surviving item of correspondence dated 25 May 1950, between BR and Brown-Boveri, suggests the builders were concerned as to the possible ingress of smoke into the turbine should the engine be assisted at any time by a steam locomotive coupled ahead. Accordingly the suggestion was made that the gas turbine should always be in the lead. Whether this was ever necessary is unclear and the only photographs located of the engine being assisted by steam were following a failure, with the turbine shut down. Conversation with a former railwayman involved with the engine reveals its performance was not affected when passing through a tunnel where smoke from a previous train still lingered. Another railwayman though, has suggested 'the turbine' once stalled in Box Tunnel due to the shortage of air

M. Deane

opposite direction a time of 3 minutes 28½ seconds for the 2.7 miles from Plympton to Hemerdon . . . even with loads of 215 and 210 tons these are unprecedented achievements.

On several runs speeds from 80–90 mph were attained and journeys at over 60 mph from start to stop were made with loads up to 470 tons. Frequently the locomotive had to be eased to avoid running ahead of time and as yet there does not appear to have been any test of its maximum capabilities continuously over a long stretch.

Presumably the results of the BR trials on the South Devon banks had not been made public at this time. A slightly later issue of the same journal (6 April 1951) reported:

On a run from Paddington to Bristol with a load of 360 tons at 65–70 mph the turbine inlet temperature was 950°F at 4,400 rpm. Maximum generator reading at any point was 1,350 amps at 590 volts. This was not approaching its optimum power which is a continuous 2,340 amps at 675 volts. . . At the lower power output the gas turbine loses in efficiency, the consumption of oil being an average of 2.62 gal/mile or about 300 gallons on the London–Bristol run compared with 3 tons of coal for steam. But if the comparison was made at 90 mph on the level and maximum uphill then steam would probably lose its advantage.

Except when working the Plymouth turns or due to a failure, No. 18000 always returned to Old Oak Common at the cessation of the work and was diagrammed for service at that depot on Sunday of each week. During its first year the whole of the top link at that depot was trained in its operation and as such it was booked to be handled by the twelve crews who made up the Old Oak Common No. 1 link, the theory being that as the engine worked a different link from the crews the men would get an aggregate six turns per twelve weeks.

On paper at least this was an ideal arrangement as it did not allow too much time to elapse between duties so as to cause a difficulty where men forgot the method of operating the machine. Difficulties though, arose when these times were extended during the prolonged periods spent out of service.

Under normal running the duties of the fireman were considerably less arduous than that required on a steam turn and as such the engine was popular with the men. Besides attending to the train heating boiler, the fireman was also expected to undertake regular readings from a number of gauges within the engine compartment. As would be expected this was a particularly noisy environment although no ear protection was provided. In addition, the force of suction of air being drawn into the turbine was such that it would remove a man's hat from his head. This was demonstrated to good effect one day when No. 18000 was between Uffington and Knighton Crossing at the head of the 1.15 p.m. Paddington–Bristol train. Apparently a loose tarpaulin was sucked off a passing 'up' freight train, lodging itself against the right-hand air intake, completely blocking off the flow of air into the turbine. The effect on the engine was dramatic; a complete falling off of power accompanied by clouds of dense black smoke – a result of incomplete combustion. The remedy was swift and simple although a few minutes were lost to the schedule. No. 18000 is remembered as being a very smooth-riding engine with one former crewman recounting how it was possible to balance a cup of tea, or perhaps twelve old pennies, on the engine block even when running at speed!

Despite continued attention from the makers (Clarkson Boiler Co. with Laidlaw Drew's oil-firing equipment) it was necessary to return the complete train heating boiler to the manufacturer for modification and in this form, minus its facility to heat a train, a new duty working was arranged. Accordingly, on 31 January 1951, No. 18000 was rostered for a train of milk tanks between Swindon and London. As such the non-working of the train heating boiler did not matter although it must remain conjecture as to why such a tour of duty had not been considered beforehand. These duties continued until 25 April, by which time the mileage had reached 24,432, but were interrupted on two occasions, the first when the combustion chamber lining was replaced and also when four days were lost owing to necessary repairs to the light fuel tank.

Commencing on 30 April the engine worked a London and Bristol passenger duty, the 7.30 a.m. ex-Paddington (this was a Paddington–Plymouth train which ran via Bristol and was loaded to fourteen vehicles) returning with the 12 noon (9.07 a.m. Exeter–Paddington via Bristol, eleven vehicles) from Bristol. One exception to this occurred on 4 May when for an unknown reason it returned light from Bristol. From 21 May an additional duty involved the 6.35 p.m. Paddington to Cheltenham Spa train, comprising ten vehicles, which it hauled as far as Swindon where a steam engine was substituted. The return to Paddington was usually at the head of the 3.50 p.m. Whitland–Kensington

Possibly taken not long after its entry into service, No. 18000 draws an appreciative crowd of onlookers at Paddington station. Based on a weekly total of 1,750 miles and involving approximately fifty hours turbine running time, the following quantities of oil were used: diesel engine sump, $1\frac{1}{2}$ gallons; compressor exhauster, 1 gallon; traction motor gears, 1 gallon; traction motor armature bearings, 2 pints; various grease points, $4\frac{1}{2}$ lb. Every three months the main lubricator tank for the turbine required ten gallons for topping up, while the sump of the diesel engine and exhauster/compressor would use 20–22 gallons. In total the consumption of oil (not including greases) may be averaged at 2.5 to 2.8 pints per 100 miles

Tom Middlemas

milk train which No. 18000 hauled from Swindon to Southall, working thence light to Old Oak, arriving at approximately 11.30 p.m. The engine was prohibited from working through to Kensington itself although if an alternative milk train destined for West Ealing was substituted the engine did work through to that destination. Another alternative was on a parcels train from Swindon to London. The total mileage worked in a week on such runs was an aggregate of 2,058 miles.

Part of the the agreement governing the purchase of the engine was that a guarantee would exist relating to its first year's running, commencing at the time No. 18000 operated its first revenue-earning train. As this had occurred on 10 May 1950 the guarantee therefore expired on 9 May 1951, sole responsibility for the maintenance of the machine then being with British Railways. (It later transpired that BR requested an extension of the guarantee period until 9 May 1952. Brown-Boveri was sympathetic and, although not agreeing to a 'cover-all' policy, promised to examine favourably any failure which did occur. This proposition, which was dated 16 November 1951, was sent to R.A. Smeddle at Swindon and then passed on to Riddles for approval. Sanctioning by the Railway Executive was given shortly afterwards.)

Although dates are not given, it is known that a number of minor faults occurred during the first year, which included a faulty indicator light (a date of 19 April 1951 is given for this problem), the light fuel tank, the diesel engine radiator, some of the thermostats and the heavy fuel oil pressure system. Another difficulty occurred on 21 May 1951 when the engine failed at Reading due to a broken quartz rod in the thermostat after turbine. On this occasion repairs were quickly carried out and the engine returned to Old Oak ready for its booked turn on the 6.35 p.m. service. None of these failures were regarded as particularly serious although a number contributed to the odd days the engine spent out of service. Taken as a whole the first year may be summarized as follows:

Days in service	161
Days on trials	11
Days lost for operating reasons	66 (primarily Saturdays and Sundays)
Days lost due to failures	121
Days lost due to maintenance	6
	365

From the official records it is clear that Swindon was still learning about the machine for an entry of 20 April refers to the fact that a detergent which had been used to clean the compressor blades had been found to result in accumulations of sludge and a new method was to be tried.

Hurrying along on what is purported to be a Cheltenham–Paddington service, No. 18000 is seen approaching Twyford West. One of the technical problems to be overcome in burning a heavy grade oil was in the quantities of ash that tended to be produced. These would be expected to lodge on the turbine blades but this problem had been overcome at the expense of the lining of the combustion chamber which required changing at regular intervals. The exhaust from the engine was generally clear under normal working conditions

Maurice Earley/National Railway Museum

Whether a similar compound was used elsewhere is unclear and so, with no undue worries from the expiry of the guarantee, it was a considerable shock when less than three weeks later, on 29 May, the worst failure so far occurred, with a fire in the heat exchanger. The incident occurred at Bristol after the engine had arrived at the head of the 7.30 a.m. from Paddington and had such a devastating effect that within seconds the complete heat exchanger was damaged beyond repair. Not surprisingly, the engine was a total failure, necessitating a tow to Swindon for examination, although at the time the effects of the damage were not fully appreciated.

Upon examination at Swindon it was discovered that the whole of the centre nest of 1,000 steel tubes was severely wasted and fused. The cause was believed to have had its origins in a catalytic effect occurring due to the presence of vanadium and sulphur compounds which then set up a chemical reaction, in turn damaging the tubes. The mileage total at this time was 39,912.

Fortunately a full set of correspondence has survived on this first serious difficulty, commencing with the report of Insp. C. Pullen. This is reproduced in its original note form and gives the impression that even the inspectors were wary of both the machine and, perhaps more importantly, the wrath of Swindon should they not follow its instructions to the letter:

> Inspector Wiltshire and myself having interviewed Driver P. Matthews (OOC), who was the driver in charge . . . I now wish to report on the experiences of Matthews and myself prior to the arrival of Inspector Wiltshire at Bristol at 4.30 p.m. Matthews states he had quite a normal run from Paddington to Bristol; after leaving Paddington during acceleration the 'temperature before turbine' red light lit up and he reduced from notch 4 to 3, when red light went out, and no further trouble was experienced in this way although during the journey he used all notches from 1 to 6. At the time the red light lit up the indicated temperature was only 1,000 degrees and I would point out that this has been quite a normal occurrence for a long time.
>
> On arrival at Bristol Matthews fully disposed of the locomotive and was quite satisfied at that time that no excessive temperature had been recorded *en route* or up to that time 10.35 a.m. Matthews locked up the locomotive and went to the cabin for half an hour and returned in ample time to restart the turbine at 11.35.
>
> The turbine started without any difficulty but when he went to move off, the 'before turbine' red light lit up, although the temperature indicator was not showing high temperature. Matthews decided he would not proceed off shed under these conditions so he shut down the turbine and noticed the red light did not immediately go out. When turbine revolutions had dropped to 200 and red light gone out, he again restarted the turbine without difficulty but again when he moved off the red light lit up and he finally decided he could not work train and asked for another engine to be provided and for Swindon to be advised of the circumstances. Matthews then set locomotive back clear with the auxiliary generator and completely shut down including the battery switch and the reverser handle, after which he would get no recording of temperatures at the driver's panel at either end, but I would add that Matthews could not say with assurance what the heavy oil pre-heater temperatures were during the time he was twice starting the turbine. Matthews realising he was going to be very late finishing now locked up and went to the canteen for food after which he returned to No. 1 cab and waited

The results of the fire in the heat exchanger at Bristol on 29 May 1951. Distortion in the tubes is obvious, which had changed consistency due to chemical effects on the metal. Repairs involved a complete new set of tubes and it was not until 20 August 1951 that the engine was able to resume working. The large circular item visible in the aerial views is the top of the combustion chamber

for my arrival and it was only about half an hour before my arrival that he first smelt and saw any signs of oil fumes and smoke, and these he could not locate as on the gas turbine.

At 9.10 I was at Swindon station and saw the turbine arrive and depart and also inspected cab and observed that all meters and gauges were reading normal and train left without any evidence of smoke from turbine exhaust.

I was advised at 12.32 p.m. by Mr Willmott that the turbine had failed at Bristol and then spoke to Matthews on the phone and as no one else was available and symptons seemed to indicate faulty thermostat, I caught the 1.00 p.m. train to Bristol leaving a message for Inspector Wiltshire to follow.

I arrived at Bath Road Shed at 2.55 p.m. Matthews on seeing me started to prepare for starting up turbine and when he started diesel engine from No. 2 cab the red light lit up immediately so I went into the engine room (where I found it to be very hot but smokeless) and popped up thermostat when red light went out. I was now called away to the phone and on my return found Matthews was unable to start turbine and then observed that temperature recorded in pre-heater was right round beyond the meter readings and decided there was something serious happening so instructed Matthews to shut down completely. On first arrival on locomotive I had noticed some smoke and fumes in No. 1 cab but these did not seem of serious nature but on examination of generator and engine room I found that smoke and fumes were extensive, heat in corridor very hot and some evidence of smoke actually coming out of compressor inlets. By this time I realised how serious the failure was and came to the conclusion that it would probably be an advantage to turn over turbine and compressor to circulate cool air but although I made the necessary contacts the shaft failed to revolve, and after repeated efforts decided to wait Inspector Wiltshire's arrival before taking any more action. An important point as regards the actual time the excessive heat had occurred in the heat exchanger is the fact that the Running Foreman and others had noticed the discoloration of the heat exchanger covering plates soon after his booking on at 2.00 p.m. and pointed it out to me on the first practical occasion after my arrival and this with my other observations was handed on to Inspector Wiltshire on his arrival.

Inspector Wiltshire reported thus:

> I arrived on the locomotive shed at 4.30 p.m. on the day of the incident.
> My immediate examination of the locomotive with the unit shut down revealed the condition as follows;
> Temperature of heavy fuel oil after preheater reading at the maximum of the instrument 400°F.
> Heavy fuel oil temperature in tank reading 100°F.
> Thermometer for temperature before 'Gas Turbine' 650°F.
> The 'Flame Burning' pilot lamps were showing an intermittent light.
> No heavy or light fuel oil pressures were showing on the instruments.
> The interior temperature of the locomotive was excessively high and there was a strong smell of exhaust gases, but none visible.
> I viewed the combustion chamber through the inspection glasses and observed the dark orange flame burning upwards from the bottom of the chamber and a heavy shower of sparks falling from the top.
> Opening the combustion chamber drain cocks about an egg cup of fuel oil drained from each side.
> On examination of the outside of the roof section above the heat exchanger, I found the paint burnt off, also the plates slightly buckled, but I did not consider it advisable to open the exchanger inspection covers.
> I was now of the opinion that the heat exchanger had been on fire, with the possibility of some remaining pockets of fire still burning, although there was no smoke visible through the exhaust outlets. The sparks in the combustion chamber signified that some air tubes had been destroyed.
> My first concern was to reduce the high temperature and extinguish any remaining pockets of fire in the heat exchanger.
> I tested the turbine shaft alignment with the hand ratchet. I started the diesel auxiliary generator and motored over the unit to 800 rpm to induce a sufficient volume of air through the exchanger tubes to extinguish the fire in the combustion chamber, and reduced the fuel oil preheating temperature to 200°F, also the locomotive interior to a normal temperature.
> At 6.30 p.m. I opened the heat exchanger inspection covers and as far as could be seen the tubes were badly distorted . . .

Not unnaturally a full report of the incident was requested by R.A. Riddles at the Railway Executive Headquarters at Marylebone. This was compiled by K.J. Cook from Swindon.

Photographs taken at the time of the first change of combustion chamber lining in June 1950, with the internal and external surfaces visible

The report at first deals with the same ground as that referred to by the two inspectors and then continues:

> The following day the locomotive was towed to Swindon for examination . . . Messrs Brown-Boveri's representative, who flew over from Baden, was present when the unit was dismantled, and I have asked the firm to let me have a full report on his investigations as soon as possible. [This report has not been located.]
>
> It was at first supposed that the fire had been caused by a leakage of heavy oil fuel in the pre-heater tubes which pass through the heat exchanger. This proved not to be the case, however, and on cutting away the tubes, it was appreciated that the damage was of such a nature that could not have been caused by an oil fire.
>
> It was the opinion of Messrs Brown-Boveri's representative that the trouble started by local generations of heat, probably due to deposits of soot around the tubes. The fuel oil contains compounds of sulphur as well as vanadium, and the exterior of the tubes was coated with iron oxide. The close association of these substances under high temperature conditions can result in the formation of iron sponge, which has free-burning characteristics.
>
> The Swiss Engineer was also of the opinion that these conditions were accelerated by incomplete combustion of the fuel oil. It appears from an examination of the burner that a leakage of oil had occurred through a faulty joint in the burner assembly. Carbonisation of this oil might well have affected the atomisation of the oil in such a manner as to increase the proportion of droplets which pass through the flame zone in a partially burnt state to be finally deposited on the relatively cool walls of the heat exchanger tubes.

This burner, which had been installed on the locomotive for about a fortnight, had recently been received from Switzerland, where it had been sent at the request of Messrs Brown-Boveri for modification and adjustment. During this period, I received no reports of unsatisfactory performance, nor was any reference made to visible signs of poor combustion.

My Metallurgist is closely investigating the matter in conjunction with the Area Chemist . . .

Messrs Brown-Boveri on their own initiative made immediate arrangements to manufacture a new heat exchanger at their works in Baden, and this should arrive at Swindon tomorrow, Wednesday, the 20th instant, when work on re-assembly will be commenced.

A copy of the report was also sent to the Western Region General Manager, Mr K.W.C. Grand, at Paddington.

A replacement heat exchanger was not one of the items carried at Swindon as a spare, so Mr Cook's timings were slightly optimistic, as the new unit did not arrive via Dover until 25 June 1951. While awaiting the new unit the opportunity was taken to give the engine a 'Heavy Casual' overhaul. It was generally hoped that all the repairs could be effected before the start of the annual works holiday although in the event the engine was not ready to re-enter service until 20 August, after which it resumed work on express passenger trains between Paddington and Bristol.

The new heat exchanger differed slightly from the old one in that a spray tube was fitted beneath the tube nest which was intended to facilitate cleaning out as well as helping to extinguish any fire which might occur in future. Larger access doors were also fitted to the unit. These preventative measures were based on experience with the earlier Swiss engine which it was discovered had previously suffered a similar fire; the question must be: Why was this change not effected earlier? Despite the speed at which Brown-Boveri acted in arranging for the new unit to be manufactured there is no reference as to whether at this stage the firm also took a financial stake in the repairs.

While out of service the accounts section took time to analyze the fuel consumption figures for the first months of running. This was disappointing as it had been assessed on the maker's guaranteed efficiency of 16.9 per cent when working at full load although in practice the figure returned was just 7 per cent. In part this was thought to be caused by the engine not running continually at full power and accordingly the Swiss engineers were instructed to adjust the burner so as to improve the efficiency rating when working at three-quarters loading on the turbine. Unfortunately this adjustment was found to increase the production of smoke and soot, the latter of course at the heart of the heat exchanger fire earlier in the year. Around the same time complaints began to be heard at Paddington as to the smell which invaded the coaches behind. Again adjustments were made, with an attempt to lift the exhaust higher from the roof. Indeed a re-design of the roof was even suggested although in the event this was ruled out as the engine was already almost up to the maximum limit of the loading gauge.

As a result of the failure the normal servicing procedures scheduled to be carried out after 300–400 turbine hours running time were re-assessed to half that figure, 150–200 hours, and involved the following:

a. Dismantle and clean fuel injection nozzle
b. Examine combustion chamber
c. Examine compressor, wash out at every 3–4 examinations
d. Wash out heat exchanger

A Bristol–Paddington express hauled by No. 18000 passing Moreton Sidings, east of Didcot, on 22 September 1951; note the stump where the whistle was previously located. The engine appears to dwarf its train, being built to the maximum limit of the generous GWR loading gauge. Internally the engine was divided into a number of compartments, the dirtiest of these being the 'clean air' compartment, where air for the turbine was admitted. Externally too the engine appears none too clean. It was said a dog near Didcot could hear the engine coming for some distance, though the noise the engine emitted under power was no worse than a modern day HST set. Speed-wise, the maximum rating was 90 mph with the turbine designed to cut out if 92 mph was reached

J.F. Russell Smith/National Railway Museum

Interestingly, there was no requirement to clean the actual turbine blades which showed no signs of attracting any deposits.

Drivers and shed staff were also given new guidelines as to operating the engine:

1.   The turbine should never be started up and run under its own power for less than 15 minutes.

2.   When shutting down the turbine, the fuel control lever must be moved quickly from position 2, to position 0, without halting on position 1.

3.   At the same time, the flame in the combustion chamber should go out immediately and the driver should view the combustion chamber through the three inspection glasses to see that the flame is extinguished, and the exhaust from the roof should be clean and free from smoke or white fuel vapours (as the turbine runs down); at night after shutting down, observe for sparks from the roof.

4.   If it is noticed that smoke begins to form after the turbine has been shut down normally, *the turbine should be started up immediately and kept running under its own power for 15 minutes at the upper idling speed (position 'high').*

5.   If, despite the above measures, after the turbine has been shut down, smoke or sparks come from the roof, showing that there is burning in the heat exchanger, the turbine must be put into motion without ignition or fuel, and turned by means of the diesel engine auxiliary generator at 800–1,200 revs, for 15–20 minutes, in order to cool the plant down. In the meantime the Fireman should be sent to obtain the services of a mechanic, and according to the conditions at site, the following measures are to be taken:

If possible, the engine should be placed over a pit, the cover (painted red) over the turbine drain outlets underneath the engine, removed, also the heat exchanger inspection covers in the roof opened and water sprayed over the tubes.

The hose carried on the locomotive connected to a hydrant and the heat exchanger fire extinguishing pipe connection on the side of the engine and water supply turned on.

On 4, 6 and 11 September 1951 the engine worked the 3.30 p.m. down Paddington–Plymouth train which on each occasion was loaded to twelve coaches including the dynamometer car. Scheduled stops were at Taunton and Exeter. The usual return working of the 7.15 a.m. London train was used calling at Totnes, Newton Abbot, Teignmouth, Exeter, Taunton and Westbury. (There appears to be a degree of conflict over the actual dates of the dynamometer car trials, for in a letter dated 4 February 1952 covering failures of the engine during the previous months, the dynamometer car trials are reported as having taken place from 8 to 15 September. Another anomaly concerns 5 September when, according to the report, the engine failed to start at Old Oak due to a faulty rectifier valve in the flame indicator unit.)

The official BR report pertaining to the tests, No. W14, is of little use to the non-technical reader. A far more readable assessment of events appeared in a number of contemporary journals from which, by piecing together various snippets, it is possible to ascertain a number of facts relevant to the trials. These have been assimilated into the log on p. 51 which itself was published in the magazine *Diesel Railway Traction* for July 1952. No official reason for the tests is given although it may well have been partly due to the poor fuel and efficiency figures previously referred to.

Following the trials No. 18000 resumed normal working, although on 20 September records show the engine was declared a failure on reaching Paddington at 2.40 p.m. which necessitated running back to Old Oak on the diesel engine only. The cause was an electrical fault on the earthing of the ignition rod circuit and its associated contactor and was fully repaired the following day.

On 28 September Brown-Boveri wrote to BR suggesting that a boost device be fitted for short-term use to assist when climbing gradients. This was obviously based on the experience so far gained on the South Devon banks. 'It should be possible to draft some simple instructions for the benefit of the drivers to ensure the safe use of this "extra power device". Incorrect working might have serious consequences.' Presumably the latter comment is a reference to overheating of the traction motors.

Despite now running reasonably satisfactorily the usual evening duty for the engine was cancelled on 4 October 1951 in order to allow Mr Kind from Brown-Boveri to make certain adjustments to the generator excitation.

The engine was again out of service from 8 October until 16 November, although this period had been previously scheduled for the refitting of the modified train heating

Trains—Down. 3.30 p.m. Ex Paddington to Plymouth. Slipping 1 coach at Heywood Rd Jcn. and stopping at Taunton and Exeter.
Up. 7.15 a.m. Ex Plymouth to Paddington. Stopping at Totnes, Newton Abbot, Teignmouth, Dawlish, Exeter, Taunton and Westbury.

		1	3	2	4*
Run number	..	1	3	2	4*
Date		11.9.51	13.9.51	12.9.51	14.9.51
Direction		Down	Down	Up	Up
Weight of locomotive	.. Tons	119·2	119·2	119·2	119·2
Load and No. of vehicles—					
Paddington-Westbury	Tons tare/No. of vehicles	395 for 12	395 for 12	—	—
Westbury-Exeter	,,	359 for 11	359 for 11	—	—
Exeter-Plymouth N. Rd.	,,	239 for 7	239 for 7	—	—
Plymouth N. Rd.–Newton Abbot	,,	—	—	228 for 7	227 for 7
Newton Abbot-Exeter	,,	—	—	388 for 12	356 for 11
Exeter-Paddington	,,	—	—	388 for 12	386 for 12
Distance—Actual	.. Miles	225·2	225·2	225·2	153·2
Under power	,,	182·2	189·4	185·6	120·2
Ton miles—excluding loco.		78,000	78,000	82,400	53,600
Time—Booked running	.. Min.	259·0	259·0	275·0	—
Actual	,,	252·3	251·4	269·0	186·1
Overall (including stops)	,,	265·5	264·4	296·3	220·0
Actual less drifting and idling (under power)	,,	209·9	204·0	213·4	175·6
Average speed	.. m.p.h.	53·6	53·7	50·2	49·4
Work done	.. d.b.h.p.-hr.	2,520	2,824	2,621	2,135
Average d.b.h.p.		721	831	736	729
Average d.b. pull	.. Tons	2·25	2·59	2·46	2·47
Oil—Total used : Heavy	.. lb.	4,960	5,230	5,450	4,340
Light	,,	224	223	250	186
Total	,,	5,184	5,453	5,700	4,526
lb./d.b.h.p.-hour		2·05	1·93	2·17	2·12
Oil—Total used under power: Heavy	.. lb.	4,496	4,727	4,759	3,970
Light	,,	177	172	180	148
Total	,,	4,673	4,899	4,939	4,118

Oil rate section — each run shown as Overall total | Under power:

		Run 1 Overall	Run 1 Under power	Run 3 Overall	Run 3 Under power	Run 2 Overall	Run 2 Under power	Run 4 Overall	Run 4 Under power
Oil rate—Heavy	.. lb./hr.	1,121	1,282	1,210	1,350	1,102	1,337	1,181	1,353
Light	,,	50·6	50·6	50·6	50·6	50·6	50·6	50·6	50·6
Total	,,	1,176·6	1,332·6	1,260·6	1,400·6	1,152·6	1,387·6	1,231·6	1,403·6

		1	3	2	4*
Oil rate, drifting and standby, H & L—Total		550·6	550·6	550·6	550·6
Gross calorific value of fuel oil—Heavy	.. B.Th.U./lb.	18,530	18,580	18,680	18,740
Light	,,	19,610	19,590	19,530	19,490
Oil/mile	.. lb.	23·02	23·20	24·2	28·3
$\dfrac{\text{Work done at drawbar}}{\text{Total heavy fuel oil used}} \times \dfrac{100}{1}$	Per cent	6·95	7·42	6·56	6·68
$\dfrac{\text{Work done at drawbar}}{\text{Heavy fuel used under power}} \times \dfrac{100}{1}$	,,	7·67	8·20	7·51	7·29
$\dfrac{\text{Work done at drawbar}}{\text{Total heavy and light fuel oil used}} \times \dfrac{100}{1}$	,,	6·66	7·09	6·25	6·39
$\dfrac{\text{Work done at drawbar}}{\text{Total heavy and light fuel oil used under power}} \times \dfrac{100}{1}$	,,	7·40	7·91	7·22	7·02

(*) This test terminated at Savernake because of defect in dynamometer car

boiler. This item was to be replaced yet again at a later time. It was entirely due to the restrictions placed upon the effective sphere of operation by the inadequacies of the train heating boiler that involved the engine's use on the Paddington–Bristol services; the relatively short duration of running within the boiler's capabilities insofar as heating a twelve-coach train was concerned. It was a different matter however on a 4½- or 5-hour Plymouth schedule. Much of the problem was because of the limited quantity of water carried. (At the same time a recurring difficulty with the fuel pump(?) was finally resolved.)

The subject of train heating had by now also involved the operating department which had been requested to provide stock fitted with thermostatically controlled heaters whenever possible, the advantage of such stock being that once a set temperature had been reached there would be a reduced demand upon the train heating boiler. In addition a steam engine could heat the vehicles to the set temperature before the train's departure. Today such thermostatic equipment on coaching stock is of course normal, though at that time there were few vehicles so equipped and those that existed were allocated to the prestigious 'Riviera' and 'Torbay' services. Naturally then the Operating Superintendent was reluctant to give up these vehicles just to run behind No. 18000 and despite continued pressure for some months in 1951 it appears no special stock was used.

In connection with modifications to the train heating boiler a special trial run was arranged for 26 October, with the engine hauling twelve empty coaches, comprising a brake compo, ten thirds and another brake compo. An 'A' headcode was to be used with the run being to the following times:

An up test train on Goring troughs during 1950, with the Churchward dynamometer car coupled next to the engine. It had been announced in February 1950 that No. 18000 would work a four-hour Paddington to Plymouth service, similar to that revised shortly afterwards as the best timings for steam traction. (The 3.30 p.m. down train, later worked on a semi-regular basis, occupied a 4½-hour schedule.) Against these times it is rather unfair to attempt comparisons with 1989 schedules. An HST is able to complete the same run in considerably less than 3 hours although a number of essential criteria must be considered in such a comparison, including the power/weight ratios as well as improvements that have taken place to track and signalling

Maurice Earley/National Railway Museum

	Arr.	Pass.	Dep.
Swindon (Stratton Park)			11.58 a.m.
Wootton Bassett		12.09 p.m.	
Badminton		12.33	
Stoke Gifford	12.48	E	1.00
Filton Jct.		M1.02L	
Stapleton Road		1.07	
North Somerset Jct.	1.12		1.17
Bath Spa		1.44	
Chippenham		2.03	
Wootton Bassett		2.19	
Swindon (Stratton Park)	2.30.		

E = Engine examination

The programme for the run stated:

> The coaches to be berthed 30 minutes before the departure of the special train. A steam engine will be provided during this period for steam heating purposes.
>
> A clear road to be kept for the special train as far as possible but it should not be allowed to delay other passenger trains.
>
> If the test is successful, the Gas Turbine will run 'light' from Swindon to Old Oak Common at the following times;

G Headcode	Arr.	Pass.	Dep.
Swindon			5.23 p.m.
Steventon		5.50	
Foxall Jct.		ML	
Didcot		5.55	
Reading		6.17	
Maidenhead		6.32	
Slough		6.40	
Southall		6.53	
Friars Jct.		RL	
Old Oak Common	7.05		

The 1.50 p.m. (Saturdays only) Bristol–Paddington train at St Anne's Park on 2 September 1950. Some time later, on 15 December 1951, the broadcaster Raymond Baxter made the first live radio commentary for 'Children's Hour' from the footplate of No. 18000 when working a Plymouth–Paddington service between Reading and London. For the purpose a coach was specially fitted by the BBC with a roof aerial and transmitter. The train was met by Wynford Vaughan Thomas upon arrival at Paddington

R.J. Leonard. Courtesy Mr & Mrs R. Webber

With oil headlamps instead of route indicator discs, No. 18000 approaches Southcote Junction, Reading, heading west on a six-coach test train some time in 1950. For a time certain drivers trained on the engine saw themselves as superior to their colleagues and would not allow non-authorized men to enter the cab even for a brief look around

Maurice Earley/National Railway Museum

Unfortunately the timings for a run light to Old Oak were somewhat presumptuous as the changes made were not at this time totally successful and it was not until 17 November that the engine took up regular work between Paddington, Swindon and Bristol, remaining on this route through to the end of the year. The same timings and duties as previously were used.

For 16 November 1951 an interesting letter exists in the files as to a planned modification to the existing duties then scheduled to be worked by No. 18000. This involved plans for a service between Paddington and Cardiff although the correspondence referred mainly to ensuring the engine carried sufficient supplies of heavy fuel and water. It stated that the maximum distance the engine was able to run on one load of heavy fuel – 3 tons – as being approximately 240 miles. With only the limited re-fuelling points available, careful planning was thus necessary to ensure sufficient leeway was allowed for out of course delays such as permanent way slowings and signal checks. It is worth mentioning that even on the Paddington–Bristol runs this limited fuel capacity was sometimes an embarrassment, the engine having to have sufficient fuel on leaving Old Oak for the round trip. Former Locomotive Inspector Tony Tyler, who was then a fireman in the gas turbine link, recalls one occasion when due to delays the driver switched to a mixture of heavy and light fuel at Maidenhead on the way up to

No. 18000 seen departing from Swindon with a fine example of a Western signal gantry alongside
A.C. Sterndale

Paddington. With supplies of heavy oil totally exhausted at West Drayton, light fuel was used for the remainder of the journey.

Although slightly out of sequence at the present time it is known that around 1957 No. 18000 did work through the Severn Tunnel on empty stock from Bristol to Newport on just one occasion, originating as an extension of the 1.15 p.m. arrival from Bristol. The return was in time for the scheduled 4.15 p.m. to London. This is thought to have been the only time this occurred while it is alleged the fumes from the machine caused ill effects to some permanent way men working in the tunnel at the time.

The failure record of No. 18000 for the last weeks of 1951 shows a machine still plagued by minor defects although these were not always the engine's fault.

30.11.1951 Boiler feed pump failed, wiring to motor loose.

8.12.1951 General maintenance, cleaning compressor, heat exchanger.

9.12.1951 Changing combustion chamber lining.

10.12.1951 Changing combustion chamber lining.

11.12.1951 Engine returned to service on 6.35 p.m. service.

12.12.1951 Failed to work morning turn due to steam heating failure of fuelling point.

21.12.1951 Failed at Chippenham, diesel engine filter trouble.

22.12.1951 Repairs to diesel engine.

24.12.1951 Did not work evening turn due to convenience of staffing over Christmas period.

26.12.1951 Not working.

27.12.1951 Diesel engine failed at Swindon, fuel blockage.

Brown-Boveri had in the meanwhile found that by some relatively minor modifications to the main generator exciter panel the load haulage capabilities of the engine could be increased and the necessary materials were despatched to Swindon for 18 October. There then followed an amount of technical correspondence on the same subject, with the actual alterations being carried out at Old Oak Common by an electrical fitter from Swindon over the period 8–10 December 1951. Following static electrical tests, No. 18000 was then authorized to take 350 tons un-aided over the South Devon banks.

Despite what appears to be a depressing record, No. 18000 was about to enter into one of its most prolific periods in service, while for such a unique and, it must be said, complicated machine, it had stood up to its first complete calendar year in service reasonably well. The focus of attention at Swindon meanwhile now moved away towards the new Metropolitan Vickers gas turbine engine although No. 18000 would continue to give sterling service. To emphasize this the mileage run between 2 November 1951 and 14 June 1952 reached an average of no less than 312 miles for every day the engine was in service. It could only be hoped No. 18000 would continue to achieve such a high performance.

No. 18100

The Metropolitan Vickers Machine

Despite being ordered before the Brown-Boveri engine, No. 18100, the Metropolitan Vickers gas turbine, was the second of the two engines to take to the rails. Why this should have been the case is not completely clear although it appears that the builders were limited as to the time they had available for what involved much new research. Certainly Metropolitan Vickers approached the project fully aware of its implications, while its technical experience of turbines in a railway environment had previously involved the development of the steam turbine as fitted to the LMS Pacific No. 6202.

Erection of what was No. 18100 began some time around 1948 although, as referred to above, progress was at first painfully slow. So far as the actual turbine unit was concerned the design followed that already developed for use in a number of naval applications which in turn were based on the F2 aircraft jet propulsion unit. Often minor changes in design took place as the assembly of the engine proceeded. One of these alterations affected the external front end superstructure, early plans clearly showing a design with just two windows very similar in appearance to the SR diesel-electrics Nos. 10201 and 10202.

While full details on the building of No. 18100 are not unfortunately available some odd snippits have survived from BR files, including the fact that at Swindon the engine was referred to as an 0–6–6–0 'Leader'!

This lack of information is explained in two ways. Firstly, BR, by the terms of the agreement with regard to construction, was to leave the design work of the engine to Metropolitan Vickers. Secondly, the Metropolitan Vickers company no longer exists as a separate concern and, although its successors have been more than cooperative, full records do not always survive such upheavals.

Certainly BR was informed and consulted in a variety of areas, one of which was the choice of train heating boiler to be used. Three options were suggested; a 'Clarksons' – thimble tube, 'Sentinel' – inclined cross tube, or 'Spanner' – vertical tube, the latter type eventually being selected. Another set of correspondence concerned the proposed fuel tank filling time which the manufacturer had stated to be 2,000 gallons per hour. Swindon considered this to be excessive, as based on the 940 gallons of fuel estimated to be used on a run from Paddington to Plymouth, the engine would take twenty-eight minutes to be re-fuelled.

A more serious concern was voiced by Riddles in July 1948 in relation to the bogie design. With regard to this he states, '. . . we are frankly accepting these without too much enthusiasm . . .' An attempt was even made to substitute the Metropolitan Vickers bogie design with one similar to that used on the LMS diesel-electric No. 10000, but for an un-reported reason this was not proceeded with. Events would later prove Riddles' scepticism to have been well founded.

The brand-new No. 18100 outside the Manchester Trafford Park works of Metropolitan Vickers in late 1951. Shortly after the photograph was taken the engine was towed to Swindon and officially handed over to the Western Region. A total of four works plates were fitted, two at each end of the engine. The two circular portholes provided light in the engine compartment, with bulkheads at the rear of each cab, as well as amidships, enclosing the air intake louvres. Some of the louvres were dummies, provided to ensure visual symmetry on each side. The central bulkheads were intended to prevent the compressor swallowing air which might have been circulating in the large engine compartment and therefore could have become polluted or pre-heated. Also, it was possible to examine much of the equipment without danger from the powerful suction of the machine

In November 1950 the actual power unit was tested at the Trafford Park works of Metropolitan Vickers in Manchester with a number of BR representatives present. Here too, an interesting comment arises, for in the Swindon account of the visit there is a reference to, '. . . disappointment that the expected 3,500 hp was not developed although in every other way the unit was very satisfactory'. This is certainly strange as it has always been understood that No. 18100 was only ever intended as a 3,000 hp machine.

No doubt prompted by what they had witnessed, an approach was made by BR to Metropolitan Vickers to have the locomotive completed and ready for display at the Festival of Britain exhibition scheduled for March 1951. Metropolitan Vickers replied that this was unlikely. It transpired the only event of March 1951 to be reported concerning the new engine was when Swindon supplied, 'Six ash trays for use in the cabs of the gas turbine locomotive.'

Completion of No. 18100 was eventually achieved in the autumn of 1951 and a number of successful short trips were made within the confines of the Trafford Park works during November. A deliberate attempt appears to have been made to keep the

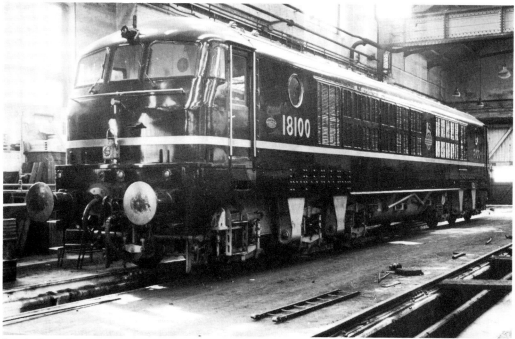

Inside Swindon works on 10 February 1952. In order to acquaint staff with the new engine a series of lectures was given on maintenance, while it is known that Metropolitan Vickers engineers travelled on a number of the trial trips, usually in the engine compartment. Stan French recalls that on more than one occasion the turbine 'blew out' due to fiddling by these travelling engineers
Les Elsey

engine out of the public eye at this time although a number of official photographs were taken. Following these preliminary tests No. 18100 was despatched to Swindon, leaving the Trafford Park works at 10.43 p.m. on 15 December.

For the journey south, the new engine was hauled dead in the middle of a mixed formation consisting of a steam locomotive – the number of which is not reported – passenger composite, goods brake van, No. 18100 and another goods brake van at the rear. The route taken was via Colnbrook West Junction, Sale, Altrincham, Knutsford, Middlewich and Crewe Gresty Lane, where a stop was made for a number of hours. It was also a slow trip as for the first five miles speed was restricted to 10 mph, increasing then to 20 mph and finally a maximum of 30 mph for the remainder of the journey. This was to allow bearings, etc. to 'bed-in'. After Crewe the route was via Market Drayton, Wellington, Cosford, Wolverhampton, Birmingham Snow Hill, Banbury, Oxford, Didcot, Steventon and finally Swindon. Arrival at the Wiltshire workshop was at 8 p.m. on 16 December and reputedly twenty minutes later than scheduled. Official records state the WR paid for the haulage of the engine from the manufacturers at a cost of £423 11s.

Meanwhile an amount of discussion had taken place behind the scenes as to the likely field of operation for the new engine, which was eventually decided by the Chief Civil Engineer to be the same as for the 'King' class. It was also decided to restrict initial use to the Paddington–Bristol line where, '. . . there are steam depots every few miles able to supply a replacement engine if required . . .' Clearly the Western Region had learnt from its earlier experiences.

At Swindon No. 18100 was taken straight into the works for inspection after which a number of trial trips were undertaken within the confines of the works sidings. Perhaps mindful of earlier experiences with No. 18000 there was no urgency to introduce the new engine to traffic and consequently No. 18100 spent the period 21 to 29 December 1951 in store in 'AE' shop at Swindon.

Following a return to work after Christmas, No. 18100 recommenced running in the works sidings while WR-type ATC was also installed. No troubles had so far been experienced and so, no doubt impressed by the engine, a main-line trial was arranged. This took place on Thursday 3 January 1952, running light engine between Swindon and Stoke Gifford. The trial was not without incident as official reports state the turbine had to be shut down four times during the return run to Swindon due to the fuel filter being blocked.

The day before this first main-line run a meeting had taken place at Swindon on 2 January to consider services suitable for working with the new engine. Four men were present, Messrs H.G. Kerry (Chairman) and R. Spencer representing the Motive Power Department, Mr W.A.L. Creighton from the Mechanical and Electrical Engineers Department and Inspector C.J. Pullen. The following minutes were recorded:

SUGGESTED TRIPS

First two weeks during preliminary runs:

11.15 a.m. Paddington to Bristol
 4.15 p.m. Bristol to Paddington

It was considered that this service would be more suitable than the 3.30 p.m. Paddington to Plymouth one day, returning with the 8.30 a.m. Plymouth to Paddington the next day for the following reasons:
a) There are Motive Power depots at frequent intervals along the road, and in the event of failure there would be no great difficulty in providing a steam engine.
b) It would be easier to manipulate one or two men to work the engines on a 'single home' turn than to find men to work 'double home'.
c) The 11.15 a.m. to Bristol and back would be convenient for Railway Executive or Chief Officers to ride, if required.

    After, say, two weeks on the Bristol run and engine performing satisfactorily, it was suggested that the engine could be rostered to work one of the following alternative schedules:

1.	12.15 a.m.	Newspaper	Paddington to Plymouth	5.00 a.m.
	8.30 a.m.	Passenger	Plymouth to Paddington	1.40 p.m.
	Mileage 462 per day			
2.	2.20 a.m.	Newspaper	Paddington to Bristol	MWF
	7.45 a.m.	Passenger	Bristol to Paddington	10.00 a.m.
	3.30 p.m.	Passenger	Paddington to Plymouth	MWF
	8.30 a.m.	Passenger	Plymouth to Paddington	1.40 p.m. TThS
	Miles averaging 352 per day			
3.	11.00 a.m.	Passenger	Paddington to Plymouth	M–F
	7.54 p.m.	Parcels	Plymouth to Paddington	2.20 a.m. M–F
	9.05 a.m.	Passenger	Paddington to Bristol	Sat
	1.50 p.m.	Passenger	Bristol to Paddington	4.30 p.m. Sat
	Mileage 462 per day M–F, 243 per Saturday			

Inside 'AE' shop at Swindon on 3 March 1952 and No. 18100 is being partly dismantled for inspection. Notice the air horns beneath the framing by the left-hand buffer. The following day the engine commenced trials between Swindon and Plymouth

If sufficient fuel can be made available for working Paddington to Reading and back and then to Plymouth it is suggested that after arrival at Paddington at 2.20 a.m. on suggestion No. 3 the engine can work the 4.30 a.m. Paddington to Reading and back then 11.00 a.m. Plymouth making a mileage of 535 per day.

With regard to link working it was suggested that initially there should be two turbine links, i.e. one of four men to work Brown-Boveri, one of eight men to work the Metro Vickers, as it is considered that the Brown-Boveri is more difficult to handle and more complicated to learn than the Metro Vickers. Later on the two links might be amalgamated into one link of twelve men. Such a link to be regarded as being on a par with the top Passenger Steam Link.

Drivers in a link immediately below these two links to have option as to whether they will progress with the Turbine or Steam link and men who opt for Turbine who prove unsuitable for such work to progress into No. 1 Steam Link.

Firemen to progress through both No. 1 links, the Turbine to be regarded as the senior of the two for their promotion.

Drivers Bert Jones, Walter Harris and possibly Percy Matthews in present No. 1 link know the Brown-Boveri and if they would transfer to the Turbine link this would allow the two senior men in present No. 2 Link who do not wish to work the turbine or are unsuitable for same to go immediately into the new No. 1 steam link. Seven or eight men from No. 2 plus Bill Pither and Arthur Gould who have gone back from No. 1 to present No. 3 Link plus Harris and Jones to form the Turbine Link.

By this arrangement we should lose the experience men in the present No. 3 Link have gained of the Brown-Boveri but it is gathered that apart from Pither and Gould there is only one capable of working on his own, i.e. Bert Lang; in any case it is hoped that Pither, Gould, Jones or Matthews would form the Brown-Boveri Link for a start.

By 14 January the engine was working additional trial trips; unfortunately on this particular day a failure is reported with a flash-over in the bus bars – electrical return or common feed equipment – which warranted seven days out of service. The cumulative mileage at this time was 524. Interestingly, official records refer to this incident having occurred in Avington Tunnel although this was probably a misprint for Alderton Tunnel on the Badminton line. It is unlikely that Swindon would be prepared to allow its new machine to wander too far from home at this early stage. (Unofficially Alderton Tunnel was sometimes known as Hullavington Tunnel.)

To rectify the defect the aluminium bus bar system which had been installed to carry current between main generator, traction motors and battery, etc. was replaced with conventional insulated conduit. Un-insulated aluminium had originally been used for reasons of weight-saving.

Despite the earlier experiences with No. 18000 the Press Department at Paddington arranged to show off its new acquisition at the London terminal on Tuesday 29 January 1952 with representatives from most of the leading newspapers, magazines and film media invited to attend. This time luck was on the side of the railway and No. 18100 was stabled next to the buffers on Platform 4 where it attracted an admiring audience.

No. 18100 at Ranelagh Bridge depot just outside Paddington on the morning of 29 January 1952, prior to the press inspection. A set of electric indicator lights together with a red tail lamp were provided at each end of the locomotive although these were rarely used on their own and instead recourse was made to oil lamps or headcode discs. Unusually no official views of the completed engine appear to have been taken at Swindon itself, although a number of detail photographs were taken of the various components. Of the three steam engines visible only one can be positively identified, No. 6975 *Capesthorne Hall*

British Railways

No. 18100 against the buffers of Platform 4 at Paddington with the Press in attendance, 29 January 1952. The press release from Paddington emphasized that this was the first British-built gas turbine and also the most powerful locomotive running on BR. (Presumably Paddington conveniently forgot the LNER 'Garrett' and LMS 'Duchess' class steam engines!)

Hulton Picture Company

PRESS RELEASE 29.1.1952
THE FIRST BRITISH-BUILT GAS TURBINE LOCOMOTIVE

The first British-built gas turbine locomotive has been delivered to British Railways by the designers and manufacturers, Messrs Metropolitan Vickers Electrical Company Ltd. of Manchester.

The locomotive, No. 18100, has a maximum tractive effort of 60,000 lb – sufficient to start the heaviest passenger train on the steepest gradient – a maximum speed of 90 mph and weighs 129 tons 10 cwt. It is 66 ft 9½ in long, 9 ft 0 in wide and 12 ft 10 in in height above rail level.

The construction of the locomotive is an experiment initiated by the Great Western Railway and carried forward by the Railway Executive under the direction of Mr R.A. Riddles, CBE, MIMechE, MILocoE. The financial and technical responsibility for the project is shared by British Railways and the manufacturers.

Whilst being suitable for use on any of the British Railways main lines, the new locomotive is primarily intended for work on the London to Plymouth route of the Western Region.

The morning of the Paddington press inspection and No. 18100 receives some minor attention alongside the platform. The engine would later disgrace itself by dislodging an amount of soot from the station roof onto the guests below! Interestingly there was no press trip at this time and the engine returned light to Swindon

The Keystone Collection

Of the 3,000 hp continuously available from the turbine, approximately 550 hp is taken up in transmission losses and in providing power to the auxiliary machines, thus giving a continuous output of 2,450 hp available at the rails for traction purposes, over the greater part of the range of operating speeds. The locomotive, will, therefore be the most powerful on British Railways.

Some idea of the capabilities of No. 18100, which uses the same fuel as is used by diesel locomotives and buses, can be obtained from the sustained speeds which could be achieved when hauling a load of approximately 650 tons, viz:

on level track	85 mph
up a 1 in 100 gradient	41 mph
up a 1 in 50 gradient	23 mph

To obtain the performance required six driving axles are necessary, to each of which is geared an electric motor, of the type used in ordinary electric locomotives. Each pair of motors is fed from one of the three main generators which are driven, through gearing, by the turbine.

The most interesting and novel feature of the locomotive is, of course, the gas turbine. This comprises three main components built together as a single unit. These components are a rotary compressor in which air is compressed to 60 lb per square inch, a combustion chamber in which the burning fuel oil heats air to 700 degrees centigrade (1,300 degrees Fahrenheit) and a turbine in which this intensely heated air develops 9,000 hp by its expansion.

The compressor, requiring 6,000 hp is driven by the turbine, leaving the balance of power of 3,000 hp available for driving the electric generators.

Temperatures of the order quoted are essential for good thermal efficiency, but they involve the use of special heat-resisting materials for the combustion chamber and turbine. In this machine, the thermal efficiency of which is 19% at full power, the special materials used are nickel and alloy steels containing nickel and chromium.

The turbine, reduction gear and electric generators are mounted on a

Driver Arthur Gould poses in the cab of No. 18100 at Paddington. As with the Brown-Boveri engine, the controls were laid out for right-hand drive and were similar to those on the EM1 class of electric engine which possessed Metropolitan Vickers electrical equipment. Notice the leather strap to the drop light in the driver's door

The Keystone Collection

bedplate as a single unit carried on three supporting points on the locomotive underframe.

The power plant and auxiliary equipment required for such purposes as train heating are also housed in the body of the locomotive, carried by means of suspension links on the two 6-wheel bogies. The flexibility of this arrangement is designed with the object of obtaining safe and comfortable running at all speeds.

At each end of the body is an enclosed driving cab so that there is no necessity to turn the locomotive round at terminal stations.

The case for using this type of locomotive in preference to steam traction rests mainly on economics from its higher efficiency and anticipated lower maintenance costs for equal work done.

In relation to diesel traction its case rests largely on operating economics. Furthermore, experience has shown so far, that in higher powers, gas turbines can be built with approximately half the weight and half the length of diesel locomotives of the same power.

Following the press inspection, fifty invited guests went on to a cocktail reception. Paddington was no doubt keen to play down the only untoward incident of the occasion when No. 18100, as had No. 18000 previously, dislodged an amount of soot from the cavernous roof of the station onto the waiting guests below. On a more serious note though, BR was distinctly concerned as to the effect the exhaust blast from the engine might have on some of its more delicate items of infrastructure and, in particular, smoke-plates fitted to bridges, etc. There is no official evidence to later confirm such a fear although privately a number of enthusiasts who monitored the engine's performance themselves expressed similar misgivings.

The comments as to the speed and load haulage capabilities are certainly of interest for at this time trials had certainly not taken place. The figures must have been gauged on the estimated performance although in practice they would later prove to be extremely accurate.

In the final paragraph of the press release the comment on the experience gained so far must be taken as a direct reference to No. 18000, yet as the reader will no doubt recall, 1951 could not really be regarded as an unqualified success for the earlier engine.

Following the press inspection No. 18100 returned light engine to Swindon and was noted passing Southall at a far higher speed than most steam engines achieved at this stage. Metropolitan Vickers had expressed a desire to see the locomotive operating both passenger and freight services as soon as possible although Swindon was understandably reluctant to do this until further trials had been carried out.

Accordingly a further meeting was held at Swindon on 12 February 1952 to decide upon the future test programme. Appropriately this took place following the return of a trial with the engine from Swindon to Badminton:

PRESENT

Mr W.A.L. Creighton	–	Western Region
Mr A.W.J. Dymond	–	Western Region
Mr Mundell	–	Western Region
Mr Pullen	–	Western Region (Part-time)
Mr F. Wyman	–	Metropolitan Vickers
Mr H. Kemp	–	Metropolitan Vickers
Mr J.H. Seager	–	Metropolitan Vickers
Mr J.K. Brown	–	Metropolitan Vickers
Mr G.R. Higgs	–	Metropolitan Vickers

The following tentative programme was discussed and it was agreed that arrangements would be made to follow it as closely as practicable:

During the next $2\frac{1}{2}$ weeks the setting and adjustment of the control equipment will be completed and the special run on 20 February for filming the locomotive will be made.

On 4 March the locomotive will haul 12 coaches from Swindon to Plymouth and back to Swindon.

On 6 March the locomotive will haul 18 coaches from Swindon to Plymouth and back to Swindon.

On 8 March the locomotive will haul 18 coaches from Swindon to Plymouth and on the 8th and 9th tests will be carried out with that train on the heavy gradients in the Newton Abbot district.

On 10 March the locomotive and train will return to Swindon.

The period from then till 22 March is allocated to certain modifications to be carried out in the shops, and during that period the body will be lifted off the bogies for a general inspection (the Railway will prepare the necessary lifting tackle in the meantime).

During the week following this any check tests and adjustments found necessary will be carried out and the locomotive will be offered for commercial traffic commencing 31 March.

For the first few weeks the commercial service will probably consist of working trains of 360 to 400 tons between Paddington and Bristol (stopping at Bath) to the following schedule;

Leave Paddington 11.15 a.m., arrive Bristol 1.32 p.m.
Leave Bristol 4.15 p.m., arrive Paddington 6.35 p.m.

Thereafter the locomotive will be transferred to the Plymouth route and the programme will probably be as follows;

11.00 a.m. Paddington to Plymouth (arrive 4.35 p.m.)
7.52 p.m. Plymouth to Paddington, followed by a round trip Paddington to Reading, daily from Monday to Friday
9.05 a.m. Paddington to Bristol
1.50 p.m. Bristol to Paddington on Saturdays

On that service the train weight to Plymouth will probably be about 500 tons, the weekday mileage about 535 miles and the Saturday mileage about 243 miles.

Locomotive Riding

The locomotive riding was discussed in some detail and general satisfaction with it was expressed. It was agreed that a final assessment could not be made until the effect of tread and flange wear could be observed.

Train Performance

The Railway proposes to assess the locomotive's capabilities in the following terms:
a) What is the best timing for hauling a 500 ton train to Newton Abbot and 350 tons from Newton Abbot to Plymouth? [Note: The original document refers to 500 tons to Plymouth and 350 tons thence to Penzance. These entries are however crossed out.]

b) What is the maximum train weight on the present steam schedule? [A statement showing train loads and speeds for the Summer of 1952 compared with the summer of 1939 is given in Appendix I.]

To assist them in these assessments we agreed to send to Mr Seager the run curves which we have already carried out on the basis of 3,500 hp available from the turbine. [1]

Braking

After considerable discussion it was agreed that;

a) we would fit a vacuum chamber release valve in each driving cab in a location out of reach of the driver's normal driving position.

b) we will design and reconstruct the driver's vacuum brake valve push button in the form of a trigger grip.

c) we shall take the operating circuit for the locomotive brake cylinder cut-out valve from a special 'essential services' circuit independently fused from the battery.

Mr Pullen agreed that these measures would meet his criticisms of the present arrangement and he undertook to instruct the drivers that the vacuum chamber release valves are to be used only for their designed function and not as a service means of brake control.

We informed the Railway that we were still dissatisfied with the proportionality obtained between the vacuum brake and the corresponding application of the locomotive brake and that we had arranged with the Westinghouse Brake Co. to supply new relay valves of the piston ring type to replace the existing 'Gaco' packed type which should not have been used in this application. It is expected that they will greatly improve the locomotive brake application at small vacuum reductions.

We said that we had been given to understand that there was some criticism of the failure of the locomotive brake (and the vacuum brake) to respond adequately to the operation of the ATC equipment. We also pointed out the incompatibility of sensitive response and fast brake release, except with the addition of more equipment.

Mr Dymond confirmed the information we had already been given by the Railway that any application of the brake by the ATC equipment was entirely incidental to its prime function of giving a warning. He also explained that when full effect had been given to British Railways' standardisation plans, there would be little or no brake application from ATC on any of their trains. [This of course is totally at variance with the ATC/A'''S principle and could well be an accidental misprint.]

We referred to our letter of 5 December last on the subject of parted couplings protection. Mr Creighton said that the letter would be replied to agreeing with our recommendations. [Note: neither the original correspondence nor its reply have been located. Pencilled in against this paragraph in the report is the word 'No'.]

---

1. Official records are very clear on the fact that the Metropolitan Vickers engine was rated at only 3,000 hp and not the 3,500 hp stated. This error has been perpetuated in the past although contemporary technical journals state it would be possible to upgrade the turbine to produce the higher figure by means of exchanging the turbine blades with those having a differing profile. There is no evidence to suggest this modification was ever carried out.

Locomotive Weight

It was agreed that the last weighing carried out at Swindon would be regarded as the official weight of the locomotive. The relative figures were as follows and were based on approximately 980 gallons of fuel and 600 gallons of water in the tanks, sand boxes almost full, and the boiler part filled.

The total weight is 130 tons 2 cwt made up as follows:

No. 1 End	T.	Cwt	T.	Cwt	T.	Cwt
	10	18	10	16	10	15
	10	10	10	14	10	12
No. 2 End	T.	Cwt	T.	Cwt	T.	Cwt
	11	1	10	14	11	0
	10	16	11	6	11	0

Boiler

The Railway was anxious to get experience with the boiler soon and Mr Kemp explained that it would be working on trial runs commencing from Monday next. It will also be in use on the running schedules commencing 4 March.

Turbine Exhaust Pressures and Temperatures

We gave a verbal reply to the enquiry which the Railway had addressed to us on 5.2.1952, as far as the conditions at roof level are concerned. For the conditions above roof level Mr Kemp will arrange to make measurements at turbine idling speed. We shall then give a written reply to the whole enquiry.

In the meantime, it would appear that the pressures obtained in service will cause no damage to the smoke plates.

Cab Light

After some discussion on the circuit feeding the cab light from the battery, it was agreed to leave the matter to be settled between the Railway engineers and our engineers on site.

Lubrication Chart

We agreed that, in line with the Railway's request, we would prepare a lubrication chart for the locomotive, and that it would be cross referenced with the schedule of lubricants already submitted.

Spares

We agreed to submit a schedule of the spares which we have manufactured for this locomotive but are retaining here.

The document was signed on behalf of the Traction Projects Engineering Dept. of Metropolitan Vickers.

Unfortunately the day's filming on 20 February was marred by a slight problem when a flat battery caused a delayed start to the work. The cumulative mileage at this time is reported as 1,250. Further information on the filming is regretfully not given.

Following on from the 20th, No. 18100 spent the last five days of February 1952 operating further trials from Swindon, for which full details are available:

		Miles	Actual running time
25.2.1952	Swindon Factory to Swindon Jct. (light)	1	10
	Swindon Jct. to Badminton (Empty Stock)	23	1.02
	Three trips Badminton to Little Somerford and return	60	1.38
	Badminton to Swindon Jct. (Empty Stock)	23	30
	Swindon Jct. to Swindon Factory (light)	1	20
		108	3.40

Total engine time: 6 hrs 30 mins

		Miles	Actual running time
26.2.1952	Swindon Factory to Swindon Jct. (light)	1	10
	Swindon Jct. to Badminton (Empty Stock)	23	34
	Two trips Badminton to Little Somerford and return	40	1.04
	Badminton to Swindon Jct. (Empty Stock)	23	27
	Swindon Jct. to Swindon Factory (light)	1	20
		88	2.35

Total engine time: 5 hrs 25 mins

		Miles	Actual running time
27.2.1952	Swindon Factory to Swindon Jct. (light)	1	5
	Swindon Jct. to Badminton (Empty Stock)	23	30
	Three trips Badminton to Little Somerford and return	60	1.38
	Badminton to Swindon Jct. (Empty Stock)	23	25
	Swindon Jct. to Swindon Factory (light)	1	25
		108	3.03

Total engine time: 6 hrs 55 mins

		Miles	Actual running time
28.2.1952	Swindon Factory to Swindon Jct. (light)	1	5
	Swindon Jct. to Badminton (Empty Stock)	23	38
	Two trips Badminton to Little Somerford and return	40	1.03
	Badminton to Swindon Jct. (Empty Stock)	23	25
	Swindon Jct. to Swindon Factory (light)	1	20
		88	2.41

Total engine time: 6 hrs 10 mins

29.2.1952	Swindon Factory to Swindon Jct. (light)				1		10
	Swindon Jct. to Swindon Jct. out via Box				80		2.00
	Home via Badminton						
	Swindon Jct. to Swindon Factory				1		10
					82		2.20

Total engine time: 4 hrs 10 mins

No problems were reported as a result of the runs although two points emerge very clearly from the week's trials. The first was that there was no attempt made at speed trials at this time and the second that the reliability of the engine was such that the planned tests for March could go ahead. Indeed the trials of March 1952 are the next confirmed moves recorded for the engine, although it is known that on 1 and 2 March No. 18100 was resident in 'AE' shop at Swindon.

Based on the previous reliability of the engine it may be reasonable to assume that the Plymouth route trials with No. 18100 commenced as scheduled on 4 March 1952. From the present writer's point of view the intention of this book is naturally to provide an as accurate record as possible of the gas turbines and it is therefore a matter of regret that an assumption as to the start of the trials has to be made. The information though is given on the basis that no evidence has been found to contradict such a statement.

Accordingly then on 4 March, No. 18100 left Swindon at the head of twelve coaches, destined for Plymouth. Two days later a seventeen-coach train of 532 tons was taken over the same route. On both occasions no difficulties were reported. Speeds of up to 85 mph were recorded. Fortunately a log of the run of 6 March has survived:

6 March 1952
6.45 a.m. Empty Stock, Swindon to Plymouth via Reading
Drivers; Pither and Wilton
Weather; heavy rain

Miles from Swindon			Booked times		Actual times		Remarks
m.	c.		arr.	dep.	arr.	dep.	
		Swindon Rodbourne Lane		6.45		6.45	
21	31	Steventon	7.12		7.13		
40	75	Reading West	7.38	7.39	7.34	7.42	Gain by loco
70	30	Bedwyn	8.14		8.12		Gain by loco
98	42	Heywood Road	8.44		8.40		Gain by loco
119	25	Castle Cary	9.10		9.04		Gain by loco
146	69	Taunton	9.38		9.30		Gain by loco
177	50	Exeter	10.12		10.09		Gain by loco
197	65	Newton Abbot	10.37		10.33		Gain by loco
206	43	Totnes	10.52		10.49		Gain by loco
213	32	Brent	11.05		11.01		Gain by loco
229	54	Plymouth	11.30		11.25		Gain by loco

The first time No. 18100 visited Plymouth, 4 March 1952, and seen entering North Road at the head of a twelve-coach train which had been worked from Swindon, via Reading and Westbury. In charge of the engine were drivers Pither and Wilton. Evidently the railway 'grape-vine' was working well judging by the number of observers. Unofficially it was said the engine successfully took a train of twenty-three sleeping cars from a dead stand on Hemerdon Bank and passed over the top at 30–35 mph

Maurice Dart

No. 18100 comes off its train at the west end of Plymouth North Road station prior to running back to Laira for servicing on 4 March 1952. No. 1006 *County of Cornwall* is alongside, while the station-master, Mr G. Anthony, can be seen stepping onto the board crossing

Maurice Dart

Miles from Swindon m. c.		Booked times arr.	dep.	Actual times arr.	dep.	Remarks
	Plymouth	2.57		2.57		
6 56	Hemerdon	3.13		3.17		Flood water at Plympton Bridge
16 22	Brent	3.26		3.31		Loss by loco
23 11	Totnes	3.35		3.29		Gain by loco
31 70	Newton Abbot	3.49		3.55		ROS Aller Jct.
52 04	Exeter	4.14		4.20		
82 64	Taunton	4.49		4.53		ROS Taunton
110 28	Castle Cary	5.16		5.18		
159 23	Bedwyn	6.20		6.11		Gain by loco
188 59	Reading West	6.55	6.56	6.46	6.50	
204 76	Didcot	7.19		7.10		
229 10	Swindon	7.46		7.37		
229 54	Swindon Rodbourne Lane	7.48		7.43		

The timings were recorded by an observer from Swindon who was on board the train and although no other information of the run other than that reproduced is given, it would certainly appear that No. 18100 was capable of substantial improvement on the schedule laid down. The possible exception to this was on the climb up Hemerdon on the return journey which would be mirrored in the load trials a few days later.

The actual load trials then took place from Plymouth on Sunday 9 March, with special instructions issued to the various signal-boxes concerned as to the working of the train. A report of the day's event was written the following day which is worth quoting in full:

Five trials were held, two in the morning and three in the afternoon; on the first trial 14 coaches were taken out of Millbay station brought to a stand at Plympton Up Starting Signal and restarted from this point and again brought to a stand at the Telephone Box at the middle of the incline and again restarted. At this second restarting, two or three abortive efforts were made and on each of these the overload switches on the Traction Motors came out, eventually however, the train was successfully restarted and taken to the top of the bank.

While the coaches and engine were being remarshalled for the second trip with 17 coaches the setting of the overload relays for the Traction Motors was increased from approximately 1,150 amps to 1,400 amps, at this new setting the 17 coaches were taken into the bank from Tavistock Junction, again stopped at Plympton and subsequently the Telephone Box, at both of which points the engine restarted the train without any difficulty whatsoever. After lunch another run with 17 coaches was made straight from Millbay Station to Hemerdon Box, stopping at North Road Station. Owing to a check at Plympton, however, the purpose of the trial was defeated as it was intended to take the time passing Hemerdon Box from starting at North Road. On the fourth trip 18 coaches were taken from Tavistock Junction, stopped at Plympton and again at the Telephone Box and from each of these places a restart was made with conspicuous ease. On the fifth and final trip the 18 coaches were again taken from Tavistock Junction to Hemerdon Box without stopping, the speed passing Plympton Box was approximately 40 mph and the time of the ascent from Plympton Box to Hemerdon Box was 8 minutes, the minimum speed on the bank being 15 mph rising to 18 mph at the summit.

The weights of the train respectively were;

14 coaches – 478 tons

17 coaches – 577 tons

18 coaches – 609 tons

The weather was dry throughout.

The report also makes mention of a number of checks which were made in order to check the condition of the couplings both before and after the tests, one elongated link being subsequently found. This had lengthened by as much as $\frac{9}{16}$ in, the component later being forwarded to Swindon for examination. (In the summer of 1953 a series of load trials took place between Stoke Gifford and Reading in which a 'King' class steam engine hauled trains of twenty-three and twenty-five coaches. It would be interesting to know if similar coupling difficulties occurred on these tests. It should also be mentioned that at an unknown date, although thought to be around this time, there was a gradual change from the previous standard 56 lb GWR coupling to a heavier, and therefore stronger, 78 lb type. Little further information is available on this point.)

Although not confirmed from official reports the *Railway Observer* reported a further test run involving No. 18100 from Bristol to Birmingham comprising a trailing load made up mainly of restaurant and kitchen coaches. No date for this run is given; neither is it clear which route, GWR or LMS, was used.

After such success it was only a matter of time before No. 18100 was handed over to the Operating Department for normal running and accordingly, following the scheduled works visit planned to start on 22 March 1952, arrangements were made to work the engine to Old Oak depot. Evidently this was arranged for 31 March 1952 but the engine failed to start at Swindon, where examination showed the burner isolation valve had failed to close properly. The result was that the combustion chamber was flooded with fuel. Records show the total mileage at this time as being 3,346.

It was a simple matter to resolve the problem, so just three days later on 2 April, No. 18100 worked a stock train of ten restaurant and kitchen cars from Swindon, arriving at Old Oak at 6.10 p.m. (A correspondent's report in *Trains Illustrated* for June 1952 also has the engine working a trial to Wolverhampton on 1 April 1952 although this is not confirmed elsewhere.)

The first public passenger train worked by the engine was on 4 April 1952, comprising the 11.15 a.m. Paddington–Bristol service returning to London on the 4.15 p.m. up working.[2] Again no difficulties were encountered although No. 18100 was not rostered for passenger work again immediately in order that time could be spent on crew training. In this latter guise No. 18100 next operated on 16 and 17 April when it worked a twelve-coach empty stock train from Paddington to Plymouth. The formation included a restaurant car, with an observation saloon at the rear. Departure time from Paddington was 9.30 a.m. with a return at 7.33 p.m. daily.

---

2. Chris Leigh, in what is probably the best account of the gas turbines previously published, 'The Western's "Big Blow"', (*Steam Days*, Nos. 2 and 3, 1986), quotes the engine as having worked an alternative duty roster for the beginning of April 1952, with the source of his information stated as the *Railway Observer*. A study of this publication however reveals a different duty and accordingly this chapter contains references from the original source material. Information as to duties for April 1952 is taken from the *Journal of the Inst. of Loco. Engineers* for the same period.

No. 18100 was formally handed over to the Motive Power Department on 18 April 1952 and just six days later, on 24 April, was in charge of the up 'Bristolian' express from Bristol to Paddington, seen here passing over Goring troughs. At this time the engine was insured by BR against accident or damage for an annual premium of £250. Of the 9,000 hp produced by the gas turbine, 6,000 hp was absorbed by the compression and a further 550 hp in transmission and auxiliary equipment. This left approximately 2,450 hp available at the wheels, equal to an overall thermal efficiency of 19 per cent.

A.C. Cawston/National Railway Museum

Officially No. 18100 was handed over to the Motive Power Department the following day, 18 April, up to which time £4,968 18s. 8d. had been spent on repairs and modifications. On 20 April the engine was noted as being out of service in the repair shop at Old Oak. No reference is found of a defect having occurred around this time and so it may be concluded that the visit was for planned maintenance.

Shortly afterwards No. 18100 entered regular passenger service between Paddington and Bristol on the 'Bristolian' and 'Merchant Venturer' trains. It was not to be a long spell in revenue-earning operation for on 19 May the first failure on a public train occurred when, with a cumulative mileage of 12,895, the engine failed at Ladbroke Grove due to a faulty control circuit-coil in the output regulator. One day was sufficient to effect repairs.

Public workings were then resumed on the Paddington–Bristol route although on 31 May the turbine failed to start at Bath Road depot in time for the return working to Paddington. The fault, which was not defined, was resolved when the engine was successfully started at 3.40 p.m., with the engine then proceeding light to Swindon via

Engine-changing at Bristol, with No. 18100 being replaced at the head of the 'Merchant Venturer' by No. 7813 *Freshford Manor*. The steam engine was provided to work the train the last few miles from Temple Meads to Weston-super-Mare. Overall No. 18100 was a generally reliable machine although an official BR report admits that, 'The maintenance and running of the locomotive has been supervised by Metropolitan Vickers Engineers and there is no doubt that their presence has prevented a number of breakdowns which otherwise might have caused delays or stoppages'

Adrian Vaughan Collection

Bristol Temple Meads, 31 May 1952, on which day No. 18100 failed to start in time for its regular duty on the 4.15 p.m. up 'Bristolian'. The engine was successfully started a little later and is seen about to run light to Swindon where it took over its scheduled duty

T.E. Williams/National Railway Museum

No. 18100 alongside the platform at Bristol Temple Meads, 31 May 1952, after arrival from Paddington. The uniform worn by the schoolboys is a particular memory to all of us who were once forced to endure wearing a cap! Notice that windscreen wipers were provided at the windows of both the driver and fireman on this engine. By this time Swindon had discovered small cracks in certain areas of the bogie frames although the matter was being kept under wraps for the time being. In the background are an early series 44xx tank and 10xx 'County' 4–6–0
T.E. Williams/National Railway Museum

Badminton where it took over its scheduled train from the former station. In addition to the service trains referred to, official reports state that there was a number of additional trial and demonstration runs around the same time although dates are not given. These are thought to have involved a variety of destinations including Bristol, Plymouth and Wolverhampton. The trial to Wolverhampton is known to have been a train of thirteen bogie vehicles, mainly restaurant cars.

On 5 June 1952 a serious problem showed up while No. 18100 was under examination at Old Oak, this time when a lubricating oil pipe feeding one of the main bearings of the turbine fractured. As the amount of dismantling necessary to correct this was considerable it was decided to anticipate a projected week's stoppage in the shop by a few days and the engine was accordingly withdrawn from service temporarily.

The late A.J. Dymond of Swindon in his paper, 'Operating Experiences with Two Gas Turbine Locomotives' – Paper No. 521 (1953) – *Journal of the Inst. of Loco. Engineers*, quotes the following as the reasons for the withdrawal: 'The intention to withdraw the engine for a week arose from the desire to carry out simultaneously some modifications to the exhaust trunking, the motor traction gear cases, and the main side frames of the bogies. None of these modifications was the result of any serious defect but each was deemed necessary in the endeavour to secure the maximum degree of reliability . . .' The cumulative mileage at this time was 16,313.

Pictured at speed near Ruscombe, just east of Twyford, with the 11.15 a.m. Paddington–Weston-super-Mare express, 'The Merchant Venturer', due in at Bristol at 1.28 p.m. and stopping *en route* at Bath. Some crews experienced difficulty in not running ahead of schedule with No. 18100 while from logs of runs reproduced both in this book and in various contemporary railway periodicals, it was obvious the engine could easily have managed the pre-war 105-minute 'Bristolian' timings with a standard eleven-coach load instead of the shortened seven-coach train. Several men involved with the engine felt that it was never tested to its limit and that it was on a par with today's HST sets with regard to power. Speed-wise an unofficial 100 mph was recorded near Dauntsey

J.F. Russell-Smith/National Railway Museum

It would be perfectly understandable if at this stage the reader were to form the conclusion that No. 18100 was a basically successful machine. But behind the scenes the first problems had occurred that would eventually be taken into consideration with regard to the future of the engine. These involved problems with the bogies and showed up as one or two small fatigue cracks on the inside of the main frame plate bottom flanges. These were first identified towards the end of May 1952 and at the time of a routine examination. Matters were corrected by welding in the corners at the bottom of the flanges where they joined the bottom flange of the vertical cross-stiffeners. Understandably Mr Dymond was not prepared to divulge these problems in detail at the time.

Other than a scheduled test run from the works to Badminton on 18 June, which was cancelled at Swindon station due to the turbine stalling, a return to regular traffic did not take place until 25 June. The following day however, another turbine stall occurred, this time at Paddington shortly before No. 18100 was due to leave at the head of the

'Merchant Venturer' express. The control log for the period reports the train as three minutes late in departing. Cumulative mileage at this time was 17,251 miles.

Regular working then continued until 12 July, with the following day spent out of service. Certainly at this stage there was no reason to suspect anything further was amiss and so on 14 July No. 18100 was rostered for a double return trip to Bristol, this consisting of the 2.30 a.m. down and 7.45 a.m. up trains as well as the down 'Merchant Venturer' and up 'Bristolian' trains. Similar duties followed which related to some 2,900 miles weekly.

A further stall took place at Paddington on 31 July, again at the head of the 'Merchant Venturer' express. As before three minutes were recorded against the engine.

Such problems were evidently insufficient to mar the reputation of the engine in the eyes of the Traffic Department and accordingly plans were made to fit the engine into a link allowing for a daily return trip to Plymouth. The last Bristol duty was worked on 2 August after which two days were spent out of service. The Plymouth turn commenced on 5 August with the 11.00 a.m. down train, returning on the 7.04 p.m. up train (3.45 p.m. ex-Penzance) and due in at Paddington at 2.00 a.m. Saturdays involved working the down 'Merchant Venturer' from Paddington to Bristol, returning with the 2.57 p.m. up duty. As before Sunday was for scheduled maintenance.

This arrangement continued until 23 August when a further broken oil pipe, this time on the fuel supply, was diagnosed just before leaving Paddington. The fault was corrected with one day out of use. Interestingly another former locomotive inspector, Stan French, who was at the time a 'fireman' rostered to the turbine, recalls similar faults having occurred on the road while running. On one occasion Stan had to spend part of the journey with his finger covering a hole in another fuel pipe!

The same period of working to Plymouth was interrupted a second time on 28 August at the more inconvenient location of Tigley incline between Totnes and Brent. This time a 'faulty control' was to blame which necessitated the presence of a banking engine to assist No. 18100 to a fifty-minutes' late arrival in Plymouth. Other than a recorded mileage at the time of 37,626 no other details are given as to any time spent out of service and it may be assumed that the defect was rectified at Laira.

How long it was originally intended to keep the engine working to Plymouth is not recorded although in the event the duty was dramatically curtailed as from 9 September when a flash-over occurred on the turbine starting contactor panel while the engine was in Somerton Tunnel between Castle Cary and Taunton. A small fire in the electrical components followed although this was quickly extinguished by the crew.

No. 18100 was then towed to Swindon, although it is thought that it didn't arrive until 13 September. Repairs involved considerable renewal of the wiring together with components in the control gear. During the stoppage the bearings at the pinion ends of the traction motors were changed from oil to grease lubrication. This was necessary as it had been found the oiling system required fairly considerable replenishment due to persistent loss of lubricant. Records show the mileage at this time was 42,021, with 1,237 turbine hours run. Six weeks were spent out of service and No. 18100 was not ready to resume work until 26 October.

At the same time as the electrical fault was being dealt with a number of other modifications and changes were carried out to the traction motor bearings as well as the installation of an additional fuel tank and associated fuel pump.

The inclusion of the last two named items is of particular interest at this stage, for up to this time there is no reference in any document to any shortfall in fuel capacity. Certainly later on it is well known that one of the significant features in the premature demise of the engine was its excessive fuel consumption, so this measure may be taken

No. 18100 rounding the curve near Teignmouth between Exeter and Newton Abbot *en route* to Plymouth at the head of a twelve-coach train. To cover for emergencies a most comprehensive set of tools was carried on the engine. Its train heating boiler was somewhat more reliable than that of its sister engine No. 18000, although the men recall having to light it with a device similar to a Roman candle. According to the crews the riding of the machine was not as good as the Brown-Boveri engine

Colin Marsden Collection

as a reference to the problem. As will also be recalled the underslung tanks of the main frame held fuel and water respectively – the latter for the train heating boiler. It is not clear if the additional fuel capacity at this stage referred to a conversion of both tanks to hold fuel as was allowed for on the original plans, although this would appear unlikely. The most likely location for this additional fuel tank was in part of the engine room.

According to the movement log for 1952, No. 18100 was returned to service on 27 October, although it is known that at least one trial run had occurred during the latter stages of the Swindon repair. This was on the 22 October when the engine worked to Badminton (presumably from Swindon) and a faulty starting valve and weak battery were noted.

Neither was the first day back in service, 27 October, particularly successful, for at Paddington the turbine shut down twice due to a faulty control, although the engine was able to undertake its planned turn on the down 'Merchant Venturer' and up 'Bristolian'. This single return duty to Bristol continued for four days until 31 October when the engine was stopped in preparation for a further series of trials on the South Devon banks.

From 3 to 22 November 1952, No. 18100 was reported as being based at Laira and working 'heavy trains' between Plymouth and Newton Abbot. (A correspondent in *Trains Illustrated* for December 1952 reports the engine working the 11.00 a.m. Paddington to Plymouth on 1 November 1952. Although this is at odds with official information it may have been the means utilized to deliver the locomotive to Plymouth in anticipation of the forthcoming tests.) These trials involved two return workings daily, the 11.10 a.m. and 3.45 p.m. up services, returning with the 1.12 p.m. and 5.40 p.m. respectively. All were normal service trains worked by steam before and after Newton Abbot and Plymouth and the trains for No. 18100 were specially strengthened to between fifteen and seventeen coaches. On one occasion the formation included a six-coach ex-Southern set which still sported its pre-nationalization green livery. No difficulties with haulage were reported although perhaps understandably the train heating boiler was taxed beyond its limit. The operation of such lengthy trains required slow stops at the intermediate stations in order to bring the correct coaches in line with the platforms.

Logs from certain runs appeared in the *Journal of the Stephenson Locomotive Society* for December 1958 in an article by P.W.B. Semmens:

Train		8.00 a.m. Penzance–Paddington					12.00 noon Penzance–Crewe					
Date:		18.11.1952		19.11.1952			18.11.1952		19.11.1952			
No. of vehicles		15		17			16		16			
Load tons tare/gross		493/530		556/590			465/500		469/505			
	Dist. Miles	Sched. Min	m.s	mph	m.s	mph	Dist. Miles	Sched. Min	m.s	mph	m.s	mph
PLYMOUTH N Rd.	0.0	0	0.00	–	0.00	–	0.0	0	0.00	–	0.00	–
Lipson Jct.	1.5	4	3.56	41	4.32	42	1.5	4	4.28	40	4.01	41
Tavistock Jct.	2.8	–	5.44	45	6.21	46	2.8	–	6.19	43	5.49	43
Plympton	4.0	–	7.02	51	7.40	51	4.0	–	7.41	48	7.13	47
Hemerdon	6.7	15	13.32	16	13.58	18	6.7	15	13.11	22	13.17	20
Cornwood	8.4	–	16.06	45	16.27	47	8.4	–	15.26	51	15.42	48
Ivybridge	10.8	–	19.11	51	19.26	54	10.8	–	18.09	55	18.38	53
Wrangaton	14.1	–	23.07	48	23.21	47	14.1	–	22.00	49	22.33	48
		Sig. stop										
Brent	16.3	30	29.05	–	27.06	–	16.3	28½	24.40	43	25.10	51
Rattery	2.3	–	4.31	49	4.10	54	18.6	31	27.40	47	28.02	49
TOTNES	6.9	11	10.09	–	10.50	–	23.1	37	32.50	52	33.29	47
Milepost 219¾	3.1	–	6.04	42	5.16	47	26.2	–	36.53	49	37.33	45
Dainton	4.8	–	9.49	17	8.06	23	28.0	–	39.36	26	40.24	25
Aller Jct.	7.6	–	14.27	–	12.17	–	30.8	–	43.37	45	44.32	38
									Sig. slight			
NEWTON ABBOT	8.7	16	16.44	–	15.28	–	31.9	51	45.55	–	48.00	–
Net time Plymouth–Brent (mins):			27		27							
Net time Plymouth–Newton Abbot (mins):									45.00		45¾	

Date:				18.11.1952		19.11.1952	
No. of vehicles				15		11	
Load tons tare/gross				491/520		341/355	
	Dist. Miles	Sched. Min		m.s	mph	m.s	mph
NEWTON ABBOT	0.0	0		0.00	–	0.00	–
Aller Jct.	1.1	–		2.58	35/45	2.50	39/48

Driver Arthur Gould and Chief Locomotive Inspector Charlie Pullen alongside the Metropolitan Vickers gas turbine. In order to assist the maintenance staff working on the gas turbines, the fuel pipes of both were colour-coded, with heavy fuel identified as red and white, light fuel red and blue and common pipes blue and white, all in bands every 4–6 in. The engine was fitted with Western Region ATC and two air horns. The latter items were located underneath the buffer beams

Kenneth Leech

	Miles	Min	m.s	mph	m.s	mph
Dainton	3.9	–	8.03	23	7.02	32
TOTNES	8.7	16	15.27	–	14.20	–
Tigley	2.7	–	7.22	26	6.13	31
Rattery	4.6	11½	10.50	36	9.05	43
Brent	6.9	15	13.52	51	11.50	54
Wrangaton	9.1	–	16.34	47	14.27	49
Ivybridge	12.4	–	20.21	43	18.28	42
Cornwood	14.8	–	23.38	50	21.44	51
Hemerdon	16.4	30	25.32	52	23.43	48
Plympton	19.1	–	28.12	64/54	26.30	60/54
Tavistock Jct.	20.3	–	29.25	41	27.41	40
Lipson Jct.	21.6	38	31.36	31	29.46	37
			pws		pws	
PLYMOUTH N Rd.	23.1	43	36.04	–	34.41	–

It is not clear if these timings were from official statistics although what is known is that yet again the dynamometer car was not used. Indeed this lack of official data on what were clearly important load trials is puzzling – No. 18100 was destined *never* to have a proper dynamometer car trial although documents refer to these being planned for the autumn of 1953. It was almost as if BR was playing at appeasement to Metropolitan Vickers and a decision as to the future of No. 18100 had already been made.

The end of 1952 saw No. 18100 back at work on normal revenue-earning duties, commencing on 23 November. They were also some of the most demanding yet run and involved the 12.15 a.m. down Plymouth train, returning with the 7.15 p.m. up service. In addition there was a return trip to Swindon from Paddington, down at 2.15 p.m. returning with the 4.20 p.m. from the Wiltshire town. This represented a daily mileage of 622 (606) service miles, equated to 3,732 (3,636) weekly.

Four defects are reported against the engine on this duty up to the end of December 1952 at which point the cumulative mileage was 63,000.

26.11.1952	Burnham	– Electrical defect caused by a part of a windscreen wiper becoming detached and shorting two terminals in the control circuit. Turbine towed from Reading shed to Old Oak Common by engine No. 9308. Failure occurred while working the 12.15 a.m. Paddington to Plymouth.
6.12.1952	Newton Abbot	– Faulty boiler – leaking tubes. Turbine returned light to Old Oak Common. Engine No. 5079 substituted.
13.12.1952	Old Oak Common	– Air cock to traction motor contactors was closed. Worked light engine to Plymouth. Took 8.30 a.m. ex-Plymouth instead of 7.15 a.m. Fifty-five minutes late at Paddington due to exhaust gas temperature control resistance burnt out.
29.12.1952	Old Oak Common	– Fuel cock closed. Missed Plymouth run.

Fuel consumption figures, together with other related costs for No. 18100 during 1952 and 1953, where known, are given in Appendix J. It should be noted though that the complex methods of accounting used by the railway mean that although the figures quoted in the appendix are as taken from official files they do not necessarily reflect every amount of expenditure on the locomotive. This was probably not assisted by the financial agreement with Metropolitan Vickers.

The new year, 1953, started badly for No. 18100 as a failure of control equipment on board the engine meant a late arrival on its allocated duty. Records are not clear which turn this was although the incident is referred to as having occurred at Swindon.

Four days later on 5 January the engine was on a return working from Plymouth and this time became a casualty at Exeter while at the head of the 8.30 a.m. ex-Plymouth. The cause was a frozen steam pipe between the engine and the first coach which, although counted as a failure, was hardly the fault of the gas turbine. Accordingly No. 18100 returned light to Old Oak Common.

Although there had been previously little trouble with the train heating boiler and its associated workings another fault was to occur on 22 January while at the head of the 12.30 a.m. Paddington–Plymouth service. This time there was difficulty in getting any water into the boiler and two minutes were lost in getting to Reading with a further six minutes' delay at the same station. Arrival at Plymouth was eventually eighteen minutes late with No. 18100 again returning light engine to Old Oak. Such difficulties could well have been exaggerated by the exceptionally cold spell of weather prevalent at the time

Cautiously threading its way over the maze of pointwork at the west end of Swindon station, No. 18100 is seen running light on one of its many trial runs. Full power from the engine could be taken after approximately ten minutes idling on low power, while on shutting down an automatic barring gear rotated the turbine for a few seconds every three minutes to equalize the cooling forces. Despite its physical size the engine was quite manoeuverable and could negotiate curves down to a five chain radius

R.H.G. Simpson

which was obviously considered by the Operating Department prior to subjecting passengers to a long train journey in unheated stock.

In describing the above defects we have moved slightly out of chronological sequence for an additional problem occurred on 10 January when a starting valve on the engine gave trouble at Paddington prior to No. 18100 working the 12.15 a.m. to Plymouth. The train is reported as departing eight minutes late.

Even in the most optimistic circles January 1953 could hardly be described as a good month for the engine with even worse to come on the 31st of the month. On that occasion No. 18100 had set out from Paddington for Plymouth at the head of the 12.15 a.m. service. At Hampstead crossing between Newbury and Kintbury a flash-over occurred on the main generator bus bars which left the train unable to move. Assistance was summoned in the form of 'Mogul' No. 6306 which was working the 11.10 p.m. ex-Old Oak freight to Bristol West depot (routed via the Berks & Hants line). This engine was attached at 2.08 a.m. and pushed the helpless train through to Hungerford where it arrived at 2.24 a.m. No. 18100 was then removed to a siding while another replacement steam engine, No. 7927 *Willington Hall*, was despatched from Reading at 2.05 a.m. and eventually left Hungerford at the head of the West of England train at 3.15 a.m., approximately 110 minutes late. The control log showed that the arrival in Plymouth was 101 minutes late.

Such a serious failure could hardly be kept from Marylebone and as a result Swindon was instructed to prepare a statistical analysis of No. 18100's performance set against its

With the Calne branch train in the foreground, No. 18100 hurries through Chippenham bound for Bristol with the down 'Merchant Venturer'. Records show that between 18 March 1952 and 21 March 1953, some £4,903 5s. 6d. had been spent on the engine in repairs and modifications. A further £1,253 0s. 9d. was spent on maintenance during the same period. Following the expiry of the first insurance certificate, a second policy was taken out from 23 July 1953 until it was surrendered on 14 December 1953, guarding against 'fire, damage, explosion and collision'. The cost of the premium was reported as £99 6s. 4d.

Kenneth Leech

failure rate. The result was nothing short of alarming for against a cumulative mileage total of 75,595 there had been twenty-five failures or, as Swindon was forced to concede, '. . . an average of 3,024 miles per failure'.

Not surprisingly No. 18100 was towed to Swindon where it was to remain under repair until 19 May.

At Swindon official records state the bus bar chamber was replaced with insulated cables in conduit. It should be stressed that this information was taken from official sources, in the full knowledge that these same official reports refer to the previous replacement of the bus bar conductors as a result of the failure on 14 January 1952 which was caused as a direct result of similar difficulties.

While at Swindon the tyres were also examined and evidence of flaking was found on all wheels. Accordingly each was turned and the diameters reduced by $\frac{7}{16}$ in.

The bogies were also subjected to another minute examination, with a number of further fatigue fractures being located. Some of these had developed in similar

Following the dramatic failure of No. 18100 at Hampstead crossing (near Newbury) on 31 January 1953, the engine was towed to Swindon for repair to the electrical equipment where at the same time modifications were undertaken to the bogies in an attempt to resolve the problem of cracks that had appeared. In this view taken at Swindon on 13 March 1953 the bogies have been wheeled out from underneath the engine and are awaiting repair. Cracks had been found in the side frames to the right of the left-hand spring hanger and also in the top gusset plates at the top corners of the bogies. These gusset plates were felt to be inflexible and were removed

locations as before although this time they also extended into the main frame plates in places. A number of repairs were effected which included new stiffener beams as well as additional gusset strengthening. New horn liners were also fitted to the sides opposite the trunions. A side effect of this work was that after the repairs the horns were found to be out of alignment and accordingly were reset with the aid of Zeiss optical equipment.

The problems with the bogies were serious enough to warrant a limited issue report of the difficulties being prepared, which was restricted to just eight copies. Fortunately one has survived in the archives at the National Railway Museum.

Records state the cost of the repairs at this time as follows:

	£	s.	d.
Main Bogies;	677	6	6
Skimming up wheels;	209	1	3
Replacing bus bar chamber with cables in conduit;	60	7	4

New inside and outside stiffening bars were added, with bolts being used to secure the new items in preference to welding. Inside the frames – although out of sight in this particular photograph – a number of new strengthening gussets were also added. In the background is 'Britannia' Pacific No. 70022 *Tornado* with the fitter temporarily distracted from his work on the engine. Most of the time between eight and ten men were engaged on the bogie modifications supervised by a Metropolitan Vickers engineer

An amazing collection of taxis forms the imposing background to this view of No. 18100 drawn up against the buffers of Platform 8 at Paddington. Somehow the engine hardly seems to fit in with such a scene which belongs to another age. Certain railway writers have in the past compared a mediocre performance from one of the new units with a one-off outstanding example of steam work. In theory either gas turbine could have easily beaten almost any of the steam timings then in use, although fuel and timetable constraints often prevented the best results being obtained

B.Y. Williams

(The accounting system means these figures are not assimilated with those in Appendix J.)

A series of control logs for No. 18100 from late May until December 1953 indicate the engine resumed running on a test basis from 20 May, though this could in fact be one day adrift. Whatever the date, the first trials were light engine followed by an increasing load. As before the route was from Swindon westwards on the South Wales Direct line to Badminton, from which point a number of 'shuttle' runs were made between the latter station and Little Somerford before returning to Swindon.

These tests continued for a week without difficulty with No. 18100 then set for its heaviest ever test; Swindon to Plymouth on 27 May with fourteen vehicles of 502 tons followed by a return the following day with nineteen vehicles of 659 tons from Plymouth to Newton Abbot. Both runs were accomplished without apparent difficulty although for an unknown reason the load back from Newton Abbot to Swindon was restricted to fifteen vehicles of 535 tons. A further three days' trials were then undertaken before No. 18100 returned light engine from Swindon to Old Oak Common on Saturday 6 June in anticipation of taking revenue-earning trains.

On Sunday 7 June No. 18100 reappeared on the 12.15 a.m. Paddington–Plymouth duty, returning the following day on the 7.15 a.m. Plymouth–Paddington. After arriving in London and having its train drawn off, No. 18100 was stabled at Ranelagh Bridge for just fifty minutes before returning to Paddington ready to work the 2.15 p.m. to Swindon. Again there was a quick thirty-two-minute turn-round at the Wiltshire town before returning at the head of the 4.20 p.m. Back in London No. 18100 now retired to Old Oak for service and re-fuelling ready to work the 12.15 a.m. down train.

This duty ensured as high a usage as possible of the engine throughout the twenty-four-hour period and equated to a theoretical weekly mileage of over 2,500 miles. Apart from the necessary light engine mileage to and from Ranelagh Bridge, Old Oak and Laira, all of these turns were passenger workings; No. 18100 was never known to work freight or milk duties.

Full details of the runs around this time are reproduced in the control logs at the end of this chapter.

The Plymouth turns continued until 17 June, on which day No. 18100 was at Plymouth working the 7.15 a.m. Paddington train. Unfortunately at Newton Abbot the record states the engine to have failed although the reason is not recorded. Evidently it was a minor difficulty for the following day No. 18100 returned light engine to Old Oak. It was destined never to work to Plymouth again.

No. 18100 is next heard of on 25 June when it worked light engine from Old Oak Common to Reading shed and return. The implication then is that the previous failure was dealt with at the London depot without recourse to Swindon; this is also believed to be the only time the engine actually visited the shed at Reading. The cumulative mileage prior to the Reading test run was 80,185.

Unconfirmed from the control log is a report that No. 18100 was stabled outside Swindon works on 27 June 1953. The same source, the *Railway Observer*, also states that during the following week the engine was observed passing Bath in the down direction about 1.30 p.m. on empty stock. This took place on 29 and 30 June and involved a ten-coach train.

If it was but then known, No. 18100 was now entering into the final part of its working life, on a diagram for a twice-daily trip from Paddington to Bristol. Apart from the necessary light engine working to and from sheds and a short trip to and from the Malago carriage sidings at Bristol, all the duty was spent on a revenue-earning service equal to a daily mileage of 483. Thus, twenty-six days of July were spent operating the

Gathering speed after the Bath station stop, No. 18100 approaches Twerton Tunnel with the down 'Merchant Venturer'. In locations such as these it was common for a steam engine to use its sanding gear as leaves might cause the rails to be slippery. Sanding equipment was fitted to No. 18100 although it is recollected as rarely being needed. For some weeks between 14 July 1952 and 2 August 1952, the engine was diagrammed for a very quick turn-round at Paddington after working in with the 7.45 a.m. up train from Bristol, being allowed just sixty-five minutes for servicing before leaving at the head of the 11.15 a.m. departure

G.F. Heiron

A superb photograph of No. 18100 pulling out of Bath Spa station with the down 'Merchant Venturer' in the summer of 1953. The various advertising hoardings are worthy of some study

G.F. Heiron

One of the last photographs taken of No. 18100 at Swindon, seen outside the works on 22 November 1953. It was destined never to work a train on the Western Region again and was moved to Dukinfield just three weeks later on 15 December

N.E. Preedy

same roster, with 12,558 miles covered in this way. No faults whatsoever were reported.

A log of part of the first up Bristol duty for 21 July 1953 was recorded by Mr G.J. Jefferson:

8.26 a.m. Chippenham to Paddington (7.45 a.m. ex-Bristol)
Thirteen coaches 424 tare to Didcot, thence twelve vehicles – 392 tons

	m.	s.	mph
Dauntsey	8	50	54
Wootton Bassett	14	36	55
Swindon	20	04	68
Shrivenham	24	49	78
Uffington	28	39	80
Challow	30	39	80/15 pws
Wantage Road	33	36	53
	38	38	sig.
Didcot	46	04	64 (one coach slipped)
Cholsey	50	08	76
Goring	53	05	79
Pangbourne	55	36	79
Tilehurst	57	71	79
Reading	60	06	58
Twyford	65	04	62
Maidenhead	71	53	75
Slough	75	34	75
West Drayton	79	52	76
Southall	83	21	75
Ealing Broadway	86	16	70
Acton	87	43	62
Westbourne Park	92	12	
Paddington	95	40	
Arrived 10.10 a.m.			

An interesting aspect of the turn was in connection with the first down run from Paddington to Bristol which took the form of the 2.25 a.m. service. This was regularly loaded to just six vehicles, of which three were removed at Swindon. No. 18100 left to haul a featherweight train of between just seventy-two and ninety-eight tons with almost an hour to cover the forty-odd miles to Bristol.

The same duties were worked in August 1953, apart from on the 3rd of the month, when there was just a single return trip to Bristol. In this way a further 12,320 miles were run. Once again no failures were reported and so this may be taken to be another very creditable performance. The only disadvantage was the equivalent fuel cost, over £2,290, based on a consumption of 3.46 gallons per mile at a time when the fuel oil was but 1s. $\frac{7}{8}$d. per gallon.

September commenced with the same turn although records come to an abrupt end after 7.25 p.m. on 8 September, at which time No. 18100 was back at Old Oak Common shed after completing its scheduled duty.

According to the *Railway Observer* No. 18100 had failed after working the 7.45 a.m. ex-Bristol. Its place on the down 'Merchant Venturer' that day was taken by No. 7036.

This of course is in conflict with the official records. The *Railway Observer* also reports that, '. . . No. 18100 worked its full roster again the following day but has not been seen since'. Official records fail to confirm this last day's working.

It is known though, that an official notice had been issued to withdraw No. 18100 from service – from whom this emanated is unclear and the reason why is discussed in a later chapter. Suffice it to say that No. 18100 languished out of use at Old Oak for some weeks. The only information regarding the period is a comment in Chris Leigh's article in which he states spring failures were a problem in 1953.

On 2 November 1953, No. 18100 took part in a light engine trial from Old Oak to Reading station and on the following day left Old Oak for the last time, working light to Swindon.

At Swindon the engine appears to have entered the works although it emerged again on a test the next day, 4 November, at the head of a ten-coach test train to Stoke Gifford. The purpose of this test was unofficially reported as a high-speed trial, with the engine uncoupled and arriving back at the Swindon factory at 1.30 p.m. The mileage at this time was slightly in excess of 109,000.

The course of events now moves away from Swindon to the Metropolitan Vickers factory at Dukinfield near Manchester, No.18100 leaving the Western Region for this new location on 15 December 1953.

All references, both contemporary and official, now record the same statement from BR, to the effect that the engine had been withdrawn for conversion to burn heavy fuel in accordance with the original programme.

While this may have been an acceptable comment in 1953, today it is worthy of considerable investigation, for despite extensive research into the history of this locomotive, nowhere can there be found any reference to such a supposedly planned conversion referred to before this time. The inference then may be taken that this may well have been a rapid decision.

At Dukinfield, Metropolitan Vickers commenced preparatory work on the necessary conversion to the alternative fuel and at the same time started a re-design of the electrical control circuits.

Smeddle visited the engine in Manchester in the course of its conversion in February 1954, at which time both the WR and Metropolitan Vickers were optimistic over a rapid return to duty. (The *Railway Observer* states that No. 18100 spent 1954 under overhaul at Swindon. This though, was an unfortunate error in an otherwise excellent record of railway activities.)

In a report of his visit, Smeddle hoped the final running tests of the engine could be carried out on a branch line although no specific location is mentioned. Certainly at this stage Swindon was cooperating fully with Metropolitan Vickers and several specialist tools were forwarded to Manchester from Wiltshire as requested.

The months now began to drag on and on 30 August 1954 Smeddle again wrote to Metropolitan Vickers with regard to progress. No reply was forthcoming from Metropolitan Vickers and the impression is clearly gained that Manchester was stalling for time. An acknowledgement was finally sent on 13 November although this only stated, '. . . a full report was being compiled and would be forwarded shortly'.

Meanwhile the railway accountants forwarded a statement showing the WR share of expenditure incurred on joint trials and modifications to date, a total of £18,810 10s. This amount was approved for payment to Metropolitan Vickers.

Not surprisingly Marylebone was by now enquiring as to the situation on the locomotive which, for the moment at least, represented an expensive investment upon which there was no return. Such pressure from headquarters was directed at Pad-

A rare view of No. 18100 at the Dukinfield, Manchester, works of Metropolitan Vickers, showing the engine under static test while burning heavy fuel oil. The cables took the output from the main generator to a number of water resistances

dington, with the WR General Manager, K.W.C. Grand, in turn enquiring of Smeddle.

Smeddle then wrote to Metropolitan Vickers, although again a reply was not immediately forthcoming. When it did arrive, Metropolitan Vickers stated it would be at least May 1955 before the conversion work was finished and tests completed. The delay was stated as being caused by difficulties in obtaining the necessary electrical and measuring equipment from outside suppliers. Smeddle was thus caught in the middle of a situation over which he had no control, his personal feelings probably not helped by Metropolitan Vickers referring to him as Mrs Smeddle in the letter!

More pressure from Marylebone came on 30 October 1954 in a letter to Grand from S.B. Warder, the Chief Officer at the Railway Executive for Electrical Engineering. Smeddle's reply reiterated the previous Metropolitan Vickers comments although adding his own rider over the time-scale, in that '. . . this may be rather optimistic'.

Towards the end of 1954 Metropolitan Vickers finally provided a report to Swindon on No. 18100 which listed in detail the modifications being carried out. This dealt with the various technical aspects of the conversion, with particular reference to alterations made to the electrical control system intended to reduce the risk of a turbine stall. Also referred to in detail were further changes to the bogies, on which topic Metropolitan Vickers stated the following; 'The modifications made before the locomotive came out of service appear to be accurate.'

At Swindon this latest correspondence was digested carefully although an unknown individual has underlined the Metropolitan Vickers comment regarding the bogies and added his own comment, 'How do they know?' The inference then was that Swindon was rapidly losing patience – and interest – in the whole affair, hardly surprising with the engine already out of service for over a year.

Shortly afterwards Smeddle relayed the contents of this latest Metropolitan Vickers report to Grand without adding any written comments of his own.

The next move in what can only be described as a saga came in late February 1955 when W.L. Creighton visited Manchester on behalf of Swindon. Metropolitan Vickers informed the visitor that it was still hoped to keep to the previous estimated time-scale.

Again though, Metropolitan Vickers' timing was grossly optimistic, for on 22 April a further letter to Smeddle informed him that again delays in delivery of equipment meant tests had not yet started. Smeddle acknowledged the letter in a positive sense, at the same time requesting that two Swindon fitters be permitted access to the locomotive, 'when appropriate', in order to become familiar with the modifications being carried out. This was approved by Metropolitan Vickers.

Despite the references to an ever-increasing amount of displeasure between the parties involved it must be made clear that Metropolitan Vickers was indeed attempting to modify the engine as promised. The work was eventually sufficiently advanced for No. 18100 to be taken to the nearby test sidings on 26 April 1955 and where ten days were spent in preliminary tests and adjustments to the oil supply and oil circulating mechanisms. A further ten days were then occupied in adjustments to the combustion chamber, with the turbine being started for the first time on its new fuel on 16 May.

Little official evidence is available of these first trials, although they may be assumed not to have been fully successful, for on 14 June an internal memorandum from Metropolitan Vickers states it had postponed full load testing due to a leakage of oil from the main turbine bearings. Curing this involved a full strip down.

Testing recommenced on 21 June, although a further memorandum to BR referred to the fact, '. . . that the design for the combustion chamber had yet to be finalized and there were several types to try. Tests have been commenced with that which shows the most promise.' These tests eventually evolved into full load trials, though with the engine remaining static, the generator output being dissipated through a number of water resistances.

At this stage progress on what was basically a technical conversion hardly warranted reference in magazines. The exception was *The Oil Engine and Gas Turbine Review* for August 1955 which reported, '. . . that the turbine was started on light fuel – for which purpose 200 gallons is carried, before being switched to heavy fuel. . . At this stage 30 hours of full load testing has been carried out. The light fuel is carried in the additional tank previously installed in the engine room.'

As before Swindon was kept fully informed of developments, with the latest communication from Smeddle to Grand and Warder referring to the fact that no work would be undertaken during the period 22 July to 6 August 1955 due to the Metropolitan Vickers works holiday. 'It is to be hoped that testing will finally be completed on 4th September after which there will be a further 2–3 weeks checking and testing of the control circuits.'

No doubt under pressure from Marylebone, Grand again wrote to Smeddle on 2 September enquiring when the engine would be ready to return to traffic. Swindon in turn directed the enquiry to Metropolitan Vickers which responded with the answer that, '. . . the static tests were nearly finished and hopefully should appear satisfactory'.

This last reply from Metropolitan Vickers must be the understatement of the whole story, for on 6 September Smeddle was forced to inform Grand that he had received notification that there was trouble with the linings of the combustion chamber, which were lasting for only 25–30 hours' running.

The combustion chamber life was later improved to a figure approaching 100 hours, although Metropolitan Vickers was then forced to concede another difficulty had occurred, this time involving the main turbine outlet bearing. The cause was soon diagnosed as due to the weight of a new exhaust system which resulted in distortion of the turbine bedplate and, in turn, the actual turbine bearings. It was a relatively simple matter to resolve although it naturally added further delay.

In early November 1955, and no doubt following a good deal of pressure from Swindon, Metropolitan Vickers prepared a summary of the events to date which included the information that the total running time on heavy fuel was just fifty-nine hours twenty-nine minutes, added to which 10,435 gallons of heavy oil had been consumed. This was against a total running time since overhaul of 106 hours 46 minutes. The latest estimate for completion was that the engine would be transferred back to Swindon around the end of January 1956.

After so many setbacks Swindon was clearly not prepared to accept this date and a serious suggestion was made to Metropolitan Vickers that the engine be converted back to light fuel in order to test the new control equipment. Metropolitan Vickers was quick to respond by stating the conversion work had already gone too far.

As such the implication is clear that the Western Region was rapidly coming round to the opinion that No. 18100 would never run for it again. This theory is given credence in a letter from Grand to Smeddle in which the former says, 'I should not regard a maximum life of 100 hours for the combustion liner as being acceptable and assume you would share this view. Although the modifications are being carried out at the firm's expense, I feel that unless this locomotive can be made to work efficiently and reliably at a relatively early date, we shall need to consider whether we are justified in going on with this project.'

Despite the problems now admitted by Metropolitan Vickers, Smeddle at least was not yet prepared to give up all hope and on 9 December wrote to Manchester, 'I agree with your views that a life of 100 hours for the combustion chamber cannot be accepted. However it seems to me to be a pity at this stage to terminate the project and I would recommend for your consideration that we should wait until the end of January next to see what progress has been made with trials . . .' (One hundred hours' turbine operation was the equivalent of only about one week's operation.)

Metropolitan Vickers in replying to Smeddle was somewhat more reticent, for in a letter of 22 December, reference is made to 'further difficulties', although without any other elaboration. Not surprisingly a pencilled note at Swindon questions what these were.

A resumé at the start of the new year, 1956, revealed it was already over two years since No. 18100 had left for Dukinfield and in reality Swindon was no nearer knowing when the engine might return. Pressure from above no doubt contributed to Grand having to reveal to Marylebone on 5 January 1956 that already £169,300 had been spent on the project, £93,000 of this since the end of 1952.

Accordingly on 31 January Smeddle was instructed to contact Metropolitan Vickers for a 'detailed report'. Metropolitan Vickers was hesitant, and replied that it was at present, 'unable to complete this'. Such a reply was naturally unacceptable to Paddington which wrote again on the 14 February to the effect that it was 'very concerned'.

A note from Metropolitan Vickers shortly afterwards suggests a meeting with a representative from Swindon at the forthcoming Institution of Locomotive Engineers meeting in London on 29 February, to which Swindon responded by saying this was, 'totally unacceptable'. Clearly what Metropolitan Vickers was attempting was to hold a meeting to act as a 'sounding board' as to which way to proceed. An alternative venue was then arranged, this time for 9 March 1956 at Swindon.

It is a matter of considerable regret that no BR record of 9 March meeting has been located, although a letter from Metropolitan Vickers dated 12 March 1956 is no doubt an accurate record of events.

Dear Sir,

We would confirm the discussions which we had in your office on Friday last when Mr Whyman and the Writer spoke to Mr Smeddle and Mr Creighton concerning the results of modifications and tests which we have been making on the above locomotive in order to simplify the control gear and convert the gas turbine to run on heavy fuel oil.

With regard to the control gear, this has been modified and simplified in such a way that although it will call for more attention from the driver, we feel it would be more reliable in operation.

A very considerable amount of work has been done in converting the turbine to run on heavy fuel and a large amount of testing has been carried out over a considerable period. As far as load running on heavy fuel is concerned a fair measure of success has ensued, but we regret to have to inform you that the achievement of a performance which would justify returning the locomotive to you for service running on heavy fuel would involve a re-arrangement of the basic units of the prime mover – an undertaking of greater magnitude than we can justify from our own point of view in the conditions existing today.

The purpose of such a re-arrangement would be to provide a greater combustion volume, more in keeping with that which contemporary development has shown to be necessary for heavy fuel burning in other applications, by this and other firms.

The two basic heavy fuel troubles with space restrictions have prevented us from solving on the existing arrangement are the relatively short combustion chamber liner life and turbine blade fouling during idling. This fouling was mainly carbonaceous and not at all related to vanadium deposits, and was quickly dispersed by a spell of load running. If, however, load running were not forthcoming at the appropriate time the build-up would eventually cause a compressor stall, or would interfere adversely with the next start. In this connection we note that in Western Region service with maximum loads limited, as Mr Smeddle has indicated, to King class tonnages, the ratio of load to idling to near idling running would be unfavourably low.

In the circumstances outlined above the only course is to offer to return the locomotive reconverted to gas oil burning and with the improved control system.

Mr Smeddle requested that these matters be confirmed in writing for discussion with his General Manager prior to reaching a decision. We requested that the decision should be made known to us early, within the next two weeks if possible, on account of the difficulty and delay in re-starting a job on which work has been halted and continuity and interest interrupted.

It was agreed that if you elect to have the locomotive returned as a gas oil burner, you would take it over completed as envisaged in the existing agreement, subject to the satisfactory completion of a period of about 2 months' working to cover load running adjustments of the governor control, and the demonstration of the satisfactory operation of the modified control system.

Should you, however, decide otherwise, the procedure would be that provided in the agreement for such a contingency.

Yours faithfully,

Metropolitan Vickers Electrical Co. Ltd.

BR's full reply is not recorded, although a brief summary on the file states, 'that a reconversion to light fuel would be unsatisfactory and this will p-lace the engine at a disadvantage compared to the Brown-Boveri machine'.

Quite what this meant is perhaps a little unclear, although it was in effect an academic comment, for the next paragraph contained the final damning statement; 'Serious consideration should therefore be given to terminating the project.'

The remainder of the story is briefly told. On 1 May 1956, Smeddle informed Metropolitan Vickers that Mr Grand had referred the matter to the British Transport Commission, the result of which was Board sanction to abandon the gas turbine venture with Metropolitan Vickers. The agreement between the two parties was formally cancelled on 18 December 1957. BR records show the total cost of the project to have been £347,880 19s. 3d. divided equally between the two participants. Fuel and lubricants were naturally not included in this amount.

And what then of No. 18100? It would appear perhaps others already had their eyes on the machine for another purpose, for on 11 May 1956 a letter exists on file from the Chief Mechanical Engineer at Marylebone, R.C. Bond, asking Smeddle to submit the engine's drawings with a view to proposed clearance for working underneath overhead AC electrified lines. In the event the engine was destined to have a further lease of life although this was hardly a success story. It is referred to in more detail in the next chapter.

The story of No. 18100 and the Western Region finally ended on 1 January 1958 with its official withdrawal. It was then towed dead from Dukinfield to Stalybridge and thence via Diggle, Huddersfield, Morley and Farnley Junction Leeds to Stockton. It was over four years since it had last been seen at Swindon.

CONTROL LOGS FOR NO. 18100, 20 MAY–4 NOVEMBER 1953

20. 5.1953	Return trip Swindon to Badminton. Light engine.
21. 5.1953	Return trip Swindon to Badminton plus Badminton to Little Somerford. Six vehicles of 128 tons.
22. 5.1953	Return trip Swindon to Badminton plus two trips Badminton to Little Somerford. Six vehicles of 177 tons.
26. 5.1953	Return trip Swindon to Swindon out via Bath and back via Badminton. Fourteen vehicles of 502 tons.
27. 5.1953	Swindon to Plymouth and then Laira. Fourteen vehicles of 502 tons.
28. 5.1953	Laira to North Road and then Nineteen vehicles of 659 tons to Newton Abbot. Thence Fifteen vehicles of 535 tons to Swindon.
3. 6.1953	Return trip Swindon to Badminton plus Badminton to Little Somerford. Light engine.
4. 6.1953	Return trip Swindon to Badminton plus three trips Badminton to Little Somerford. Six vehicles of 181 tons.
5. 6.1953	Return trip Swindon to Badminton plus two trips Badminton to Little Somerford. Six vehicles of 181 tons.
6. 6.1953	Light engine Swindon to Old Oak Common.
7. 6.1953	Paddington to Plymouth. Max. load of 428 tons.
8. 6.1953	Plymouth to Paddington. Return trip Paddington to Swindon. Paddington to Plymouth. Max. load of 348 tons.
9. 6.1953	Plymouth to Paddington. Return trip Paddington to Swindon. Paddington to Plymouth. Max. load of 378 tons.

10. 6.1953	Plymouth to Paddington. Thence Paddington to Reading – FAILED. Max. load of 366 tons.
11. 6.1953	Return trip Paddington to Swindon. Plus Paddington to Swindon. Max. load of 318 tons.
12. 6.1953	Plymouth to Paddington plus return trip Paddington to Swindon. Max. load of 387 tons.
13. 6.1953	Return trip Paddington to Swindon. Max. load of 274 tons.
14. 6.1953	Paddington to Plymouth. Max. load of 372 tons.
15. 6.1953	Plymouth to Paddington. Return trip Paddington to Swindon. Paddington to Plymouth. Max. load of 416 tons.
16. 6.1953	Plymouth to Paddington. Return trip Paddington to Swindon. Paddington to Plymouth. Max. load of 367 tons.
17. 6.1953	Plymouth to Newton Abbot – FAILED. Max. load of 189 tons.
18. 6.1953	Newton Abbot to Old Oak Common. Light Engine.
25. 6.1953	Return trip Old Oak Common to Reading shed. Light Engine.
29. 6.1953	Return trip Old Oak Common to Bristol. Max. load of 311 tons.
30. 6.1953	Return trip Old Oak Common to Bristol. Max. load of 311 tons.
2. 7.1953	Two return trips Paddington to Bristol. Max. load of 425 tons.
3. 7.1953	Two return trips Paddington to Bristol. Max. load of 419 tons.
4. 7.1953	Two return trips Paddington to Bristol. Max. load of 425 tons.
6. 7.1953	Two return trips Paddington to Bristol. Max. load of 423 tons.
7. 7.1953	Two return trips Paddington to Bristol. Max. load of 432 tons.
8. 7.1953	Two return trips Paddington to Bristol. Max. load of 426 tons.
9. 7.1953	Two return trips Paddington to Bristol. Max. load of 427 tons.
10. 7.1953	Two return trips Paddington to Bristol. Max. load of 427 tons.
11. 7.1953	Two return trips Paddington to Bristol. Max. load of 451 tons.
13. 7.1953	Two return trips Paddington to Bristol. Max. load of 426 tons.
14. 7.1953	Two return trips Paddington to Bristol. Max. load of 419 tons.
15. 7.1953	Two return trips Paddington to Bristol. Max. load of 427 tons.
16. 7.1953	Two return trips Paddington to Bristol. Max. load of 432 tons.
17. 7.1953	Two return trips Paddington to Bristol. Max. load of 423 tons.
18. 7.1953	Two return trips Paddington to Bristol. Max. load of 454 tons.
20. 7.1953	Two return trips Paddington to Bristol. Max. load of 428 tons.
21. 7.1953	Two return trips Paddington to Bristol. Max. load of 420 tons.
22. 7.1953	Two return trips Paddington to Bristol. Max. load of 425 tons.
23. 7.1953	Two return trips Paddington to Bristol. Max. load of 481 tons.
24. 7.1953	Two return trips Paddington to Bristol. Max. load of 425 tons.
25. 7.1953	Two return trips Paddington to Bristol. Max. load of 425 tons.
27. 7.1953	Two return trips Paddington to Bristol. Max. load of 457 tons.
28. 7.1953	Two return trips Paddington to Bristol. Max. load of 418 tons.
29. 7.1953	Two return trips Paddington to Bristol. Max. load of 419 tons.
30. 7.1953	Two return trips Paddington to Bristol. Max. load of 418 tons.
31. 7.1953	Two return trips Paddington to Bristol. Max. load of 445 tons.
1. 8.1953	Two return trips Paddington to Bristol. Max. load of 480 tons.
3. 8.1953	Return trip Paddington to Bristol. Max. load of 415 tons.
4. 8.1953	Two return trips Paddington to Bristol. Max. load of 454 tons.
5. 8.1953	Two return trips Paddington to Bristol. Max. load of 422 tons.
6. 8.1953	Two return trips Paddington to Bristol. Max. load of 430 tons.
7. 8.1953	Two return trips Paddington to Bristol. Max. load of 434 tons.

THE RAILWAY EXECUTIVE – WESTERN REGION.

Office of the Chief Accountant,
SWINDON, Wilts.
24th June, 1953.

GAS TURBINE LOCOMOTIVE No. 18,100.

W.E. 13th JUNE, 1953.

Booked Working:-

Date	From	To	Dep	Arr	Actual Running Time Hrs.Mins	Miles	Load Veh.	Tons
June 7th	Shed	Paddington	11.40	12.5	25	3	-	-
	Paddington	Taunton	12.15	2.50	2. 35	143	13	428
	Taunton	Newton Abbot	3.2	4.5	1. 03	51	12	396
	Newton Abbot	Plymouth	4.12	5.5	53	32	11	365
	Plymouth	Shed	5.10	5.20	10	2	-	-
	Total Engine Time – 5 hours 40 mins.				5. 06			
June 8th	Shed	Plymouth	6.40	7.0	20	2	-	-
	Plymouth	Newton Abbot	7.15	8.7	52	32	6	198
	Newton Abbot	Paddington	8.18	12.13	3. 55	194	11	348
	Paddington	Shed	12.30	12.55	25	3	-	-
	Shed	Paddington	1.45	2.5	20	3	-	-
	Paddington	Swindon	2.15	3.48	1. 33	77	9	Not
	Swindon	Paddington	4.20	6.20	2. 0	77	11	Shown
	Paddington	Shed	6.40	7.15	35	3	-	-
	Shed	Paddington	11.40	11.55	15	3	-	-
	Paddington	Taunton	12.15	2.36	2. 21	143	8	232
	Taunton	Newton Abbot	2.50	4.2	1. 12	51	7	205
	Newton Abbot	Plymouth	4.8	4.55	47	32	6	178
	Plymouth	Shed	5.10	5.25	15	2	-	-
	Total Engine Time – 17 hours 30 mins.				14. 50			
June 9th	Shed	Plymouth	6.30	6.45	15	2	-	-
	Plymouth	Newton Abbot	7.15	8.8	53	32	6	199
	Newton Abbot	Paddington	8.16	12.15	3. 59	194	12	378
	Paddington	Shed	12.30	12.45	15	3	-	-
	Shed	Paddington	1.45	2.0	15	3	-	-
	Paddington	Swindon	2.15	3.47	1. 32	77	9	Not
	Swindon	Paddington	4.27	6.20	1. 53	77	11	Shown
	Paddington	Shed	6.45	7.20	35	3	-	-
	Shed	Paddington	11.40	11.55	15	3	-	-
	Paddington	Taunton	12.22	2.50	2. 28	143	11	351
	Taunton	Newton Abbot	3.0	4.0	1. 0	51	10	321
	Newton Abbot	Plymouth	4.6	5.0	54	32	9	291
	Plymouth	Shed	5.15	5.25	10	2	-	-
	Total Engine Time – 17 hours 35 mins.				14. 24			
June 10th	Shed	Plymouth	6.40	6.55	15	2	-	-
	Plymouth	Newton Abbot	7.15	8.8	53	32	6	198
	Newton Abbot	Paddington	8.16	12.15	3. 59	194	11	366
	Paddington	Shed	12.15	12.30	15	3	-	-
	Shed	Paddington	1.45	2.0	15	3	-	-
	Paddington	Reading	2.15	3.10	55	36	9	Not Shown
	FAILED AT READING							
	Total Engine Time – 7 hours 35 mins.				6. 32			

8.	8.1953	Two return trips Paddington to Bristol. Max. load of 457 tons.
10.	8.1953	Two return trips Paddington to Bristol. Max. load of 426 tons.
11.	8.1953	Two return trips Paddington to Bristol. Max. load of 415 tons.
12.	8.1953	Two return trips Paddington to Bristol. Max. load of 406 tons.
13.	8.1953	Two return trips Paddington to Bristol. Max. load of 415 tons.
14.	8.1953	Two return trips Paddington to Bristol. Max. load of 416 tons.
15.	8.1953	Two return trips Paddington to Bristol. Max. load of 421 tons.
17.	8.1953	Two return trips Paddington to Bristol. Max. load of 454 tons.
18.	8.1953	Two return trips Paddington to Bristol. Max. load of 416 tons.
19.	8.1953	Two return trips Paddington to Bristol. Max. load of 425 tons.
20.	8.1953	Two return trips Paddington to Bristol. Max. load of 422 tons.
21.	8.1953	Two return trips Paddington to Bristol. Max. load of 415 tons.
22.	8.1953	Two return trips Paddington to Bristol. Max. load of 484 tons.
24.	8.1953	Two return trips Paddington to Bristol. Max. load of 431 tons.
25.	8.1953	Two return trips Paddington to Bristol. Max. load of 415 tons.
26.	8.1953	Two return trips Paddington to Bristol. Max. load of 431 tons.
27.	8.1953	Two return trips Paddington to Bristol. Max. load of 418 tons.
28.	8.1953	Two return trips Paddington to Bristol. Max. load of 415 tons.
29.	8.1953	Two return trips Paddington to Bristol. Max. load of 478 tons.
31.	8.1953	Two return trips Paddington to Bristol. Max. load of 451 tons.
1.	9.1953	Two return trips Paddington to Bristol. Max. load of 419 tons.
2.	9.1953	Two return trips Paddington to Bristol. Max. load of 423 tons.
3.	9.1953	Two return trips Paddington to Bristol. Max. load of 424 tons.
4.	9.1953	Two return trips Paddington to Bristol. Max. load of 418 tons.
5.	9.1953	Two return trips Paddington to Bristol. Max. load of 450 tons.
7.	9.1953	Return trip Paddington to Bristol. Max. load of 452 tons.
8.	9.1953	Two return trips Paddington to Bristol. Max. load of 418 tons.
2.11.1953		Return trip Old Oak Common to Reading shed. Light Engine.
3.11.1953		Old Oak Common to Swindon. Light Engine.
4.11.1953		Return trip Swindon to Stoke Gifford. Ten vehicles, load of 300 tons to check the motor suspension bearings and springing at high speed.

No. 18000

Zenith and Decline

As previously recounted at the end of Chapter 2, No. 18000 commenced 1952 as a reliable and useful member of the motive-power fleet on the Western Region.

Such behaviour was destined to be brief although it did show the sceptics, and there were still those at Swindon, Paddington and most importantly 222 Marylebone Road, that this form of traction was worthy of consideration as a possible replacement for steam in future years.

According to the four-weekly reports of mileage run for the early part of 1952, No. 18000 was averaging a figure of nearly 1,700 miles for a number of weeks and this despite a succession of minor faults. The first of these was on 11 January, when the engine was reported a failure at Old Oak prior to taking its booked turn of duty, the 7.30 a.m. Bristol train. The cause was nothing more serious than the ignition rod current being too low, thought to have been accidentally caused by a cleaner who in the process of carrying out his duties, turned the adjustable resistance potentiometer. Fortunately an electrical fitter was quickly on hand and the engine was made available for working the later 9.05 a.m. Bristol service.

Just three days later, on 14 January, yet another problem occurred, this time when a leaking oil pipe was discovered when the engine arrived at Swindon at the head of a train. The defect was serious enough to warrant a temporary withdrawal from traffic although the necessary repairs were undertaken at the works and the engine resumed service the next day.

The 16 January saw one of those annoying defects which although not the fault of the engine were counted against it in relation to reliability. Apparently there was trouble at the Old Oak Common fuelling point and accordingly No. 18000 was unable to take up its booked duty.

There was now a week without difficulty although this abruptly terminated on 24 January with a fire in the underframe of the engine while it was approaching Corsham west of Chippenham on a Bristol-bound train. Fortunately the incident was quickly dealt with although examination showed an accumulation of dirt and grease around the undersides of the engine which was evidently ignited by a spark from the brake blocks. It would appear the engine was back in service very quickly. The photographs on page 104 were taken to illustrate the problem of accumulated dirt around the underframe and clearly show up this particular hazard. (The problem of underframe fires due to dirt and grease was common in the early days of mass dieselization.)

According to official reports there were three other difficulties, the first on 26 January when a faulty contactor was found on the boiler feed pump, then on 31 January a faulty valve was reported and finally on the very next day, when difficulty was reported in starting the turbine. In each case no other information was given.

No. 18000 passes the east end of Didcot station on 1 January 1952 at the head of a Paddington-bound service. While photographs of the Bristol line services operated by the engine are relatively common, this is not the case for its newspaper, milk or later Hungerford–Paddington trains, the likely explanation for this being the unsocial hours such services operated. Despite the fitting of electric headcode lights it would appear they were seldom used on their own and instead recourse was made to the archaic oil lamps which dominated the steam age

Colin Marsden Collection

When read purely as a fault record the behaviour of No. 18000 for the start of 1952 was indeed suspect although as previously stated, the cumulative mileage between 29 December 1951 and 26 January 1952 was no less than 6,599 miles. Even so a report of each failure, together with the occasions when the engine did not take up its booked working and the weekly mileage run, had to be sent to Marylebone and there it would appear that at least one individual chose to ignore the mileage figures and concentrated on the failure record instead.

It was a question then of apparently 'passing the buck' for there was certainly correspondence between Paddington and Swindon over the various figures given, although regretfully the first letters on the subject are missing from the files. The inference is that this was Marylebone telling Paddington of its displeasure, with Gilbert Matthews writing to Pellow at Swindon over the matter.

Pellow evidently passed the correspondence to Smeddle at Swindon who, in a letter dated 27 February, clearly attempted to defend the engine:

> Between 21 May 1951 and 1 February 1952, there were 12 occasions when the engine may have caused delay to trains; this was out of 27 occasions when the engine did not not run as scheduled. Nine of these 12 were when the engine was withdrawn from service either at short notice or on a run. 2 at Old Oak Common, 1 at Reading, 1 at Chippenham, 1 at Bristol, 4 at Swindon. Four of these occasions might have been avoided if an electrical fitter had been available either at Old Oak Common or on board. No one defect has occurred more than once . . .

These photographs were taken to illustrate the problems of accumulated dirt, particularly around the traction motors, which was a common problem. Conditions such as these were the cause of the fires that occurred on No. 18000 in January and May 1952

British Railways

A little later in the same letter Smeddle continues on the theme of a requirement for an electrical fitter and states:

> More maintenance staff are required at Old Oak Common to deal with the complicated nature of the turbines and the increasing number of diesel shunters. I suggest an inspector plus one each electrical and mechanical fitter. [A number of the GWR/WR diesel shunters were by this time allocated to Old Oak.]

The correspondence was intended to refer to both No. 18000 and its later sister No. 18100 which had by now appeared upon the scene. The comment made by Smeddle as to a travelling fitter is particularly interesting, although there is no evidence to suggest that other than in the early days when a representative of the manufacturers was present on most of the runs, was a travelling fitter ever used on a regular basis.

Interestingly however, over thirty years later the Eastern Region of British Rail has introduced the use of such an individual under the guise of a travelling Technical Riding Inspector, whose job it is to attempt to ensure maximum usage on a number of the HST sets running out of King's Cross. The 1950s though, were a difficult time for BR in relation to the employment of staff and it is known that on some occasions Swindon men were sent to either Old Oak or Bristol if the gas turbines required the presence of a specialist. This type of arrangement continued for some years into the 1950s. Against the background of low pay and poor conditions for artisan staff on BR compared with those offered by outside industry, it is unlikely that Smeddle's request for additional staff was acted upon.

Privately Paddington was evidently concerned as to the effect on public relations caused by delays the turbine caused to passenger trains and accordingly there is a brief note around the same time suggesting the engines might be better employed on express freight work. In practice, however, the difficulty of arranging suitable rosters for this type of duty was stated to be insurmountable, although bearing in mind the number of milk trains that were hauled it would surely not have been beyond the realms of possibility to secure additional freight turns of the type involving fully fitted trains. In the event there is no evidence to suggest either engine ever worked any regular freight duties.

During March and most of April No. 18000 remained a regular performer on the main line to Bristol, undertaking the following duties:

    7.30 a.m. Paddington–Bristol
    12.00 p.m. Bristol–Paddington
    6.35 p.m. Paddington–Swindon
    10.05 p.m. Swindon–Southall Milk. SX

Loadings varied on a day-to-day basis and while figures for March and April are not given, in June it was reported that the 6.35 p.m. would sometimes involve as many as fifteen vehicles, equal to 487 tons, while the milk train is known to have regularly reached 505 tons.

These are among the highest tonnage figures No. 18000 is known to have hauled in normal service.

During the same period, March and April 1952, official records refer to only the occasional minor fault having occurred, although for the first time records become generally less concise and, as a result, it becomes more and more difficult to piece together the engine's movements and its failures.

What *is* known is that on 23 April 1952 No. 18000 brought the 12.00 p.m. ex-Bristol

The 12 noon Bristol to Paddington service was one of those to omit a stop at Reading, calling instead at Bath Spa, Chippenham and Swindon, after which it was non-stop to London. This was a regular duty for No. 18000 in its early days, with the train seen here passing a line of engines alongside Reading locomotive shed some time in 1952

Maurice Earley/National Railway Museum

into Paddington fourteen minutes early, having run the 77¾ miles from Swindon in seventy-six minutes. This represented a start to stop average speed of just over 61 mph and, allowing for the leisurely schedules of the day, was still a creditable achievement. Surprisingly perhaps, officialdom frowned on such a performance.

In April 1952 there was a brief visit to Swindon works on the 20th of the month, followed by a re-arranged roster on the Paddington–Plymouth duties, No. 18000 working down with the 3.30 p.m. service on the 26th and returning with the 7.00 a.m. train the next day. The up train was specially loaded to 400 tons over the South Devon banks to test the abilities of the engine, now fitted with its climbing boost. These were the first load haulage trials since the modifications of the previous December.

Despite the importance of such a test little is known other than the run was entirely successful, No. 18000 arriving back at Paddington five minutes early, after which it took up its normal booked working of the 6.35 p.m. passenger train, returning later with the milk tanks.

Somewhat unusually in view of the coming summer timetable and consequent reduction in need to steam heat its train, together with the recent success on the load trials, No. 18000 was not rostered immediately back to the Plymouth services and instead remained working between Paddington and Bristol. An exception to this appears to have occurred around 15 and 16 May and is referred to below. Why the Bristol route should still be preferred is unclear although a clue can perhaps be gained from a report dated 23 May 1952 in which the suggestion is made that the gear ratios of

No. 18000 'trailing' out of Paddington towards Old Oak and past the Paddington goods depot. Although un-reported in official records, the engine was the cause of a potentially serious incident at Paddington while waiting to work a scheduled passenger duty. On that particular occasion Tony Tyler was the 'fireman' working with Driver Church. The engine arrived at the terminus and backed onto its waiting train whereupon Tyler jumped down 'between engine and coach to couple up'. Unfortunately the coupling hook landed on top of his hand and with the weight of such an item in excess of 56 lb he was quite unable to free himself. Meanwhile time was ticking away towards the scheduled departure, yet Tyler dared not shout for fear his driver would hear the sound and take it to mean 'ease up', thereby crushing his hand. It was not until the intervention of an inspector investigating the reason for the late departure that the fireman could be freed, although not before his hand had become severely bruised

Collection R. Stumpf

the traction motors should be modified so as to reduce the top speed and instead improve performance on the South Devon banks. The report continues by stating that a similar change had already taken place on the Southern Region diesels, Nos. 10201 and 10202.

This is where another anomaly occurs, for the report quite clearly states that No. 18000 is still to be restricted to the same load over the gradients as a 'Star' at 288 tons, for the reason of not wishing to risk overheating the traction motors. This in itself appears to be a throwback to the very first trial of June 1950 and perhaps even came about at the behest of certain Locomotive Inspectors who wished to avoid trouble. Certainly by now the drivers had become adept at avoiding trouble either by not using full power or doing so only for short periods. Brown-Boveri was informed of the BR decision and it would appear the company was not in agreement, stating instead the engine could easily take 360 tons unaided or 400 tons provided no stop was made.

May 1952 was spent back mainly on the Bristol workings, punctuated by three known failures. The first of these was on 16 May 1952 when, according to a correspondent in *Trains Illustrated*, No. 18000 failed on the 7.15 a.m. ex-Plymouth at Reading, the train being taken on to Paddington by a 63xx 2–6–0 No. 6302, the up side pilot engine. (Reading had two pilot engines, with a 'Hall' usually available for the down side.) Official records refer only to a failure on that day without giving the location, although the cause is said to have been a loose connection on the main generator excitation.

Less than a week later on 22 May, the engine failed again, this time at Southall while at the head of the 12.00 p.m. Bristol-bound service. This time the cause was a traction motor flash-over on No. 2 motor which started a small fire, although this was quickly extinguished. Quite understandably the engine was taken off its train and towed back to Old Oak Common depot where the cause was found to be nothing more than a brush not having been replaced correctly during previous maintenance. Fortunately damage was slight and repairs were quickly effected.

The next day, 23 May, No. 18000 was booked for the 9.05 a.m. Bristol-bound train, although again fate played a part, for approaching Bath excessive oil fumes were noticed in the engine room, quickly followed by flames from beneath the combustion chamber. The cause this time was an accumulation of unburnt oil.

Movements up to the beginning of June are uncertain although by 2 June No. 18000 was certainly back in service, with two return trips between Paddington and Bristol. This time the duties continued for the whole week without difficulty.

Despite such reliable working a letter was received by Smeddle from Riddles on 22 July 1952 complaining of the recent low weekly mileage figures for the engine. This would appear to be rather strange as from the four-weekly reports (see Appendix H), No. 18000 was achieving a fairly consistent return. A further report, also from the accountant's office at Swindon, relates to fuel consumption between the beginning of April and mid-June although the mileage totals would appear to be at variance with the aforementioned four-weekly reports:

Week ending	Miles	Gallons (heavy oil)	Gallons per mile
5.4.1952	1,369	3,880	2.83
12.4.1952	968	4,060	4.19
19.4.1952	1,407	3,115	2.21
26.4.1952	1,467	4,895	3.34
3.5.1952	1,467	5,010	3.42
10.5.1952	1,467	5,100	3.48
17.5.1952	1,467	4,578	3.12
Four weeks ending 14.6.1952	3,496	12,510	3.58

The problem of limited knowledge now occurs again and there is only one reference to the month of August when, on the 10th, the engine failed due to a fire in the battery charging circuit. This is reputed to have occurred while the engine was working the 9.00 a.m. Swindon–Paddington train, itself a duty that has not been referred to previously and perhaps indicating the engine was being worked back to Old Oak after a visit to Swindon works. The fault was traced to a number of blown fuses which it was concluded had probably failed soon after leaving Swindon. Following the incident the engine resumed duties on Bristol trains until mid-September.

Sunday 14 September 1952 found No. 18000 on shed at Old Oak Common receiving attention as per its usual 600-hour examination. This took place on average every eight weeks although much was of course dependent on the general reliability of the engine. During the course of the examination it was discovered that cracks had occurred on the first row of turbine stator blades and as such it was considered unsafe to continue running.

Appropriately alongside a 'Star' class 4–6–0, No. 4049 *Princess Maud* at Paddington on 17 May 1952, No. 18000 waits after arrival with an up passenger train. The gas turbine was placed in the same load haulage category as this type of steam engine, a comparison which hardly did justice to the new design. Some forty-four years separated the two designs, with No. 4049 being withdrawn in June 1953, having run in excess of 1.6 million miles

Stanley Creer

Accordingly No. 18000 was towed to Swindon where the engine was destined to remain until the early part of the next year. Brown-Boveri was informed of the failure and undertook to supply a complete new rotor drum at its own expense, although naturally the production of such an item would take time. While waiting for the new item to be delivered from Switzerland the opportunity was taken to carry out some other work, which included turning of the tyres and overhaul of the traction motors. The diesel engine was also overhauled although repairs to this item had been scheduled at the time the engine was being examined at Old Oak.

Perhaps significantly a new train heating boiler was also fitted, this time of 2,000 lb hr capacity, double that of the previous item. The new boiler was manufactured by Spanner Boilers of London and in service was found to be a great improvement on its predecessor. The only limitation now was the amount of water that could be carried, which was sufficient for about three to four hours' steaming on a long train in cold weather. Prior to the decision on the use of a Spanner boiler an amount of correspondence had occurred over the possible use of a Vapor Clarkson boiler of the type fitted to the LMS and SR main-line diesel engines. Whether this was not used for a technical or commercial reason is unclear – or perhaps the independence of Swindon was again asserting itself.

The cause of the failure of the turbine blades was felt to be due to one of two problems, uneven gas temperature distribution or delayed ignition, and accordingly enquiries were commenced with a number of outside bodies with a view to resolving the problems.

Still sporting its '450' identification board which relates to the 7.00 a.m. Weston-super-Mare to Paddington train, No. 18000 stands outside Swindon works on an unknown date some time prior to 1957

R.J. Leonard, courtesy Mr & Mrs R. Webber

At the same time the firm of Shell UK was contacted about any advice it might be able to give with regard to the burning of residual fuel in relation to the short life expectancy of combustion chamber linings. Experiments were therefore arranged to vary both the injection pressure and temperature, those existing at the start being 40 psi at 220 °F, although naturally these could not be tested in practice until the necessary turbine repairs had been fully effected.

Thus the end of 1952 found No. 18000 static at Swindon and still some little time away from running again. It could only be hoped that 1953 would be a better year.

1952 comparisons per train mile:

Steam	18.75d.
Steam pass and freight	30.00d.
Gas turbine;	
Brown-Boveri	26.67d.
M/Vickers	50.00d. approx.
Diesel-electric shunting engine	4.48d.
LMS No. 10000	21.153d.

Repairs to the turbine, along with the various ancillary items previously referred to,

110

The new train heating boiler as fitted to No. 18000 which was of 2,000 lb hr capacity – double the output of the previous boiler. Unlike certain of the early BR diesels, neither gas turbine was ever equipped to pick up water from troughs while running and as a result its heating capabilities were dictated by the amount of water that could be carried. In addition to his duties attending to the boiler, the fireman was expected to take frequent readings of the 'temperature before turbine', meaning the heat of the gases as they passed through the fan blades of the turbine; this while the unit was running and perhaps under full power. No ear protection was provided

were completed by 24 January 1953, between which date and 21 February, five days were used for trial runs covering a total distance of 363 miles. Most of the runs involved load haulage with empty coaching stock.

Rather than return the engine directly to traffic it would appear No. 18000 was retained at Swindon pending the result of the investigations by Shell into the combustion difficulties. These finally resulted in the provision of a new burner together with a modification to the lining of the combustion chamber. The date the changes took place is not officially recorded but from a process of elimination it would appear the work was carried out between March and June 1953.

What is known is that between 21 February and 21 March just one day was spent working, when a distance of seventy miles was covered. Between March and early June the engine was back at Swindon and did not run again until 8 June, when a light engine trial was undertaken on a round trip from Swindon, travelling out via Bath and returning via Badminton. This related to a distance of sixty-eight miles.

There then followed a series of trials up to mid-August of 1953 as follows:

Date	Route	Distance (miles)	Load (Vehicles/tons)
17.6.1953	Out via Bath failed at Stoke Gifford (towed back to Swindon)	35	10 – 298
18.6.1953	Out via Bath return via Badminton	70	10 – 305
27.7.1953	Out via Bath return via Badminton	70	Light engine
28.7.1953	Out via Bath return via Badminton	70	8 – 260
30.7.1953	Out via Bath return via Badminton	70	Light engine
5.8.1953	Out via Bath return via Badminton	70	10 – 366
6.8.1953	Out via Bath return via Badminton	70	10 – 309
7.8.1953	Out via Bath return via Badminton	70	10 – 309
10.8.1953	Out via Bath return via Badminton	70	12 – 360
11.8.1953	Out via Bath return via Badminton	70	12 – 372

A note in the records states that fitter Sullivan from Swindon accompanied the engine on its trial trips between the end of July and 7 August.

(Load differences in relation to the same number of vehicles are accounted for by the use of differing types of stock having different weights. It was a common practice to use whatever vehicles were available for these types of trial.)

Despite no written evidence confirming the fact, Swindon was now undoubtedly satisfied with the condition of No. 18000 and accordingly on 14 August the engine was despatched light to Old Oak to resume its normal workings.

After a lapse of some eleven months, re-entry into revenue-earning service took place three days later on 17 August with the 7.30 a.m. Bristol service from Paddington, made up of ten coaches totalling some 321 tons. On this first outing the engine got no further than Reading where it was declared a failure, although tantalizingly no reason for the problem is given. Whatever it was however, was obviously of a minor nature for No. 18000 worked light to Old Oak Common later in the day.

After what can only be described then as a disappointing period in the engine's life, which can hardly have failed to be noticed by headquarters, No.18000 was about to enter another of its prolonged periods of use. This was fortunately well recorded from a whole series of record sheets detailing the daily duties. These are a particularly useful source of information and provide details with regard to trains worked as well as loadings and number of engine hours run. It would naturally be impractical to reproduce all the sheets although the example on page 113 is a typical record.

Following the previous day's failure at Reading the next outings were more successful with one return trip each day on 18 and 19 August between Paddington and Bristol on passenger trains. But on the 20th, while working a similar turn, the engine was declared a failure at Bristol although again it returned light to London later in the day.

Although not referred to in official reports it appears likely that combustion difficulties were the main reason for these latest problems, for though the new spill-type burner designed by Shell was certainly an improvement it had the opposite effect to what was required so far as the life of the combustion chamber linings was concerned, the component being found to require replacement at more frequent intervals than before. Old Oak had itself become quite expert at this repair and linings were sent between Swindon and Old Oak Common shed as necessary. As a result of these difficulties with the combustion chamber lining the former Brown-Boveri burner was re-fitted though retaining the Shell-designed modifications to the air director and liner cooling shell.

BRITISH RAILWAYS

XXXXXXXXXXXXXXXXXXXXXXXXXX

THE RAILWAY EXECUTIVE - WESTERN REGION

Office of the CHIEF Accountant,
SWINDON

Friday, 16th October, 1953.

GAS TURBINE LOCOMOTIVE NO. 18,000

10TH OCTOBER, 1953.

Booked Working   S dem 2517

Date	From	To	Dep.	Arr.	Actual Running Time Hrs. Mins.	Miles	Load	
							Veh.	Tons
8th Oct.	O.O.Common Shed	Paddington	6.48	7.20	32	3		L.E.
	Paddington	Bristol	7.30	10.20	2. 50	118	8	264
	Bristol	Bath Rd. Shed	10.45	10.50	5	–		L.E.
	Bath Rd. Shed	Bristol	11.35	11.45	10	–		L.E.
	Bristol	Paddington	12.0	2/32	2. 32	118	8	270
	Paddington	O.O.Common Shed	2/45	3/15	30	3		L.E.
	O.O.Common Shed	Paddington	5/50	6/25	35	3		L.E.
	Paddington	Swindon	6/35	8/19	1. 44	77	12	391
	Swindon	Wood Lane	9/45	11/45	2. 0	78	18	505
	Wood Lane	O.O.Common Shed	11/55	12.30	35	4		L.E.

	Total Engine Time - 14 hours 22 mins.				11. 33			
					======			
9th Oct.	O.O.Common Shed	Paddington	6.48	7.15	27	3		L.E.
	Paddington	Bristol	7.36	10.20	2. 44	118	8	270
	Bristol	Bath Rd. Shed	10.50	11.0	10	–		L.E.
	Bath Rd. Shed	Bristol	11.45	11.55	10	–		L.E.
	Bristol	Paddington	12/3	2/40	2. 37	118	11	366
	Paddington	O.O.Common Shed	2/55	3/15	20	3		L.E.
	O.O.Common Shed	Paddington	5/45	6/15	30	3		L.E.
	Paddington	Swindon	6/35	8/13	1. 38	77	14	457
	Swindon	Wood Lane	9/35	11/45	2. 10	78	18	505
	Wood Lane	O.O.Common Shed	12.0	12.30	30	4		L.E.

	Total Engine Time - 14 hours 27 mins.				11. 16			
					======			
10th Oct.	O.O.Common Shed	Paddington	6.55	7.18	23	3		L.E.
	Paddington	Swindon	7.30	9.7	1. 37	77	8	264
	Swindon	Bristol	9.16	10.20	1. 4	41	10	323
	Bristol	Bath Rd. Shed	10.40	10.50	10	–		L.E.
	Bath Rd. Shed	Malago	1/7	1/20	13	1		L.E.
	Malago	Bristol	1/30	1/40	10	2	13	452
	Bristol	Bathampton	1/50	2/30	40	14	13	452

	Total Engine Time - 5 hours 18 mins.				4. 17			
					=====			

FAILED AT BATHAMPTON, TOWED TO SWINDON.

Mr. L.G. Rendell,
No. 21 Accounts Office.

Duties then resumed the following day and continued as follows:

21.8.1953   Return trip to Bristol. Max. load thirteen vehicles of 419 tons.
22.8.1953   Return trip to Bristol. Max. load thirteen vehicles of 435 tons.
(Following this trip a new fuel line filter was fitted at Old Oak depot.)
24.8.1953   Return trip to Bristol. Max. load eleven vehicles of 356 tons.
26.8.1953   Return trip to Bristol. Max. load nine vehicles of 290 tons.
27.8.1953   Return trip to Bristol. Max. load nine vehicles of 286 tons.
28.8.1953   Return trip to Bristol. Max. load eleven vehicles of 355 tons.

The next day, 29 August, the engine received its usual cursory examination at Old Oak in the course of which suspicion was levelled at the body suspension arrangements and accordingly there was a further temporary withdrawal from service. It was worked light to Swindon on 3 September where a closer examination revealed that one of the helical bogie springs was also broken. This was repaired at the works and on 22 September a light engine trial was arranged from Swindon to Badminton and return. All was well and the following day No. 18000 returned light to Old Oak ready to take up its regular duties once again.

These recommenced the next day, 25 September, with a return trip between Paddington and Bristol and with a maximum loading of eleven vehicles weighing some 377 tons. Running then continued as follows. As before Sundays were spent out of service for scheduled maintenance:

26. 9.1953   Return trip to Bristol. Max. load twelve vehicles of 396 tons.
28. 9.1953   Return trip to Bristol. Max. load nine vehicles of 303 tons.
29. 9.1953   Return trip to Bristol. Max. load eight vehicles of 271 tons.
30. 9.1953   Return trip to Bristol. Max. load eight vehicles of 273 tons.
1.10.1953   Return trip to Bristol. Max. load eight vehicles of 271 tons.
2.10.1953   Return trip to Bristol. Max. load eleven vehicles of 362 tons.
3.10.1953   Return trip to Bristol. Max. load twelve vehicles of 405 tons.

Up to now records show there had only been one return trip to Bristol daily, which can hardly be described as obtaining full utilization from what was an expensive piece of machinery. This changed though with effect from Monday 5 October when the engine resumed duty on the 6.35 p.m. Paddington–Swindon train, returning as far as Wood Lane on milk tanks. In this way some 404 miles daily were covered although as before on Saturdays there was just the one return trip to Bristol.

5.10.1953   Return trip to Bristol plus return to Swindon. Max. load of 505 tons.
6.10.1953   Return trip to Bristol plus return to Swindon. Max. load of 501 tons.
7.10.1953   Return trip to Bristol plus return to Swindon. Max. load of 505 tons.
8.10.1953   Return trip to Bristol plus return to Swindon. Max. load of 505 tons.
9.10.1953   Return trip to Bristol plus return to Swindon. Max. load of 505 tons.

The same duty was scheduled for 10 October with the interesting addition that the engine ran light from Bristol Bath Road depot to the Malago carriage sidings between Bedminster and Parson Street, there to collect its return load of thirteen vehicles comprising 452 tons. This was then taken forward as the 1.50 p.m. Bristol–Paddington train although No. 18000 never got further than Bathampton where, at 2.30 p.m., it failed and was later towed to Swindon. The cause is not reported although again it must have been a minor problem because on 13 October it worked light to Old Oak, resuming normal duties on the 15th.

15.10.1953	Return trip to Bristol plus return to Swindon. Max. load of 504 tons.
16.10.1953	Return trip to Bristol plus return to Swindon. Max. load of 505 tons.
17.10.1953	Return trip to Bristol. Max. load twelve vehicles of 401 tons.
19.10.1953	Return trip to Bristol. Max. load thirteen vehicles of 455 tons.
20.10.1953	Return trip to Bristol plus return to Swindon. Max. load of 477 tons.
21.10.1953	Return trip to Bristol plus return to Swindon. Max. load of 505 tons.
22.10.1953	Return trip to Bristol plus return to Swindon. Max. load of 505 tons.
23.10.1953	Return trip to Bristol plus return to Swindon. Max. load of 505 tons.
24.10.1953	Return trip to Bristol. Max. load twelve vehicles of 398 tons.
26.10.1953	Return trip to Bristol. Max. load nine vehicles of 297 tons.
27.10.1953	Return trip to Bristol plus return to Swindon. Max. load of 505 tons.
28.10.1953	Return trip to Bristol plus return to Swindon. Max. load of 505 tons.
29.10.1953	Return trip to Bristol plus return to Swindon. Max. load of 505 tons.
30.10.1953	Return trip to Bristol plus return to Swindon. Max. load of 505 tons.
31.10.1953	Return trip to Bristol. Max. load twelve vehicles of 402 tons.
2.11.1953	Return trip to Swindon. Max. load eighteen vehicles of 505 tons.
3.11.1953	Return trip to Bristol plus return to Swindon. Max. load of 505 tons.
4.11.1953	Return trip to Bristol plus return to Swindon. Max. load of 505 tons.
5.11.1953	Return trip to Bristol plus return to Swindon. Max. load of 504 tons.
6.11.1953	Return trip to Bristol plus return to Swindon. Max. load of 505 tons.
7.11.1953	Return trip to Bristol. Max. load eleven vehicles of 370 tons.
9.11.1953	Return trip to Bristol plus return to Swindon. Max. load of 504 tons.
10.11.1953	Return trip to Bristol plus return to Swindon. Max. load of 504 tons.
11.11.1953	Return trip to Bristol plus return to Swindon. Max. load of 504 tons.
12.11.1953	Return trip to Bristol plus return to Swindon. Max. load of 422 tons.
13.11.1953	Return trip to Bristol plus return to Swindon. Max. load of 505 tons.
14.11.1953	Return trip to Bristol. Max. load eleven vehicles of 309 tons.
17.11.1953	Return trip to Bristol plus return to Swindon. Max. load of 504 tons.
18.11.1953	Return trip to Bristol plus return to Swindon. Max. load of 505 tons.
19.11.1953	Return trip to Bristol plus return to Swindon. Max. load of 504 tons.
20.11.1953	Return trip to Bristol plus return to Swindon. Max. load of 505 tons.
21.11.1953	Return trip to Bristol. Max. load eleven vehicles of 361 tons.
23.11.1953	Return trip to Bristol plus return to Swindon. Max. load of 505 tons.
24.11.1953	Return trip to Bristol plus return to Swindon. Max. load of 505 tons.
25.11.1953	Return trip to Bristol plus return to Swindon. Max. load of 505 tons.
26.11.1953	Return trip to Bristol plus return to Swindon. Max. load of 505 tons.
27.11.1953	Return trip to Bristol plus return to Swindon. Max. load of 505 tons.
28.11.1953	Return trip to Bristol. Max. load eleven vehicles of 371 tons.

Up to the latter date the 1953 mileage figure records a total of 21,839 with 672 turbine running hours. Another interesting statistical fact concerns the running costs for a number of the four-weekly periods in 1953:

Four weeks ending;	24.1.1953	£850 2s. 9d.
	21.2.1953	£947 11s. 4d.
	11.7.1953	£648 7s. 11d.
	8.8.1953	£1,224 13s. 4d.
	5. 9.1953	£359 14s. 3d.
	3.10.1953	£505 11s. 2d.
	31.10.1953	£680 1s. 10d.
	28.11.1953	£1,468 19s. 8d.

Nearing the end of its journey at Paddington at the head of the 7.00 a.m. up train, No. 18000 passes underneath the station buildings at West Ealing on 28 March 1955

B.Y. Williams

Towards the end of 1953 there is an undated report in the files suggesting a modification to the existing schedules worked, which would involve a higher utilization figure of 2,832 miles each week. The new schedule was as follows:

2.25 a.m. Paddington–Bristol
7.45 a.m. Bristol–Paddington
11.15 a.m. Paddington–Bristol
4.15 p.m. Bristol–Paddington

To achieve this however, it was commented that a heavy oil re-fuelling depot would be needed at Bristol, and as this was never installed it may be similarly concluded the diagram was never worked.

Overall the impression given by the gas turbine varied considerably between the different departments on the railway. On the plus side O.S. Nock, in his book *60 Years of Western Express Running*, recorded the comments of a Traffic Inspector who was on board the turbine-worked 7.45 a.m. ex-Bristol and was heard to remark at Chippenham: 'There; 2½ minutes through the tunnel! No steam engine could do that.'

BR, though, took a more cynical viewpoint of the engine: 'Despite this being one of the few gas turbine engines to operate with any degree of success using residual fuel . . .' This begs the question: How many engines of this type were there? The answer is just the two, the Swiss machine and No. 18100! The report also referred to the difficulties experienced with combustion and to the short life of the liner, previously 900 hours and

116

No. 18000 on display at Willesden in the early summer of 1954. Besides the gas turbine a number of other modern BR locomotives were on display including diesel, steam and electric types. Sister engine No. 18100 was not however present, instead being in the course of its abortive conversion to burn heavy fuel. Following the display it had been the intention to take over the main line out of St Pancras for a short period and run all the main line passenger services using examples of the latest non-steam motive power. This would have involved the LMS- and SR-design diesel-electrics as well as the 'Fell' diesel – not all of which were on display at Willesden. The venture was later vetoed as far as No. 18000 was concerned, as it was found to be 'out of gauge' for the route

R.A. Collection

now about 300 hours, as a result of which it was deemed preferable to keep the engine on the Bristol run where depots were more frequent and replacement steam engines easier to find.

After the end of 1953 records pertaining to No. 18000 become more scarce almost by the month. Indeed what is known often tends to refer to the breakdowns and failures that occurred and so gives a false representation of the engine's behaviour. One such failure, although due to an unreported cause, took place on 3 February 1954 when the engine was near Reading at the head of the 7.45 a.m. Bristol–Paddington service. The train continued with a steam pilot in the form of No. 9306, with the eventual arrival at Paddington some thirty minutes late.

Less than a week later there was another failure when on the same working, this time as the train approached Slough. The driver stated that he heard several loud reports which were followed by a total lack of power. Again a steam locomotive was attached as pilot with the arrival at Paddington some twenty minutes late. On this occasion the cause was a flash-over to the main generator, due to the brushes being in bad condition. The report commented that these particular components had been inspected just ten to twelve days earlier. Repairs occupied some eleven working days.

To those who were regular travellers – the word 'commuters' is a more recent addition

A cold September day in 1955 finds No. 18000 heading east towards Paddington on its morning train from Bristol and running on the up through line at Reading General. The attention of at least one passenger in the train alongside is attracted by the new form of motive power. In practice it was found that the fuel consumption of the engine varied considerably according to the load hauled and wind direction and it became the habit of several drivers to coast for long distances in an effort to effect fuel economy. The residue fuel burnt by the engine was what was left from crude oil after the various 'lighter' components had been distilled off

Len Davies

to the language – on the 7.45 a.m. Paddington service, two failures within such a short space of time can hardly have endeared the new form of traction to them. Even so, there is no record on file of a written complaint from any passenger, nor for that matter in connection with the smell the engine emitted when running. The latter in particular has been commented on by railway writers in the past.

Movements from the end of February through March and most of April are uncertain although it is known the engine was working on 19 April. Shortly afterwards, between 25 May and 4 June, No. 18000 was on exhibition at the International Railway Congress, Willesden.

Following on from the Willesden exhibition normal running was resumed on the Bristol trains. But in early July 1955 a fractured crankshaft on the auxiliary diesel engine prompted a withdrawal from service and some months were spent out of service at Swindon.

Service train operation recommenced in March 1955 and continued through until November of that year. Again duties were between Paddington and Bristol although a number of minor difficulties occurred, including a fractured body suspension spring as

Damage to combustion chamber lining No. 15 taken from No. 18000 and photographed at Swindon works on 23 November 1955. These linings were repaired for re-use whenever possible. Interestingly early correspondence suggests the use of steel bricks within the liner, but this idea was not proceeded with

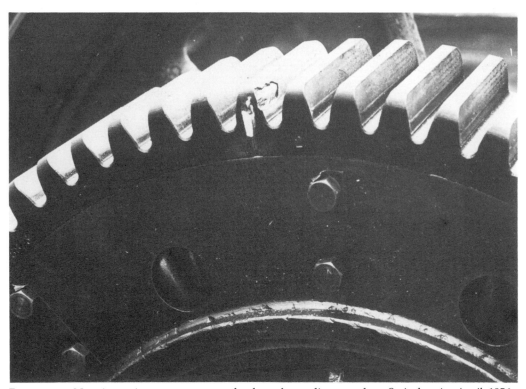

Damage to No. 4 traction motor gear wheel teeth as discovered at Swindon in April 1956. No. 18000 spent most of 1956 in Swindon works with just twenty-four miles recorded as having been run during that year

Prior to re-painting, No. 18000 is seen outside 'AE' shop at Swindon alongside a tenderless Churchward 28xx class 2–8–0, No. 2836. The steam engine was at Swindon for repair and was destined to outlast the gas turbine, not being withdrawn until June 1964

Brian Morrison

well as the more usual changes to the combustion chamber linings. After this the engine was withdrawn from service for general overhaul.

Certainly when it was running well, No. 18000 continued to give some sparkling performances, perhaps typified by its behaviour on the 4.15 p.m. Bristol–Paddington service which was routed via Bath, stopping there as well as at Chippenham. On this train it was a frequent occurrence to be held at Wootton Bassett awaiting the 4.30 p.m. 'Bristolian' express which ran via Badminton. The gas turbine also had the added handicap of the two station stops as well as the heavier gradients via Box.

Nineteen fifty-five was also the year when British Railways announced its ten-year modernization programme, intended to abolish steam traction and equip the system for the future. The fact though, that up to the end of 1955 some seventeen different combustion chamber linings had been used on No. 18000 was hardly a good omen for the use of this type of traction.

On the basis that No. 18000 was a 'one-off' its behaviour must be said to have been reasonably good, but as maintenance declined so the failures increased and eventually No. 18000 was to become very unreliable.

Perhaps typical of this was a breakdown at the head of the 1.15 p.m. down train from Paddington to Bristol, the date of which is unknown. Between Cholsey and Didcot the turbine failed to respond although it was recognized that the cause was probably electrical. The crew free wheeled to Didcot where the fault was found to be a broken resistor on the converter/motor. This was the result of a short to earth through the casing

Sporting its new green livery, No. 18000 is recorded by the official photographer at Swindon in late 1957. Notice the sand delivery pipes to the driven axles as well as the sandbox fillers located high up on the body sides. Over the years a few minor changes have been made to the external outline of the engine including a bracket for the train reporting number as well as additional steps and handrails associated with this fitment

British Railways

and hence the failure. The train was thus terminated at Didcot while a team of technicians travelled from Swindon to investigate the difficulty. They were able to afford a temporary repair and No. 18000 eventually left for Old Oak at the head of its empty stock some $3\frac{1}{2}$ hours late.

The general overhaul on No. 18000 involved the engine being out of service for the whole of 1956, indeed the official mileage for the whole of the year was just twenty-four. With No. 18000 at Swindon quite how this mileage was accrued must remain conjecture.

Despite this lack of movement some interesting details emerge from a number of photographs taken at the time of the overhaul which reveal various damaged components. These include the teeth of the gear wheels on traction motors Nos. 2 and 4 as well as views of a number of damaged turbine blades.

By this time No. 18000 was of course well out of guarantee from Brown-Boveri and so it may be concluded that the time spent at Swindon was also utilized in deciding whether to undertake what would no doubt be an expensive repair. Without written corroboration though, such a statement must only be regarded as supposition on the part of the writer although the fact that so long was spent out of service does also tend to

This time in charge of the 8.20 p.m. ex-Weston-super-Mare express, No. 18000 is seen on the up fast line shortly after entering Sonning Cutting with Earley power station just visible in the background

T.E. Williams/National Railway Museum

imply that the gas turbine project was no longer regarded as having the impetus it once commanded. Indeed the Western Region had already decided on its future traction needs using diesel-hydraulic units. The fact that no additional gas turbines had been ordered is discussed in more detail in the next chapter.

Despite the lack of official information for the period, headquarters are known to have reached an eventual decision that No. 18000 would return to service. For on 25 October 1956 there is reference to a memorandum from Smeddle at Swindon in which he states that the engine was to be re-painted in Great Western green with a number of additional embellishments:

GWR Green	–	Body sides and frame
Black	–	Battery boxes and fuel tank
Red	–	Buffer beams
Aluminium	–	Bogies, together with roof if possible. Otherwise use black. [Photographs taken after the re-painting indicate the bogies were painted black.]

There is no reference to an aluminium band around the body although contemporary observers have suggested a band did exist but painted in either red or orange.

Numbers were to remain as polished aluminium and there is again no suggestion as to any name. The BR 'cycling lion' insignia was retained although this was soon to be replaced by the newer BR emblem. Work on the re-painting commenced soon after the

A photograph which poses the interesting question: Where is it and what duty is involved? No. 18000 seen at what appears to be the head of a non-passenger working some time after 1957

Tom Middlemas

original memorandum, with a visitor to the works three weeks later recording the fact that the engine was in the course of being dealt with.

Although undated the following incident may well have been connected with the prolonged period spent undergoing overhaul, which involved former Traction Inspector Tony Tyler. He recounts that approaching Lockinge, between Wantage Road and Steventon, there was a flash and a bang from behind the cab followed by a total lack of power at the controller. The unusual fact was that the turbine was still running.

Upon examination it was found that No. 3 traction motor had seized itself solid onto the axle, which prevented the axle from turning, thereby rapidly wearing a serious 'flat' on the tyres. Not surprisingly there was nothing the crew could do under such drastic circumstances and it was not until assistance in the form of a steam engine from Didcot was summoned that No. 18000 could be removed from its train and shunted out of the way into a siding.

The cause was found to be no more serious than an oil seal which had been left off when the engine was last examined at Swindon. However, the damage was such that the decision was made not to replace the traction motor and although the wheels were re-turned, No. 18000 spent the rest of its life running on its three remaining traction motors. This itself involved a partial re-design, and as a result No. 4 motor was wired in with No. 2 for when the diesel engine was in use, and in place of Nos. 2 and 3 as had been used previously.

Sporting its new green livery No. 18000 re-entered service early in February 1957 though running-in trials were at first disappointing and involved two further incidents of traction motor flash-overs. It was not until after April that successful trials were carried out. In other areas matters were greatly improved, the life of the combustion

Steam and gas turbine meet near Goring on 19 May 1959. An unidentified 'Castle' is at the head of the down 'Cheltenham Spa Express' while No. 18000 makes towards Reading and Paddington
T.E. Williams/National Railway Museum

chamber linings being now sufficient for over 1,500 hours' running and a marked improvement on the 150 hours previously experienced. With this in mind No. 18000 was evidently considered reliable enough to be entrusted with the prestigious 'Merchant Venturer' express between Paddington and Bristol and return. In connection with the newly-relaxed regional autonomy then existing this train was one of those which had reverted to chocolate and cream coaching stock from 1 April 1957, albeit BR Mk1 vehicles, although the effect was slightly marred by the addition of a carmine and cream slip coach.

Unfortunately, in practice it was soon found that with just three traction motors working the previously arranged duties were too much for the engine and accordingly an alternative turn was found. This involved the 3.25 a.m. Paddington to Newbury newspaper train, then light engine to Hungerford for the 7.20 a.m. business train to Paddington, due in London at 9.00 a.m. This was instead of the 2.25 a.m. Bristol newspaper train as the return 7.45 a.m. up service was now too heavy a load.

After arrival in London the engine returned to Old Oak Common for fuel and then worked the 1.18 p.m. Paddington to Bristol which was restricted to about seven coaches or 230 tons, with a similar loading on the 4.15 p.m. Bristol–Paddington train. As such the milk trains were no longer hauled by No. 18000 as loads of 500 tons-plus would obviously have now been beyond its capabilities.

The new duties were evidently a success with 1957 proving a good year for No. 18000,

Assistance in the form of a freshly overhauled 'King', No. 6021 *King Richard II*, is provided for No. 18000 approaching Chippenham from the direction of Bath on 4 March 1958. Despite earlier reservations as to the ingress of soot into the turbine, this was one of the occasions when an assisting steam engine was coupled ahead, although with the turbine failed the matter was really of little consequence

Kenneth Leech

there being only one reference to it at Swindon works, during August, although how long it remained out of use is uncertain. Official records refer to just four difficulties during the year. The first when a number of thermostat tubes burnt out, then on 13 November, a ball bearing on the compressor shaft collapsed due to a blocked oil pipe and later in the year there was the first reported problem with the replacement train heating boiler – this last occurrence was sufficient to warrant three weeks out of service.

More significant perhaps, and confirming the earlier supposition that BR had almost lost interest in the engine, is that after June 1957 no official photographs appear to have been taken of defects. Prior to this the slightest problem meant a number of views were taken.

An added difficulty by the early part of 1958 was the lack of drivers experienced in operating the engine. Examples of this occurred on 3 and 4 March with two failures, both due to the inexperience of a new driver. The first was simply a lack of heavy fuel oil accentuated by the driver not shutting down the turbine at Bristol between duties. This driver was unaware that he could also operate the engine on light fuel. On 4 March lack of familiarity was again the cause of an apparent electrical defect soon after leaving Bath. Not surprisingly, there was an amount of correspondence over such incidents, with the official report stating: 'Both cases were unfortunate, but isolated cases of this kind must occur from time to time until the Drivers become fully conversant with this very complex machine . . .'

Such problems could hardly help the gas turbine cause, while the individuality of the

On what may well have been its last full day's working, No. 18000 passes Langley crossing just east of Chippenham on a Bristol-bound train, 23 September 1959, with Driver Bob Smitherham at the controls. Due to the reduction in the number of traction motors, the engine was now restricted to trains of about seven coaches or 230 tons, although on this occasion there are eight vehicles in tow, including what appears to be an ex-GWR dining car. When running normally No. 18000 was considered to be the equal of a D6xxx 'Warship'. However, it was reported as a failure the very next day, 24 September 1959, and was not seen at work again

Kenneth Leech

engine would no doubt be increasingly taken into consideration as time progressed. The total mileage recorded to 4 July 1958 was 300,500, allied to 8,060 turbine hours.

Visits to Swindon appear to have increased again during 1958 as the engine was noted in the works during April and again at the end of September. The length of time out of traffic was not recorded although it is known a fire occurred in some control cables around this time. What is certain is that on 14 August approval was given for a set of replacement stainless steel handrails to be made. The old items had become the subject of a number of complaints owing to the fact they were slippery to hold in wet weather.

As if to investigate the future of the engine on the basis of costings, Swindon prepared the following details covering the period 10 May 1950 to 1 November 1958:

Weekdays out of service	1,560
Miles run	318,995

Stored out of use at the back of Swindon works in August 1960. At this time No. 18000 was still nominally in stock although it never worked again and was officially withdrawn three months later. The engine accumulated a total mileage of some 350,000 during its life, with a 'Castle' likely to reach about 480,000 miles during the same period. The gas turbine may be said then to have achieved 75 per cent the mileage of its steam counterpart, a creditable figure for a machine which remained a 'one-off'

R.W. Hinton

Cost of maintenance:		
main works	£	49,649
depots	£	10,328
Fuel: heavy; galls		817,393
cost	£	32,282
light; galls		150,416
cost	£	8,212
Fuelling expenses	£	7,166
Lubricants; galls	£	1,971
cost	£	515
Total cost per mile		6s. 9.37d.

Based on the above figures the end for No. 18000 was surely only a matter of time and it appears to have come around September 1959. Unofficial sources reveal that the engine failed due to an unknown defect on 22 September but was back at work the next day. On 24 September however, it failed again and it appears never worked again, instead being taken to Swindon where it remained out of use until officially withdrawn over a year later in December 1960.

As far as the Western Region was concerned this was the end of the gas turbine saga, but it would indeed crop up again. Perhaps it is fitting that the steam engines No. 18000 was envisaged to replace, themselves outlasted the interloper.

FORESIGHT OR FOLLY?

Following withdrawal, No. 18000 languished for some time at the back of the works at Swindon. At this stage no BR decision as to its ultimate fate had been made although it is reasonable to assume that scrapping would probably be the next course of action.

As the reader may well be aware it transpired that No. 18000 was destined not to end up at the hands of the cutter's torch and instead would fulfill a further purpose many hundreds of miles away from its previous home on the Western Region.

Before dealing with the years subsequent to 1960 though, it is perhaps appropriate to consider instead the reasons that brought about the engine's withdrawal and indeed the conclusion of the WR gas turbine story.

To do so we must return again briefly to the 1940s and remind ourselves of the comment made by Hawksworth on 2 January 1946 that it had been decided not to proceed with a main-line diesel-electric design. Why this should be the case is still uncertain although it may well have been based on the fact that at that time the diesel-electric main-line locomotive was still some way off, though certainly for shunting the design displayed significant advantages. In a main-line context there were no equivalent designs then available as a direct comparison. What the GWR was clearly seeking was a steam substitute at least equal to existing motive power. From a production viewpoint, building cost and fuel price would also have to be comparable. It is unlikely then that even if the LMS or SR main-line diesels had been around in 1946 would Hawksworth's perception of suitable motive power for the future have altered.

Why then did he need to consider an alternative to steam? For the answer to this it is necessary to take a wider viewpoint although it would be very easy to involve government and politics at this stage. Let it be said instead that there was a need to work towards faster and heavier trains than could be handled with existing steam power. It must also be said that the trains of the late 1940s were often overcrowded and late and, while the run-down condition of the steam engine was hardly the fault of the GWR, it did little to promote the railway system to a travelling public at that time.

Accordingly, the gas turbine was seen as a potentially viable source of alternative traction allowing considerably more power from a given weight and at least equal to the most powerful types of steam traction. This is borne out by former Locomotive Inspector Stan French who recalls the Brown-Boveri as being equal to a 'King'.

So when No. 18000 took to the rails for the first time it offered a potential for power hitherto unavailable to railway operators from a self-contained power unit and as such no doubt great things were expected of it. To an extent these were realized, the ability to recover from out-of-course checks no doubt being impressive to observers.

Its reliability too may be said to have been reasonable from the outset, especially for a machine where technology was being pushed to its very limits although this was itself limited by metallurgical development. As it was, by the time the reliability of No. 18000 in service had reached a satisfactory level, so the diesel and electric lobby had advanced sufficiently to forstall any likely duplication of the design. The two factors critical to this

In store at Market Harborough. Despite a prolonged period stored out of use after withdrawal and pending its move to Switzerland, No. 18000 doesn't seem to have received the attention of vandals or souvenir hunters. Its survival was no doubt attributable to the wholesale scrapping of steam then under way which fortunately left No. 18000 forgotten. This was one of the final photographs taken of No. 18000 in England, the last of the GWR's attempts to embrace contemporary modern technology. It must be remembered that despite Swindon's apparent dislike of diesel technology, it had previously been involved with both diesel shunting engines and railcars, while there was also the electrified Ealing and Shepherd's Bush railway. Perhaps most progressive of all was a 1938 plan for the wholesale electrification of all lines west of Taunton – though a few minor branches were omitted and would have been worked by diesel. This scheme, costing some £4.3 million, would have totally eliminated steam in the West Country and so produced a considerable saving on locomotive coal together with its associated haulage costs. Unfortunately war brought an abrupt end to further planning and so it must remain conjecture as to how much of this was just an exercise in economics

Courtney Haydon

assessment were the fuel consumption of its contemporary No. 18100 and the life of the combustion chamber lining.

Of course, had the decision been made very early on for the Brown-Boveri engine to burn conventional diesel fuel, then a combustion chamber lining of the type utilized would not have been required, although offset against this would have been an increase in fuel costs. Indeed there is a certain amount of evidence to suggest that the engine was originally to have been supplied to burn conventional fuel oil and it was at the request of the GWR that No. 18000 was fitted to burn heavy fuel. The reason for this was stated to be that the conversion scheme for oil-firing steam engines was already in full swing.

Had BR considered No. 18000 sufficiently viable to develop as a replacement for steam the time to do this would have been no later than the announcement of the 1955 modernization plan. The fact that Swindon opted for diesel-hydraulic locomotives was the death knell for No. 18000. From that time on the engine was on borrowed time. But that is not to say the gas turbines did not pass on anything to the new generation of motive power, for the use of hydraulic transmission was a direct development from both Nos. 18000 and 18100, the desire being to dispense with the apparent unreliability of the electric transmission both engines possessed. In essence this was a viable and carefully considered viewpoint, for had not both engines suffered a number of electrically-derived faults ranging from generator flash-overs to traction motor failures and bogie fires? In defence of the electrical engineers though, it must be said that the last-named problems were aggravated by ignorance, the railways seemingly unaware of the essential criteria in keeping the bogies and associated traction motors free from a build-up of oil and dirt, a difficult task indeed when servicing facilities were dependent upon the conditions existing in a steam shed.

There was also a considerable degree of reluctance among engineers in relation to electric transmission, with a number of them openly stating their feelings at gatherings of the various professional and technical bodies. As an aside, this is how the 'Fell' main-line diesel engine came into being, a 2,000 hp diesel engine with mechanical transmission driving a 4-8-4 wheel arrangement, later altered to a 4-4-4-4. Regretfully it suffered a number of mechanical failures and the design was not perpetuated.

Swindon then sought an alternative to electric transmission, eventually settling on the hydraulic principle. Such a move would have to be sanctioned by the BTC and this august body was apparently willing to do this on the basis of previous BR experience with this type of transmission.

At this I can almost see the reader reaching for his pen and paper, but it must be remembered that there were already a number of diesel shunters with hydraulic transmission operating, including two types of 0-4-0, both built by the North British Locomotive Co. (BR Nos. D2700–D2707 and D2708–D2780). In addition the hydraulic principle had been used by the German Railways for a main-line unit, with the D8xx 'Warship' class being a direct derivative of this type. A number of other designs of shunter using hydraulic transmission were also built for BR after 1955, not including those constructed at or for Swindon.

Some previous railway authors have taken a slightly slanted view of the hydraulic question. It was not a question of Swindon attempting to be different; it was a genuine attempt to provide the most suitable motive power to replace steam with the full consent of Marylebone. The result was of course the various Type 2, 3 and 4 diesel-hydraulics, some of which are perhaps better known as the 'Warships', 'Hymeks' and 'Westerns', each of which owed their existence to Nos. 18000 and 18100.

To delve further into the hydraulic era is outside the province of this narrative and instead we must return to Swindon and the fate of No. 18000, now languishing disused in the works sidings.

Before doing so in detail it is necessary to explain the existence of the UIC – Union Internationale des Chemins de Fer – an international body whose headquarters are in Paris and which operates as a general forum for the exchange and standardization of railway information. A similar organization in the UK was the former Railway Clearing House . The physical location of the UIC not unnaturally affords a degree of bias towards the European railways, while a technical offshoot, the ORE – Office for Research and Development – deals with specific questions and consists almost entirely of European railways. The headquarters of the ORE is at Utrecht, Holland, where a small staff of engineers and translators seconded from the Dutch Railway system are supplemented by engineers on secondment from their own countries' railways.

In 1960 a committee was set up by the ORE to examine the problems of adhesion between wheel and rail in traction. (ORE Committee No. B44 'Adhesion of Locomotives from the point of view of their construction and operation.') Although verging on the technical the points of reference of the committee are worthy of recounting.

In relation to the problem under investigation, the great advantage of a steel wheel on a steel rail – compared with rubber on tarmac – is a very much lower rolling resistance. Against this advantage comes a problem when there is the desire to accelerate or brake sharply, as the wheels will spin or slide. It was the traction aspects of acceleration that B44 was set up to examine.

The magnitude of the adhesion coefficient, the relationship between the vertical force applied to the wheel on the rail and the tractive effort which can be transmitted by the wheel to the rail, depends on a large number of factors. These can be grouped into three categories:

1. Material Factors such as the type of steel used in the wheel and rail. Also surface contaminants, oil, water, rust, autumn leaves, living organisms (caterpillars, etc.) on the rail.
2. Shape Factors such as the cross-section of wheel and rail, and wheel diameter. These factors affect the size and shape of the area in which wheel and rail are actually touching each other.
3. Speed Factors such as the running speed of the vehicle and the relative sliding speed of the wheel surface on the rail.

No. 18000 in its new guise as a test vehicle, carrying the name 'Elisabetta', which can be discerned between the front footsteps. The photograph was taken on the Wadgassen to Ueberherrn line on 22 September 1970 and shows the engine in its livery of red oxide with white lettering. Note the alterations to the bogie as well as the extensions to the body sides. Although unconfirmed it also appears that the headlamps have been replaced

Peter Swift

Besides the adhesion coefficient itself, there are two further factors which affect the ability of a locomotive to pull. Firstly, variations in the vertical wheel/rail force, due to the tendency for the front of the locomotive to lift as traction is applied and the movement of the suspension on track irregularities. These effects can be reduced by suitable design measures. Secondly, the ability of traction control systems to make the best use of such adhesion coefficient as is available.

In the early 1960s, it was generally understood that all these factors played a part in governing the ability of a locomotive to pull, but no one really knew exactly how the different factors operated. With the development of ever lighter locomotives of increasing power, the problem was becoming more important. ORE Committee B44 was set up to find the answers, or at least some of them.

By the mid-1960s, it was apparent that in order to investigate the effects of locomotive design parameters on adhesion, it was necessary to have a locomotive on which individual features could be changed, one by one. However, even with international cooperation, finance would not run to the building of a complete new locomotive for test purposes.

The BR representative on the committee then offered No. 18000 for this use, while his Swiss counterpart offered the facilities of the Belinzona workshops at the south end of the St Gotthard main line. This offer was accepted and accordingly No. 18000 was moved from Swindon to Market Harborough and then via the Harwich–Zeebrugge train ferry to Switzerland.

At Belinzona the gas turbine power plant, generator, train heating boiler and control equipment were removed, which had the effect of reducing the weight by some fifty-seven tons. This was compensated for by placing old rails and lead weights between the frame members. The traction motors were also removed from both bogies.

Besides having the traction motors removed, the second bogie from No. 18000 was totally reconstructed, with the centre part of the bogie frame being modified to take various combinations of wheel size, traction motor and drive system for the centre axle.

The single powered axle was provided with an oleo-pneumatic suspension on which the axle load could be set and maintained at a desired figure between thirteen and twenty-two tons. This was achieved by an adjustment of air pressure. The single motor powering this axle was now mounted above the bogie frame and projected well into the locomotive body. From being an A1–A1A, No. 18000 now became a 1A1–3!

A single Alsthom TAO 646-type motor, as used on the SNCF Monomotor-drive electric locomotives, was used. Initially this drove 920 mm wheels, but 1,400 mm wheels were later substituted. During 1974, No. 18000 was rebuilt again, this time being fitted with two 10 HW 895 motors of the type used on the DB and Swiss $16\frac{2}{3}$ Hz systems.

Despite being intended for operation under overhead wires, no pantograph was provided. The traction motor took its power via cables fed in through the cab fronts from another locomotive. Besides saving valuable space this enabled the power supplied from different types of locomotive to be compared. The feeding locomotive operated as a mobile sub-station and its own traction motors were not used.

The locomotive body was still largely recognizable from the outside, although the lower part was widened towards one end so as to give more space to the modified bogie. Interestingly, a whistle was added which was operated by compressed air, its position being basically identical to the one carried by the engine when new.

Internally the two driving cabs remained although with new controls and instru-

A test train at Ueberherrn station. The formation is No. 18000, SNCF BB18665, DB test coach, SNCF BB186xx and SNCF CC14xxx

Peter Swift

ments. The rest of the locomotive was divided into three parts. Above the modified bogie was the casing around the motor together with brake and other air equipment. Next to this was a small compartment in the centre of the locomotive where the high pressure oleo-pneumatic system for suspension of the powered axle was housed together with a petrol-driven generator set. The third compartment, and nearly half the total length between the cab bulkheads, was the instrumentation compartment. This contained racking for measuring and recording instruments and also working tables. Much of the equipment was supplied by the Austrian Federal Testing and Experimental Institute (BVFA Bunde Versuchs Federal Testing Anstalt) in Vienna. Instrumentation was provided to measure continuously the tractive effort, vertical wheel load, slip and lateral position of the wheels on the rail.

During actual testing a test train was built up and consisted typically of:

No. 18000, with powered bogie leading.
The electric locomotive providing power to No. 18000.
A laboratory coach used for additional instrumentation and facilities.
A braking locomotive able to apply an electric brake load to the train and thus able to control the load on No. 18000.
An additional locomotive to take the whole convoy back to the start following each test run. This was normally another electric locomotive although on one occasion a DB class '50' 2–10–0 steam engine was provided.

Most of the tests were carried out between Wadgassen and Ueberherrn, on a DB/SNCF cross-border freight line connecting the Saar and Lorraine regions. This 9 km

133

Inside the instrumentation department. Messrs Doll (DB), Diemling and Lihl (BVFA – Vienna), discuss an aspect of the test

Peter Swift

section of line could be energized either by the SNCF 25 Kv 50 Hz system or on the DB 15 Kv 16⅔ Hz power supply – obviously though, not at the same time!

Tests were also carried out on the SNCF Annecy–La Roche sur Foron line which was used to examine the effects of severe curvature on adhesion. A final series of tests was on the DB Neubecken–Guetersloh route where the effect on new types of track structure was tested. Other sources refer to trials between Wadgassen and Hargarten and Veberherrn and Hargarten.

The trials were terminated soon after May 1975, after which No. 18000 travelled to Vienna where the instruments were removed. It was subsequently placed on a short length of track outside the Mechanical Engineering Testing building in Vienna.

The subsequent life of the Metropolitan Vickers engine, No. 18100, after 1958 is briefly told because, as recounted in Chapter 3, BR was quick to suggest a possible conversion of the locomotive to a straight electric following the manufacturer's admission that a change to burn heavy fuel was impracticable.

After its arrival at the Bowsfield works of Metropolitan Vickers/Beyer Peacock Ltd near Stockton-on-Tees, work began almost at once on the necessary conversion. This involved the removal of the gas turbine power unit together with its associated equipment and electrical equipment substituted. Two of the traction motors were also removed which altered the wheel arrangement from Co–Co to A1A–A1A. Items such as fuel tanks were also now superfluous and removed although this left the underframe with a somewhat naked appearance. To suit its new role a single Stone-Faiveley pantograph was fitted, with the roof line lowered slightly in consequence.

While the conversion work continued BR and Metropolitan Vickers were still attempting to resolve the financial implications of the project with particular reference to the original agreement for construction. (See Appendix A.) BR's first offer was to pay Metropolitan Vickers £14,000 to cover the retention of the mechanical parts of the locomotive, including the traction motors, although this was later altered, whereby BR would retain these items at no cost while Metropolitan Vickers had the actual gas turbine power plant returned.

On the face of it this was probably a better deal than the railway could have anticipated, as budgeting for a new electric locomotive would have cost some £75,000 at that time, of which £30,000 was estimated to be required for mechanical parts and £45,000 for electrical equipment. (A further figure of £27,000 appears in certain documents in relation to the actual cost of the conversion work, though there is a degree of ambiguity as to how this figure was calculated.)

In its new guise No. 18100, now re-numbered E1000, emerged from the Bowsfield works in October 1958, its overall weight now reduced to 109 tons with a total output of 2,500 hp at a maximum 40,000 lb tractive effort. Externally, it was still much as before, its appearance heightened by the retention of the original black and silver livery which later gave rise to the nickname of 'Black-Bess' – an oblique reference to the mount of the legendary highwayman Dick Turpin. Aesthetically, probably the worst aspect of the conversion was the slicing of a portion from the side of each buffer which was necessary to ensure the engine complied with the LMR loading gauge.

In its new guise the engine was used for driver training on the Wilmslow–Mauldeth Park (via Styal) line and as such performed a useful role prior to the delivery of the first producion 25 Kv electric locomotives.

Its function as a crew trainer was destined to be short-lived, for the new engines began to arrive in late 1959 and as such it was obviously impractical to continue work involving a single, totally non-standard design with different traction characteristics. For the purposes of the training programme, maintenance and stabling was at East Didsbury, although the official allocation lists show the engine allocated to Longsight depot.

A change of number occurred in October 1959, this time to E2001. A change of depots occurred shortly afterwards, with No. E2001 now being used at Allerton depot (Liverpool) as well as Crewe, and then in April 1961, at Glasgow.

As time passed however, the engine was used less and less and was subsequently stored in the open for long periods at Crewe, Goostrey, Market Harborough and Rugby. While at the last-named location, a time was spent on trial within the engine testing house there, after which No. E2001 spent four years out of use at the nearby EMU sidings.

Withdrawn for the second time in 1968, No. E2001 was sent to the former Grendon Underwood Junction–Ashendon Junction line of the former GC, where it was used for static trials based on the effect of wind on pantographs.

On 15 September 1972, the engine was sold for scrap to John Cashmore Ltd and was broken up at its Tipton (Staffordshire) site in January 1973.

With neither Nos. 18000 nor 18100 now in existence in England it would be easy to end the narrative at this point, although to do so would still leave a number of un-answered questions. One of these must be: Why was a decision made to withdraw No. 18100 from service in September 1953 when it will be recalled that at the time the reason was stated to be, '. . . in accordance with the original test programme'?

As intimated in Chapter 3 this is believed to be a totally inaccurate statement. For just a few months earlier A.W.J. Dymond, in his paper 'Operating Experiences with two Gas Turbine Locomotives', first presented to the Institute of Locomotive Engineers in February 1953, was asked this specific point: 'Col. Cantlie asked if the Metropolitan Vickers engine was to to be fitted with Bunker C oil? The Author said there was no such intention.' (Reported in the *Proceedings* of the Institution.)

The former Metropolitan Vickers gas turbine No. 18100 on test as a straight electric engine at the Rugby Test Plant and re-numbered E2001. In connection with the conversion the engine was converted from right- to left-hand drive, while its controls and instrumentation duplicated that later fitted in the first generation of AC electric locomotives used on the West Coast main line. As a gas turbine the total cost of manufacture was reported as £276,808 6s. and the cost of modifications a further £54,346 16s. 8d. to Metropolitan Vickers and £16,725 16s. 7d. to BR. On the basis of the original agreement BR paid Metropolitan Vickers £157,214 16s. 7d. for the engine which was destined to work in revenue-earning service in its original form for less than eighteen months. Following its conversion to an electric engine Swindon despatched a number of spares to Derby while other items, now redundant, were scrapped

Colin Marsden

More likely was the fact that it was already realized that the cost of fuel for No. 18000 was excessive and could not be justified. Indeed reports state the equivalent cost of fuel consumption for the engine to have been twice that of a steam locomotive. Both steam and gas turbine were also doing basically the same task, for the working diagrams of the day failed to allow for a revenue-earning train weight which could then justify utilizing such an amount of fuel.

Why not simply withdraw the engine without any pretext of a conversion? Here it is likely that BR was extremely conscious of the effect of public and press opinion. Just a few months earlier in January 1953 BR had been lambasted in the press following the 'Leader' fiasco and was no doubt unwilling to leave itself open to a further battering in this way. (See the author's book *Leader: Steam's Last Chance*, published by Alan Sutton.)

The decision then to attempt a conversion of No. 18100 to burn heavy fuel was a clever one; the fact that it failed to be achieved can only be a matter of regret, although with hindsight the conversion would have had to be completed very quickly and proven as successful immediately, to have had any appreciable effect on the locomotives ordered for the 1955 modernization plan.

A rather battered-looking E2001 at Akeman Street on 30 October 1971. It was sold for scrap eleven
months later in September 1972 and broken up shortly afterwards

Courtney Haydon

If there was a casualty in the whole affair it was surely Metropolitan Vickers, although
a tailpiece from the company's in-house journal for 1952 reporting the fact that the new
engine had just entered service, was written almost as if it knew the experiment was
already doomed:

> It is on overseas railways, rather than in this country, that the gas turbine is
> expected to make its greatest contribution to transport. Its special qualities
> can be used to advantage where train loads are heavy, gradients are long and
> severe, coal of locomotive quality is scarce and expensive, and water is of
> poor quality or has to be transported over long distances. These are
> conditions encountered in many countries abroad.

Indeed there was at first considerable interest in both engines, with some emanating
from overseas. Objectively it appears much of this was based on technical interest rather
than in relation to multiplying the type. Even so other gas turbines did appear including
one built by Renault in France around 1953. This was a 1,000 hp machine carried on two
four-wheel bogies, which ran trials for some nine years. Following on from the French
tests a proposal was made to build a 2,400 hp engine although no other information has
been found on this subject.

It was to be in America that the gas turbine railway locomotive really developed. A
prototype 4,500 hp machine was built in 1949 which, between August 1949 and March

1951, ran some 94,885 miles on freight trains, the average weight of which was 3,000 tons. As with the Brown-Boveri-built machine, the American engine used Bunker C or residue oil as fuel and burnt 1.2 million gallons during this time.

The prototype was followed in 1952 by an order for fifteen engines of basically the same type, but with a cab at only one end. All were of the B–B–B–B type, 84 ft in length, weighing 284 tons, with a tractive effort of 105,000 lb. More were delivered in 1954 and finally, thirty massive 8,500 hp gas tubines in 1958. These last-named machines gained the nickname 'Big-Blow', a distinct reference to the noise they made when warming up. Noise was indeed a problem, for within 50 ft conversation was impossible and six of the engines in a yard reportedly created bedlam! They were used on freight between Wyoming and Utah although they succumbed to the new generation of diesel locomotives in 1969.

In design all the locomotives so far referred to followed the basic principles of the gas turbine. An alternative to this was the 'Gas Generator' engine where exhaust gases from a diesel engine were used to drive a turbine. With the onward development of the diesel engine the appeal of this type of prime mover quickly diminished although it is reported that seven examples were built worldwide between 1933 and 1956.

An interesting item of correspondence has also been located for November 1952 in which a Mr Alan Muntz wrote to Swindon suggesting a joint project for the building of a 2,000 hp Pescara/Muntz turbine. Such an offer was politely declined – the WR already had its hands full!

So why did Nos. 18000 and 18100 fail to come up to expectations? No. 18100 obviously because of its excessive fuel consumption, while No. 18000 failed to show any significant advantage over the simpler diesel engine. But it was certainly not a waste of time and should hardly be regarded as a waste of effort. Indeed it must be recalled that during the early 1950s diesel fuel was comparatively cheap; the problem was that the country hardly had sufficient reserves of foreign currency to purchase its oil requirements. It was therefore a question of using the limited resources available to best advantage and this did *not* mean via a gas-guzzling No. 18100. The Suez crisis nearly threatened the introduction of large-scale dieselization and indeed, had this been followed by further conflict in the Middle East, then the 1955 modernization plan would no doubt have had to be rewritten. Ironically it was conflict among the oil producers in the early 1970s that proved a decisive factor in the development of North Sea Oil – the days of cheap fuel had gone forever.

Against such a background it is easy to undertstand how a proposal came about in the early 1950s for a coal-burning gas turbine which so nearly came to fruition. It is briefly described in Appendix K.

For comparing running costs, BR figures dealing with the fuel costs for a variety of motive power make for interesting reading:

	Year	Cost per mile (d.)
LM diesels	1951	18.887 d.
LM diesels	by June 1952	21.153 d.
Gas turbine No. 18000	1951	27.5 d.
Gas turbine No. 18100	1952	50.0 d. (approx.)
'Star' class 4–6–0	1951	22.0 d.
'Castle' class 4–6–0	1951	21.0 d.
'King' class 4–6–0	1951	20.5 d.

Availability figures also prove interesting:

1951 (Weekdays)

	Annual mileage	Days under repair	Days not required	Days in service	%
'King'	50,584	126	3	180	58.3
'Castle'	48,740	83	3	223	72.2
'Star'	40,818	62	2	245	79.3
No. 18000	40,403	137	1	171	55.3

1952 (Weekdays)

	Annual mileage	Days under repair	Days not required	Days in service	%
'King'	49,248	133	2	174	56.3
'Castle'	48,870	84	2	223	72.2
'Star'	40,285	68	2	239	77.3
Nos. 18000/18100	59,818	128	–	181	58.6

1953 – not available

1954 (Weekdays)

	Annual mileage	Days under repair	Days not required	Days in service	%
'King'	51,010	Other details not given			
'Castle'	48,972				
'Star' × 3	41,351				
No. 18000	18,872				

1955 (Weekdays)

	Annual mileage	Days under repair	Days not required	Days in service	%
'King'	48,071	Other details not given			
'Castle'	47,561				
'Star' × 3	40,019				
No. 18000	23,690				

1956 (Weekdays)

	Annual mileage	Days under repair	Days not required	Days in service	%
'King'	50,328	137	1	171	55.0
'Castle'	45,553	103	1	205	66.0
'Star'	40,272	58	2	249	81.0
No. 18000	24	Out of service 309 days			

1957 – not available

1958 (Weekdays)

	Annual mileage	Days under repair	Days not required	Days in service	%
'King'	55,291	118	1	190	61.0
'Castle'	48,879	88	1	220	71.0
No. 18000	45,640	178	5	126	41.0

1959 (Weekdays)

	Annual mileage	Days under repair	Days not required	Days in service	%
'King'	48,426	Other details not given			
'Castle'	45,879				
No. 18000	19,570				
A1A–A1A 'Warship'	72,063				
B–B 'Warship'	120,402				

1960 (Weekdays)

	Annual mileage	Days under repair	Days not required	Days in service	%
'King'	47,620				
'Castle'	42,981				
No. 18000	No information given				

There is a danger though of reading too much into the figures, especially where a steam class consisted of only a limited number of examples. Such was the case with the 'Star' class during the period in question and as such, with the examples given, the availability of the class would appear to indicate this was the best of all the steam types. A more accurate assessment however, of steam versus the more modern type of traction, is given in the single year's figures for the new 'Warship' class diesels in 1959.

The demise of the two gas turbines could hardly have been a real surprise to anyone. But they did point the way forward in many respects, not the least of which was in relation to their electric transmission. Later the electric traction motor would be blamed for a lot of the punishment given to track today, so much so that in the 1970s certain LMR West coast electrics were restricted in speed because of the effect they had on the permanent way.

The gas turbine story on BR could therefore be expected to be over, but some, it seemed, were not yet prepared to let it die. Enter GT3, the number given to the third gas turbine to take to the rails in this country. Built by English Electric at the Vulcan Foundry, here was a bold attempt to prove the gas turbine had a worthwhile future. In effect it was a lost cause from the start, though a fascinating project. Space does not allow for more than a cursory glance at GT3 in Appendix L.

Finally there was the gas turbine-powered APT which showed state-of-the-art technology as a number of individual turbines were used. These allowed for flexibility in operating costs as well as ensuring reliability. Certainly the APT was fast, 152 mph being achieved in trial running between Swindon and Reading in August 1975. Complexity was to be its downfall, although the legacy of the design may be seen in the present-day HST sets – albeit powered by diesel piston engines.

Instead of gas turbine propulsion the Western Region opted for diesel hydraulics as a replacement for steam traction. Even so the use of hydraulic transmission instead of electric traction motors was a direct throwback to experience gained with Nos. 18000 and 18100 and was far from, as has been suggested elsewhere, Swindon wanting to be different. Unfortunately the hydraulic era was destined to be short-lived because the hydraulic design eventually resulted in more complicated electrics than would have been required for a straight diesel with electric transmission. In addition, the pairing of the types of engines with the transmissions used was far from ideal. One of the good-looking 'Western' class diesel hydraulics is seen here outside Paddington when brand-new in 1962

Had the GWR survived as an independent company we may well have seen a fleet of gas turbines. Perhaps it is too much to hope that the shell of No.18000 may one day be returned to England, as a symbol of the Great Western's last attempt at maintaining its independence.

THE GAS TURBINE THEORY

A technical description of Nos. 18000 and 18100

The jet, or 'ram air' jet engine, to give it its more correct title, has been the cause of a worldwide transport revolution within the space of a single generation.

Credit for this must go to its inventor, Sir Frank Whittle, although it must be said that he has perhaps not received the recognition he really deserved. Whittle's first patent for this type of engine was logged as far back as 1930 and, while it was 1941 before the first aircraft fitted with a Whittle engine flew, a number of other inventors and companies had in the meantime taken up the idea of the jet engine and developed it much quicker than its pioneer. Brown-Boveri could well be said to have been among them. The theory of the turbine as a means of propulsion had in fact been known by several engineers for a number of years. Obstacles however, in the form of turbine and generator design, together with finding a material strong enough to be used for the blades of a gas turbine, precluded development of the principle until resolved by Whittle.

It is not proposed to go into the history of the turbine at this stage; suffice it to say that in the same way in which the railways had first revolutionized land transport in the nineteenth century, so the jet aircraft has provided a cheap and accessible means of rapid transport over long distances in the twentieth. Both the railways and ocean liners have therefore suffered the effects of competition, but while the railways have survived, where the ratio of time and distance is favourable, the ocean liner is now a relic of a past age.

At a time when the jet engine was beginning to appear as a reliable propulsion unit it made sense for its application to be attempted in a variety of ways. Some of these have already been referred to, e.g. snow clearance, the gas turbine-engined motor car and, of course, its locomotive connections.

There are several variants of the actual 'jet' engine, including the Whittle-type turbo jet, Lorin engine, Supercharged turbo jet, By-pass turbo jet, etc. In principle, all comply with Newton's third law of motion which states that, 'For every force there is an equal and opposite reaction.' One common example of this law in everyday use is the rotating garden sprinkler, where the force of the water causes the sprinkler to rotate as a result of the action of the water jets. The force is the water inlet and the opposite reaction, the rotation of the device.

In the case of the GWR-promoted engines, both Nos. 18000 and 18100 were fitted with a Whittle-type turbo jet engine and it is therefore necessary to delve into the mechanics of this type of unit which may not otherwise be familiar to the railway reader. Described in its simplest form the engine allowed air to be drawn into a compressor before passing through a combustion chamber, finally providing the power to rotate a turbine. In conventional aeronautical terms this force would then expel the air to provide forward (or reverse) thrust, although in the case of Nos. 18000 and 18100 the output was utilized to drive an electrical generator, which in turn provided power to axle-driving traction motors.

In more detailed terms, the gas turbine works by inhaling large quantities of air into a compressor and then heating this air by passing it through a combustion chamber in which fuel oil is burned. The air then emerges from the combustion chamber at high velocity to drive a turbine. The exhaust from the turbine then passes through a heat exchanger where some of the waste heat is transferred to newly-inhaled air, prior to this entering the compressor. This increases efficiency thereby saving fuel. The whole is referred to as a single-stage, open-cycle gas turbine.

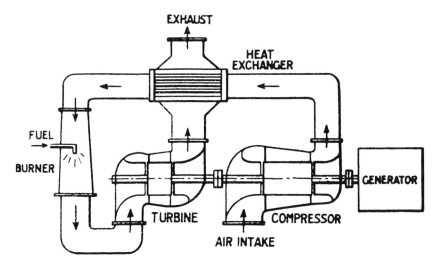

Schematic drawing of the gas turbine principle with a single-stage compressor

Although both Nos. 18000 and 18100 utilized the same basic type of propulsion unit there were a number of distinct differences between the two engines. Fortunately, both are well described in separate Railway Executive publications which, although going into the subject in some detail, are deserving of reproduction in order that the reader may become fully acquainted with the respective designs.

THE BROWN-BOVERI ENGINE

POWER UNIT

With regard to No. 18000, the Railway Executive publication included a valuable diagram:

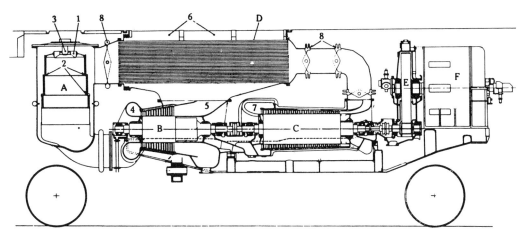

A. Combustion Chamber	1. Combustion Air Swirl Vanes
B. Gas Turbine	2. Secondary Air Inlets
C. Air Compressor	3. Burner Nozzle
D. Heat Exchanger	4. Turbine Inlet
E. Generator Reduction Gear	5. Turbine Exhaust
F. Generator	6. Exhaust louvres to atmosphere
	7. Compressor air inlet
	8. Expansion joints

A single-stage, open-cycle gas turbine (B) with heat exchanger (D) is used for the power unit, a cross section of which is shown. The air is aspirated by the compressor (C), compressed and passed through the heat exchanger (D), where it is preheated and delivered to the combustion chamber (A). There, part of the air is used for the combustion of the fuel oil injected under pressure, whilst the remaining and by far larger part serves to cool the side walls of the combustion chamber and to reduce the gas temperature at the turbine inlet (4) to the value determined by the heat resisting qualities of the blade material and the long service life demanded for such a plant. The hot gases expanding in the gas turbine (B) produce mechanical work, part of which is used to drive the compressor (C) and the rest, forming the actual useful output, transmitted to the main generator (F) through a reduction gear (E). Before escaping through roof louvres (6) to the atmosphere the turbine exhaust gases pass through the heat exchanger (D) giving up part of their heat to the compressed air on its way to the combustion chamber (A) which brings about a corresponding reduction in fuel consumption.

The air is aspirated through openings symmetrically placed in either side wall of the locomotive and connected to the air intakes (7) of the compressor (C) by two closed ducts. This has been done in order to prevent the combustion air getting mixed with oil vapours or preheated in the machine room. The casing of the multistage axial flow compressor (C) is of cast steel and rests on the auxiliary frame which also carries the gas turbine (B) and the generator (F) with gear (E). The compressor blades are of special steel. The air outlet pipe from the compressor is provided with several expansion joints (8) in order to deal with the different expansions of the gas turbine set and the heat exchanger (D). The latter consists of a great number of tubes expanded at both ends into the tubeplate.

In contradistinction to plants derived from aircraft design there is only one combustion chamber (A), which has a replaceable liner of special steel. The fuel is delivered by a separate pump set and sprayed into the combustion chamber by a single centrally locked injection nozzle of special design (3). The combustion air is admitted to the spray through swirl vanes (1). The set is started up on light fuel (Diesel) oil, and when thoroughly warmed through is changed over to heavy fuel oil for normal service. In order to obtain good atomisation in the burner nozzle the high viscosity heavy fuel oil used is preheated in a system of tubes placed in the stream of the exhaust gases. The flame in the combustion chamber is ignited at starting up of the set by an electrically heated ignition element. As the combustion gases pass down the combustion chamber they are gradually mixed with the excess air until a uniform temperature is reached at the gas turbine inlet.

The inlet casing of the multi-stage reaction type gas turbine is of special cast steel, the blades of a special heat resisting alloy.

Stainless steel has been used for the slotted roof portion over the heat exchanger through which the exhaust gases leave the locomotive.

In order to reduce radiation losses all parts of the power unit are lagged and covered with aluminium sheeting.

The gas turbine and the air compressor are each supported by two journal bearings, the compressor end bearing being a combined journal and thrust bearing to take up any residual axial forces of the set. The generator is driven from the compressor shaft through a single helical reduction gear equipped with a special collar to take up the axial thrust due to the inclination of the teeth. Pinion and compressor shaft are connected by a toothed coupling. All bearings of the thermal-electric unit are lubricated by oil under pressure supplied from a direct driven gear type oil pump located in the main gear case. Fin type oil coolers are mounted in the air intake openings in the side walls of the locomotive.

Characteristic data of the heavy fuel oil used:

Specific Gravity	: 0.95 at 60°F/60°F
Viscosity	: Redwood No.1, 950 secs at 100°F
Net Calorific Value	: 17,400 BTU/lb
Ash Content	: about 0.02 per cent (0.1 per cent maximum)

Main technical data of the gas turbine power unit as fitted to No. 18000 at full load:

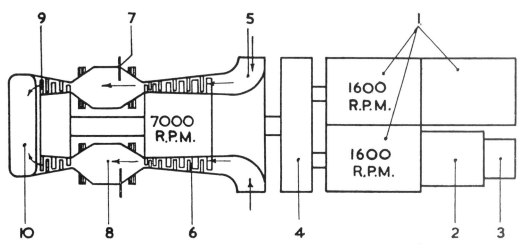

1. Three main generators
2. Auxiliary main generator
3. Exciter for main generator
4. Gear box: input shaft 7,000 rpm, two output shafts 1,600 rpm
5. Air intake for compressor
6. Compressor
7. Fuel injection nozzles
8. Combustion chamber comprising six flame tubes arranged around the main shaft
9. Turbine
10. Turbine Exhaust

Direction of Air Flow shown by Arrows

Compressor delivery pressure	: 36 lb per sq in
Gas turbine inlet temperature	: 1,100 °F
Temperature of gas at exhaust to atmosphere	: about 480 °F
Gas turbine and compressor speed	: 5,800 rpm (3 pre-set speeds – 2,800, 3,800 or 5,800 rpm)
Gear ratio	: 6.6:1
Generator speed	: 875 rpm
Input at generator coupling	: 2,500 hp
Overall thermal efficiency	: 16.9 per cent
Corresponding fuel consumption	: 0.87 lb/hp hr

Dealing again with No. 18000, its principal dimensions were as follows:

Length over buffers	: 63 ft 0 in
Maximum height from rails	: 13 ft 4 in
Diameter of driving wheels	: 4 ft 0$\frac{1}{2}$ in
Diameter of carrying wheels	: 3 ft 2 in
Continuous rating of gas turbine unit	: 2,500 hp
Tractive effort measured at wheels:	
during starting;	: 31,500 lb up to about 21 mph
continuously;	: 12,400 lb at 64 mph
	: 8,400 lb at 90 mph
Maximum speed	: 90 mph
Number of driving axles and traction motors	: 4
Weight of mechanical parts	: 52 tons 13 cwt 2$\frac{1}{4}$ qtrs
Weight of thermal parts	: 32 tons 2 cwt 3$\frac{1}{2}$ qtrs
Weight of electrical equipment	: 23 tons 13 cwt 0$\frac{3}{4}$ qtrs
Weight of stores (inc. fuel, water, sand, etc.)	: 7 tons 11 cwt 3 qtrs
Adhesive weight	: 77 tons 13 cwt 2$\frac{1}{4}$ qtrs
Fuel	: Heavy fuel oil (Light diesel oil to start)

Besides the actual power unit, the mechanics and electrics of No. 18000 were also described in the Railway Executive booklet:

The mechanical part, which was designed by the Swiss Locomotive and Machine Works, Winterthur, consists essentially of two three-axle bogies, the main frame, and the coach body supported thereon.

The main frame of the bogie is a closed box section, made of high grade steel and welded throughout. Care has been taken to avoid excessive concentration of stress.

The bogie frame rests on the axleboxes through helical springs. The axleboxes have SKF roller bearings and are guided by two vertical cylindrical pins. These pins are case hardened and ground. Screwed inside them are rods for holding the boxes in a downward position and for fixing the friction dampers. In order to damp out vertical oscillations a dry friction damping device is provided underneath, the amount of damping of which can be adjusted.

The two outer axles on each bogie are each driven by an electric motor through gears; the centre axles on each bogie being carrying axles.

The driving axles are held sideways on the driving side only, the outside race of the roller bearing being held there between the two covers of the bearing. On the outer side the roller bearing is provided with a certain amount of side play.

The arrangement for the support of the body and the transmission of the tractive and braking forces, is on this new design of three axle bogie with lateral play of the middle axle as developed by the Swiss Locomotive and Machine Works, Winterthur. The body rests at each side on two corresponding springs and through the supports lodged in buckets forming one piece with the buckle of the springs. These buckles and consequently their springs are made to move integrally with the main frame by links. The ends of the springs forming one pair are connected by equalisers which transmit their load to the frame through the inclined spring hangers. These are also joined to each other by means of the floating beams which, for sideways movements, make them move integrally with the body by means of the coupling links and the crosshead. All the articulations between the body and the bogies for controlling lateral and longitudinal motions, are fitted with silentblocs. In order to allow for side play of the middle axle, the axlebox is separated from the guides and the vertical load is transmitted from the box to the guides by means of floating beams which also exert on the axle at the same time a certain centring force.

The driving motors transmit their torque to the wheels through the Brown-Boveri Individual Axle Drive with quill stump and spring coupling. With this drive a considerable reduction in the total unsprung weight is achieved in contradistinction to nose suspended motors, because it allows the motor and gear to be rigidly fixed in the bogie frame. The unsprung weight is thus reduced to a minimum comprising only the wheels, axle, axleboxes and the carrier disc. Transmission of the torque to the driving axle is on one side only.

UNDERFRAME

The underframe of the locomotive is carried on the bogie bolsters as previously explained. The underframe girder is welded throughout and built up of constructional steel sheet. The cross stretchers and stiffeners are secured by rivets. Built into the underframe between the bogies are the tanks for water, heavy fuel oil and lubricating oil together with components for the storage battery and pump sets.

The auxiliary frame, containing a built-in tank for light fuel oil, carries the entire thermal power unit and is supported in the main frame on a three point suspension. This arrangement prevents the elastic distortions of the locomotive from being transmitted to the auxiliary frame and thus to the thermal unit and ensures a very steady riding of the locomotive.

The sections of the locomotive body, i.e. the side panels as well as the roof sections, are bolted to the ribs (continuous or in sections where necessary), thereby making the structure sufficiently elastic so that the deflection of the locomotive main frame, approximately $\frac{3}{8}$ in, will not cause the body to distort.

The coach body is sub-divided by tightly fitting partition walls into the two closed-off driving cabs and the engine room. Each cab has two side doors and a third one leading to the machine

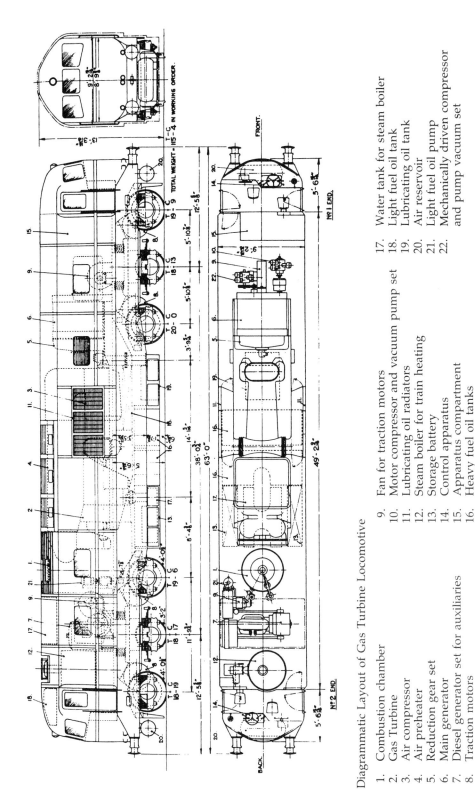

Diagrammatic Layout of Gas Turbine Locomotive

1. Combustion chamber
2. Gas Turbine
3. Air compressor
4. Air preheater
5. Reduction gear set
6. Main generator
7. Diesel generator set for auxiliaries
8. Traction motors

9. Fan for traction motors
10. Motor compressor and vacuum pump set
11. Lubricating oil radiators
12. Steam boiler for train heating
13. Storage battery
14. Control apparatus
15. Apparatus compartment
16. Heavy fuel oil tanks

17. Water tank for steam boiler
18. Light fuel oil tank
19. Lubricating oil tank
20. Air reservoir
21. Light fuel oil pump
22. Mechanically driven compressor and pump vacuum set

147

A completed bogie. The difference in springing arrangements for the driven and non-driven axles is apparent, as are the large ducts feeding air to the traction motors. The bogie itself was of tubular construction and supported the body on a centre pivot with side bearers. A feature of the design was the use of spoked wheels, with all the driven axles being interchangeable. Notice also the floating beams and helical springs

Asea Brown-Boveri

room which is provided with two side gangways. The two driving compartments are riveted to the main frame, whereas the middle part of the body is bolted for its whole length to the floor plating of the frame. With the exception of those of the train heating boiler compartment, all side panels can be removed from the body frame from the outside, so that the greatest possible accessibility to the power unit and apparatus is provided. The central portions of both side walls are occupied by the oil cooler assembly consisting of three coolers on each side. As regards the frame of the body itself, the main body ribs between the compartment for the steam heating boiler and that for electrical apparatus can also be removed in order that the complete power unit, including the generator and combustion chamber, can be placed in position from above.

The roof sections over the train heating boiler and over the power unit are removable in order to facilitate the erection of the larger parts of the equipment. The roof above the combustion chamber is provided with ventilation louvres and the part over the heat exchanger with longitudinal baffled slots which allow the exhaust to escape without permitting rain water to enter. The roof portions above the auxiliary diesel and the rear cab accommodate service tanks for water and light fuel oil.

The locomotive has a compressed air brake system for the locomotive and vacuum brake equipment for the train. This arrangement was necessary because the restricted overall dimensions to which the locomotive had to be built precluded the use of vacuum equipment on the locomotive. The two systems are so combined that by the operation of one control handle by the driver the brakes are simultaneously and proportionately applied both on the locomotive and on the train. In addition, however, the driver has at his disposal a second brake handle which only

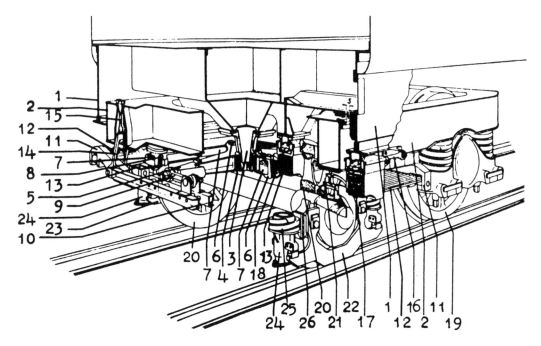

Perspective Section of Main Frame and SLM Bogie

1. Body underframe
2. Bogie frame
3. Centre pivot
4. Centre pivot silentbloc bearing
5. Cross head transmitting the tractive effort and holding the swing bolster transverse beam
6. Draw-bar link pin with silentbloc bearing
7. Draw-bar transmitting the tractive effort
8. Bogie frame link pin with silentbloc bearing
9. Swing bolster transverse beam connecting link with silentbloc bearings
10. Transverse beam for swing bolster
11. Cross equalizing beam for the body suspension springs
12. Outer body suspension spring
13. Inner body suspension spring
14. Spring hangers
15. Spring hanger adjusting bolts
16. Longitudinal connecting link for body suspension spring
17. Outer body side bearing with oil trough
18. Inner body side bearing with oil trough
19. Driving wheel
20. Carrying wheel
21. Axlebox with self aligning roller bearing
22. Outer axlebox hanger
23. Inner axlebox hanger
24. Axlebox hanger guide and spring seat
25. Helical spring
26. Thrust faces
S. Lateral play between bogie and body

acts on the locomotive pressure brakes, which affords particularly smooth and exact braking of the locomotive when shunting or running light engine.

The compressed air for the brakes and pneumatically operated apparatus and the vacuum are generated by two reciprocating compressor exhauster sets, one electrically driven, the other belt driven from an extension of the generator shaft.

The brake-rod arrangement on each bogie is divided into two independent sets each actuated by a separate brake cylinder which allows for considerable simplification and unification of the different parts. The brake cylinders are located underneath the outside cross stretchers of the bogie frame. The hand brake in each cab acts on the neighbouring brake set of the corresponding bogie. Electrically controlled pneumatic sanders are provided for the driving wheels.

The working principle of the Brown-Boveri spring drive. A quill stump (1) secured to the housing of the motor, surrounds the axle (7) with sufficient play to allow complete freedom for the relative movements of the driving axle and the underframe. The gear wheel (3), driven by the motor pinion (not shown), is carried by two spherical roller bearings mounted on the quill stump. The transmission of the torque from the gear wheel to the driving axle is flexible through eight coil springs (4), which are built into the spring cups. The lips (5) on either side of the rim of the gear wheel form the sides of the spring cups. The two ends of each coupling spring are formed by caps which are guided in the cups. A carrier disc (8) pressed on to the axle, has eight rugged spider arms which press on the spring caps to form the coupling between the big gear wheel and the driving axle which can move vertically. The coupling springs are compressed when relative movement occurs between the carrier arms and the gear wheel. Stressing of the springs due to centrifugal force can be disregarded because the springs press on their whole length against the outer wall of the spring cup. The whole gear with springs and sliding surfaces of the spring caps is protected from dust and dirt by a closely fitting gear case (6) which also allows for effective lubrication of the teeth and all moving parts. The lubricant (oil) is taken up by the gear wheel and maintained in constant circulation over all vulnerable parts. (The photograph is taken from the Railway Executive publication. No. 2 is conspicuous by its absence!)

Main generator on the Brown-Boveri engine

ELECTRICAL EQUIPMENT

The main generator supplies the four DC traction motors, which are continuously connected in parallel, through the motor isolating switches and the reversing switch which determines the direction of running of the locomotive. The motors are protected by overload relays in the main motor leads acting on the contactor of the respective motor.

The electrical equipment comprises the main generator, the traction motors, the auxiliaries and the electrical control apparatus.

MAIN GENERATOR

In order to obtain the strongly drooping characteristic essential for traction purposes the generator is equipped with three inter-acting exicition windings, namely; a counter-compound winding, a shunt winding, and a separately excited winding. The latter is fed from the auxiliary diesel-driven generator.

The rotor carrying the electrically and magnetically active part of the armature is a hollow steel casting. At the driving end the armature shaft is constructed so as to form a flange which is bolted rigidly to the flange of the reduction gear so that at this end the armature is supported by the bearing of the reduction gear. The generator itself has only one bearing at the commutator end and is of the journal type, lubricated by oil under pressure. The armature lamination assembly is pressed on to ribs on the hollow rotor.

The commutator is bolted to the hollow armature shaft. The brush holders are carried by easily

151

Traction motor and gear case assembly, unusually depicted without its associated driven axle.
There were four traction motors on No. 18000

Asea Brown-Boveri

removable brush arms of a similar construction to those of the driving motors. The brush gear can be rotated.

The generator is self-ventilating. The fan is placed on the commutator side. The cooling air is drawn in on the driving side and expelled underneath after passing over the bearing.

The main generator is a multi-polar machine with commutating pole and compensating windings.

The ratings of the main generator are as follows:

Continuous rating	: 2,340 A at approx 675V
One-hour rating	: 2,640 A at approx 760V
Maximum working voltage	: 760 volts
Maximum working speed	: 875 rpm

TRACTION MOTORS

The traction motors are entirely spring borne (i.e. free with respect to axles) and rigidly fixed to the bogie frame. The motor torque is transmitted to the driving wheels by means of the Brown-Boveri spring drive. The motors are of the series wound type and have forced ventilation. The motors have a cast steel frame containing six main poles and six auxiliary poles. The armature shaft runs in roller bearings. The six brush carriers, each carrying two brushes, are supported by a ring which can be turned to allow access to the brushes through an opening underneath the motor.

A close-up of the 'Saurer' diesel engine on No. 18000 which could be used to move the engine when running light without the need to start the main turbine

British Railways

AUXILIARIES

The locomotive is equipped with an auxiliary direct current generator driven by a six-cylinder, four-stroke Saurer diesel engine.

In addition to the separate excitation current for the main generator the auxiliary generator provides the power for all the auxiliary machinery, lighting and heating on the locomotive, either direct or through the battery which it is charging. When starting the gas turbine power unit the auxiliary generator supplies the necessary power to the main generator which runs as a motor. Finally, the auxiliary generator can be connected to two of the traction motors (one in each bogie) and thus drive the locomotive as a light engine.

The Auxiliary Generator

The construction of the auxiliary generator is similar to that of the main generator. The rotor carrying the armature stampings is a hollow steel casing which is flanged rigidly to the flange of the diesel engine. The auxiliary generator has only one bearing which is situated at the commutator end and is of the roller type. The armature lamination assembly is pressed on to ribs on the hollow rotor. The commutator is bolted to the hollow rotor. The brush gear can be rotated.

The auxiliary generator is a multi-polar machine with counter-compound and starting winding. It has one bearing shield situated at the commutator end. The frame is bolted to the diesel engine so as to form one unit.

Battery

Due to the use of the auxiliary diesel-driven generator both for starting the gas turbine and supplying the auxiliaries, the storage battery can be kept comparatively small. It serves to start the diesel set and to supply those control and auxiliary circuits which are to be operated without the diesel set running. the 'Alklum' type cadmium-nickel battery consists of 54 cells with a capacity of 200 AH.

The following auxiliaries are fed from the auxiliary generator of the battery respectively.

Voltage Converter Set

This set consisting of a motor and generator together as one unit, supplies current for the control and lighting circuits on the locomotive, the voltage being maintained constant by an automatic voltage regulator.

Control Oil Pump

This pump maintains the oil pressure in the hydraulic systems of the locomotive, as well as lubricating the bearings of the power unit until the speed of the latter is sufficient for the direct-driven lubricating pump to function.

Cooling Oil Pump

The cooling oil pump delivers oil to the bearings of the gas turbine after the latter has been shut down in order to remove the heat which they receive from the still hot turbine. The cooling oil pump set is automatically started on shutting down the gas turbine and stopped by a time switch after sufficient time has elapsed for the gas turbine to cool down.

Pumps for Light and Heavy Fuel Oil

These pumps deliver the fuel to the combustion chamber under sufficient pressure for it to be atomised at the burner nozzle. The light oil is used in the turbine during the starting-up period only, until the heavy oil, which is the normal fuel, is sufficiently preheated.

Ignition Rod Control

The ignition rod is moved in and out of the combustion chamber by a small electric motor control from the driver's desk although provision is also made for hand operation.

Builder's plate attached to No. 1 end of No. 18000 and photographed at Swindon in August 1954. Below the engine number the two items of plumbing are, left, the drain cock for the train heating boiler and right, the filler pipe for the light fuel oil

Philip J. Kelley

Automatic Barring Gear

The object of this gear is to turn the shaft of the gas turbine through 180° at intervals after it has been shut down in order to avoid a temporary deflection of the shaft while it is hot. The barring gear motor is automatically controlled by a time switch.

Blowers for Cooling Traction Motors

There are two electrically driven blowers serving the four traction motors in the bogies, each blower supplying cooling air to the two motors in the adjacent bogie. The blower sets are located in the machine room and connected by ducts and leather bellows to the traction motor cooling air branches.

Motor-Driven Compressor-Exhauster Set

Vacuum for the train brake system and compressed air for the locomotive brake system and pneumatic controls is produced by a belt-driven compressor-exhauster set. An electrically driven set is especially provided to supply compressed air when the gas turbine set is shut down and the locomotive running light on the diesel set and to boost the production of vacuum for quick release of the vacuum brakes on the trains. For this latter purpose it is switched in automatically when the driver places the brake valve in the release position.

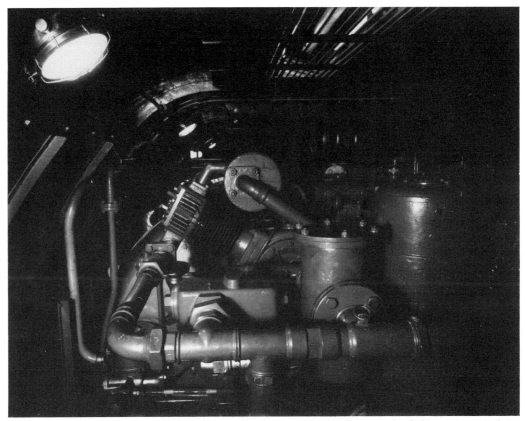

Mechanical drive exhauster and compressor set, No. 18000. The speed of this unit varied in accordance with the turbine revolutions and would later cause some difficulty in relation to the brake release time

British Railways

Train Heating Plant

For the train heating requirements the locomotive carries a Clarkson Thimble Tube Boiler of 1000 lb/hr steam capacity. The boiler is fired with light fuel and incorporates two electric motors, for the feed water pump and the burner set respectively.

LOCOMOTIVE OPERATION AND CONTROL EQUIPMENT

All operations for the starting, stopping and control of the gas turbine power unit, the diesel generator set and the auxiliaries are remotely carried out from the cabs. All controller handles, push buttons and supervising instruments are conveniently grouped on the driver's desk.

The first thing the driver will do in boarding the locomotive is to start the converter set supplying the control current, and then proceed to start the auxiliary diesel generator set by pressing a push button. This connects the storage battery to the auxiliary generator which then motors the diesel up to ignition speed. The driver can now switch the auxiliary generator on to the traction motors and in this manner shunt the locomotive at speeds up to about 15 mph. This practice has proved to be very valuable and economical in service because it provides the locomotive with an alternative source of power and makes it unnecessary to run the gas turbine for light service requirements.

A few minutes before the train is due to leave the driver proceeds to start the gas turbine set.

156

This is done by connecting the auxiliary generator which, running as a motor, accelerates the gas turbine unit. Meanwhile the fuel pumps have been started, but the light fuel is not injected through the burner nozzle nor should it be ignited until the set reaches ignition speed. After ignition the thermal unit accelerates under its own power and the diesel generator can be disconnected and switched over to supply current for the auxiliaries. As stated, starting is normally effected on light fuel oil; after a few minutes the heavy fuel oil will have been sufficiently preheated, so that the changeover can be effected.

The driver controls the starting of the train and its subsequent speed through the handwheel of the main controller which acts on the governing system of the gas turbine. Each notch of the main controller corresponds to a certain power of the gas turbine unit, this power being determined by turbine speed and fuel quantity.

The natural characteristics of the series traction motors is such that these motors do not transmit the same power at all running speeds. The governing system must allow for this fact, and it does so by means of the servo field regulator developed by Brown-Boveri especially for thermo electric vehicles. In a state of equilibrium, i.e. when the locomotive is running at constant speed and tractive effort, the power developed by the power unit corresponds to the power demands of the generator, the turbine speed remains the same and the regulation system is not brought into operation.

On the lower notches of the controller, which are used for starting the train, the rate of delivery of fuel is higher than is necessitated by the power demands so that the turbine speed somewhat exceeds the normal value. The speed governor regulates the pressure of the oil to such a low value that the driving piston of the servo field regulator is moved by the pressure of the spring into its right-hand end position so that the resistance is short circuited and the excitation of the generator brought to its maximum value. If the power demand from the traction motors is still too small to absorb all the output from the turbine, the effect is a tendency for the power unit to raise its speed still further. This is, however, prevented by a reduction in the rate of fuel delivery since, on further increase in the speed of the power unit, falling of the oil pressure in the system influences the pilot valve.

On the higher notches of the controller, which correspond to the normal speed range of the locomotive, the traction motors might impose more load on the generator than corresponds to the actual notch position. The servo field regulator now limits the load imposed on the generator by regulating the excitation current. This takes place in the following manner; if, on change of gradient, the traction motors begin to demand more power than that corresponding to the controller position, then the power unit will tend to slow down. The speed governor now causes the oil pressure to rise, so that the piston of the servo field regulator begins to move to the left, thus reducing the excitation current by increasing the resistance. The result is that the output of the generator is reduced, at the same time the reduction in turbine speed corrected and thus a new state of equilibrium reached.

When the piston arrives at its left-hand end position and the current demand from the motors has not yet been fully met, the turbine speed would again start to fall off rapidly, as the servo field regulator can have no further influence. In this case the increase of control oil pressure restricts the flow from the pilot valve and thus brings about a suitable increase in the rate of fuel delivery.

Similarly the reverse takes place when the power demanded by the traction motors diminishes.

The above explains the working of the servo field regulator and its influence on the governing system of the gas turbine when the main controller is left in a certain position. If the driver wishes to influence the speed of the locomotive by his own action he need only move the control wheel to a new position. This energizes a different electro-pneumatic valve and thus alters the power available.

On the last two notches of the controller there is no further power increase; instead the traction motor field is weakened in order to bring about the highest locomotive speeds.

Incorporated in the control system are a number of safety devices. Service safety is obtained by a number of electrical and mechanical interlocks between the controls to prevent faulty operation. Pilot lamps or instruments on the driver's desk indicate the proper working of all the components, whilst warning lamps light up should excessive temperatures occur in the gas flow. If notwithstanding such warning the driver omits to reduce the load the fuel pump is automatically shut down, thus compelling the driver to re-ignite the flame. The fuel pump is also automatically shut down if the speed of the gas turbine set exceeds the normal value by more than 10 per cent, or if the flame in the combustion chamber should go out without the driver noticing it. This latter

Driving cab of No. 18000. Two seats were provided, one for the driver on the right-hand side, with the fireman (sic) seated in front of the handbrake, the wheel of which can just be seen at lower left. Controls for the engine only and train brakes are to the right-hand side of the console. Notice the heating elements for de-mist purposes in the centre and right-hand windows. It is also only these windows which are fitted with windscreen wipers

Asea Brown-Boveri

security measure takes the form of an electronic flame monitoring device which shuts off the fuel should the flame be extinguished. Finally, the locomotive is equipped with the automatic train control apparatus which is standard on the Western Region. The shoe portion of the ATC apparatus is carried by one of the carrying axles of the locomotive.

The cab equipment comprises the driver's desk with the controls and instruments mentioned earlier. The driver's seat is on the right-hand side. In normal service the driver need only operate the main control hand wheel and when necessary the brake handle. He checks the generator load on the special cross pointer instrument developed by Brown-Boveri for thermo-electric locomotives. This instrument indicates simultaneously the generator current and voltage and the locomotive's tractive effort and further shows the driver the appropriate moment for weakening the traction motor fields by field tapping.

It is not subject to the inaccuracies inherent in a DC wattmeter particularly when dealing with the wide variations in current and voltage occurring in thermo-electric locomotives. The locomotive speed is indicated on an electric tachometer, the generator of which is driven from one of the driving axles.

The cabs are provided with indirect lighting, which can be dimmed as desired by the driver, and in addition, the main instruments are fitted with individual lighting thus permitting the cab illumination to be switched off during night runs. When in the depot, a lighting supply for the locomotive is provided from the depot mains through two standard plugs, a single phase transformer and changeover switch mounted on the locomotive.

Whilst the train heating is by steam from the Clarkson Boiler, the locomotive cabs are equipped

The basic driving controls of the Brown-Boveri machine, which were repeated at each end of the engine. On the left the two levers are respectively for 'forward–reverse' and the transition to burn heavy fuel. The 'steering wheel' acts as the master speed control and is graduated in 'notches'. To the right the two levers are for setting the turbine revolutions as well as controlling the auxiliary diesel engine and starting the main power unit. Just visible, although partly obscured by the control wheel, is the pilot lamp used for changing cabs

Asea Brown-Boveri

with adjustable electric heaters supplied from the auxiliary generator. There is also a plug for the connection of a hotplate or tea kettle. The cab windows have electrically heated double panes to prevent freezing. [At each end this applied to the centre and right-hand windows only.]

The electric identification lights at the front and rear of the locomotive are operated from and repeated on special panels in each of the driver's cabs.

THE METROPOLITAN VICKERS ENGINE

Again a full description is provided in a Railway Executive publication:

The body structure contains the power plant and a driving cab at each end; it is carried on the two bogies by swing links resiliently attached by rubber resilient universal joints to permit controlled swing bolster action and bogie pivoting, without the use of actual bolsters which would have required more space than was available between the bogie frames and within the fixed wheelbase.

Each bogie has three driving axles, each driven through a single reduction gear by a traction motor suspended on the axle and from a support on the bogie frame.

The turbine rotates at 7,000 rpm when delivering full load, and drives three main traction generators at 1,600 rpm through single-reduction gearing. The reduction gear unit has two output shafts; one drives two of the main generators in tandem and the other drives the third main

159

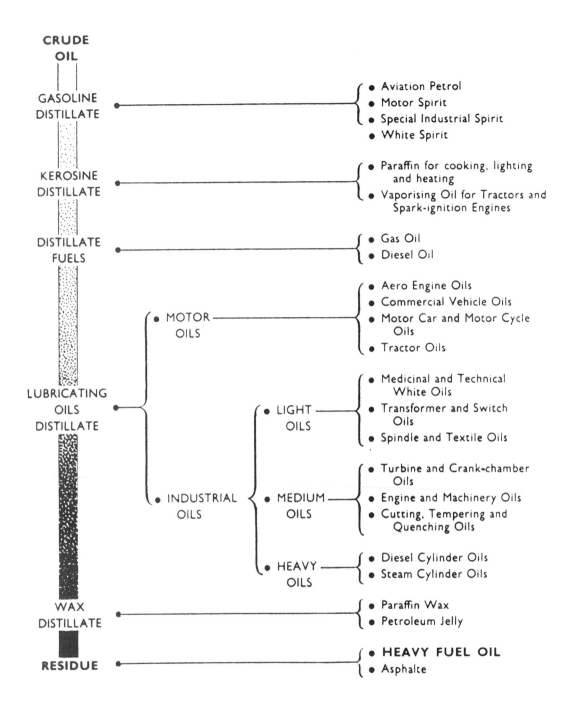

CRUDE OIL

GASOLINE DISTILLATE
- Aviation Petrol
- Motor Spirit
- Special Industrial Spirit
- White Spirit

KEROSINE DISTILLATE
- Paraffin for cooking, lighting and heating
- Vaporising Oil for Tractors and Spark-ignition Engines

DISTILLATE FUELS
- Gas Oil
- Diesel Oil

LUBRICATING OILS DISTILLATE
- MOTOR OILS
  - Aero Engine Oils
  - Commercial Vehicle Oils
  - Motor Car and Motor Cycle Oils
  - Tractor Oils
- INDUSTRIAL OILS
  - LIGHT OILS
    - Medicinal and Technical White Oils
    - Transformer and Switch Oils
    - Spindle and Textile Oils
  - MEDIUM OILS
    - Turbine and Crank-chamber Oils
    - Engine and Machinery Oils
    - Cutting, Tempering and Quenching Oils
  - HEAVY OILS
    - Diesel Cylinder Oils
    - Steam Cylinder Oils

WAX DISTILLATE
- Paraffin Wax
- Petroleum Jelly

RESIDUE
- **HEAVY FUEL OIL**
- Asphalte

generator, the auxiliary generator and the exciter. The turbine, reduction gear and group of generators are mounted on a common bedplate together with the main fuel and lubricant pumps and constitute a self-contained power unit which is installed in the locomotive body on three support points on its main underframe.

Each of the three main generators supplies two of the six traction motors; the motors of each pair are connected permanently in parallel.

The principal auxiliaries are:

160

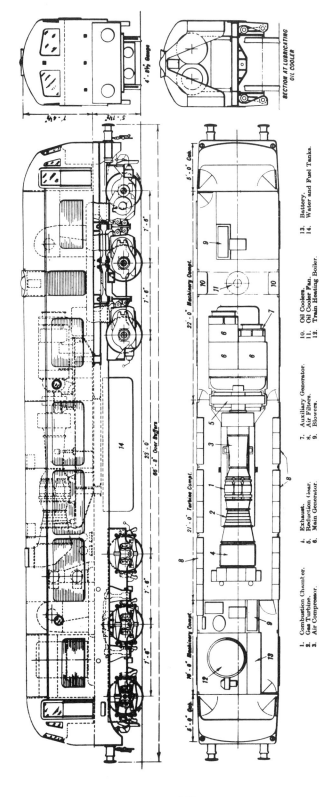

Weight diagram for the Metropolitan Vickers engine No. 18100. As with the Brown-Boveri machine the power unit and main generators were supported on a centre bedplate

1. Combustion Chamber.
2. Gas Turbine.
3. Air Compressor.
4. Exhaust.
5. Reduction Gear.
6. Main Generator.
7. Auxiliary Generator.
8. Air Filters.
9. Blowers.
10. Oil Coolers.
11. Oil Cooler Fan.
12. Train Heating Boiler.
13. Battery.
14. Water and Fuel Tanks.

1. The auxiliary generator
2. The exciter
3. The main and auxiliary fuel and lubricant pumps
4. The air-blast coolers for the turbine and reduction gear lubricant
5. The traction motor ventilation centrifugal blowers
6. The air compressor and vacuum exhausters
7. The oil-fired train heating steam boiler
8. The turbine starting battery

From the turbine output of 3,000 hp an allowance of about 150 hp provides for the loss in the reduction gear and the demands of the locomotive auxiliary equipment, leaving 2,850 hp input to the traction generators. Over most of the speed range of the locomotive an electric transmission efficiency of about 86% is achieved, corresponding to 2,450 hp at the rails. In relation to train speed, this power is sufficient to give an 18-coach train balancing speeds of 85 mph on the level, and 41 mph and 23 mph respectively when climbing gradients of 1/100 and 1/50.

A turbine full-load thermal efficiency of 19% has been demonstrated on test; when account is taken of the gear and electrical losses, the overall thermal efficiency of the locomotive becomes 16%. After deduction of the 75 hp required for the auxiliaries, the remaining traction power available at the wheels represents 15% of the heat value of fuel consumed or a fuel rate of 0.88 lb per hp hr. At half power this rate will rise to about 1.3 lb. The fuel tank has been designed to hold sufficient gas oil for the London–Plymouth run hauling the maximum tonnage trains, with a considerable reserve. It carries also the corresponding quantity of gas oil for the train-heating boiler on the same run, and another section of the tank accommodates the water supply for the train-heating boiler on the same basis. The two sections can readily be employed as a single fuel tank to give a 60% increase in fuel capacity.

The case for using this type of locomotive in preference to steam traction rests mainly on economies from its higher efficiency and anticipated lower maintenance costs for equal work done.

In relation to diesel traction its case rests largely on operating economies. Despite the turbine's considerably higher fuel consumption per horse power hour than that of the diesel engine the cost for fuel and lubricant in relation to the ton-miles hauled is only a little higher for the turbine than that for the diesel locomotive. Moreover, experience so far has shown that in the higher powers, gas turbine locomotives can be built approximately half the weight and half the length of diesel locomotives of the same power.

THE GAS TURBINE

The prime mover is a simple open-cycle gas turbine without heat exchanger, and the cycle of compression, heating and expansion of air is carried out in a compressor, combustion chamber and turbine arranged in line and built into a single straight-through unit.

The compressor is a 15-stage axial-flow machine with a pressure ratio of 5.25 at 7,000 rpm and a mass flow of 50 lb per second; it runs in two sleeve-type bearings.

The turbine is a five-stage unit running in two sleeve-type bearings and its rotor is directly coupled to that of the compressor.

The combustion chamber is composed entirely of heat-resisting steel and consists of six flame tubes with axes parallel to the machine axis and connected by flexible connection pieces at one end to the compressor outlet and at the other end to the turbine inlet.

The compressor and turbine cylinders are connected together by a tubular member surrounding their shaft coupling so that they constitute a single structural unit on which the combustion chamber is mounted. The power unit is supported from the underbed on four pillar-type supports with sufficient flexibility to accommodate expansion. A sliding key arrangement maintains the lateral location of the unit, and the inlet end of the compressor frame has its location fixed by securing it to the casing of the reduction gear which is solidly bolted and dowelled to the bedplate. The total axial expansion at the turbine end is about $\frac{3}{8}$ in. The rotors of the compressor and turbine are located axially from a thrust bearing at the compressor inlet end.

The compressor cylinder is of malleable iron and the rotor body is a forged steel drum. The

162

moving blades, machined from stainless steel bar, and fixed blades rolled from similar material, are held in dovetail slots machined axially on the rotor and circumferentially in the cylinder. The bearings are lined with white metal and are lubricated and cooled by a copious supply of lubricating oil under pressure.

A supply of compressed air is taken from an intermediate stage to a balance piston at the inlet end for the purpose of balancing the end thrust of the combined rotors.

The turbine construction employs special heat resisting materials, the cylinder being an austenitic steel casting and the rotor an austenitic steel forging, and the blades as follows:

	Fixed Blades	Moving Blades
1st stage	Nimonic	Nimonic
2nd stage	Steel (austenitic)	Nimonic
3rd stage	Steel (austenitic)	Steel (austenitic)
4th stage	Steel (molybdenum)	Steel (molybdenum)
5th stage	Steel (molybdenum)	Steel (molybdenum)

The bearings are of similar design to those of the compressor but additional cooling is provided by a flow of compressed air from an intermediate stage of the compressor.

Each of the six flame tubes of the combustion chamber is secured by quickly detachable unions to the compressor and turbine. The flame tube has an outer casing and inner primary chamber, both fabricated from austenitic heat-resisting sheet steel. By means of metering orifices the correct proportion of the air flow is introduced into the primary to give correct combustion of the fuel fed in at about 650 lb/sq in from the fuel jets. The remainder of the air is mixed with the very high temperature products of the combustion downstream of the jets so as to produce the designed temperature at the turbine inlet. Each flame tube has a double fuel injector with a small jet orifice for idling fuel and a large one fed from the main fuel valve. Two flame tubes are fitted with igniters, in the form of high tension spark plugs combined with pilot flame fuel jets. Ignition spreads to the other flame tubes through tubular connections between each pair of casings.

The bedplate of the power unit carries the two electrically driven main fuel and lubricant pump sets. Only one runs at a time but any failure of fuel or lubricant pressure immediately causes the other set to start.

To start the unit, the turbine is accelerated up to a self-sustaining speed by the main generators acting as motors fed from the starting battery, and once the driver has actuated the starting button the process is entirely automatic. The successive steps in the process are initiated by a timing or sequence controller driven at a controlled speed by an electric motor. The steps in the progression are as follows:

1. Auxiliary fuel pump starts, drawing fuel from the tank
2. Main fuel and lubricant pump starts
3. Igniters are switched on
4. Automatic starting valve commences to move, the turbine starts to rotate and by the time it reaches about 1,000 rpm, the starting valve commences fuel delivery through the idling jets of the combustion chamber

From then onwards the fuel combustion assists in the acceleration and at about 2,500 rpm, the battery is automatically disconnected from the main generators and the turbine continues its acceleration under its own power to 4,000 rpm. The time from pressing the start button until the turbine starts to turn is 10 seconds; a further 25 seconds elapse until the battery disconnects and a further 30 seconds until idling speed is reached.

Full power may be taken from the turbine after about 10 minutes' warming up at idling speed or at low power.

On shutting down after full load running it has been found beneficial to have a cooling period of about 10 minutes at idling or low power work. After stopping the turbine an automatic barring sequence comes into operation which motors the turbine round for a few seconds at intervals of about three minutes to equalize the cooling stresses. An auxiliary lubricant pump circulates oil

163

Two views of the main gas turbine power unit as installed in No. 18100 which, by means of its compact design, enabled a corridor to pass either side. Notice in particular the flame tubes as well as the various instruments on the turbine control panel

Both British Railways

round the turbine bearings throughout the cooling period, and is automatically stopped by a bearing thermostat at the appropriate time.

Throughout the operation of the locomotive, the turbine and generator are governed electrically to give the output selected by the driver on the master controller, and at the turbine speed for most efficient operation of that load. While this electrical governing deals with all normal working conditions, over-riding controls come into operation in the event of excessive turbine speed or gas temperature, excessive bearing temperature, or low fuel or lubricant pressures.

THE REDUCTION GEAR

The three shafts of the reduction gear lie in a horizontal plane, the middle one carrying the pinion and each of the others a gearwheel. The pinion is made from case-hardened steel, the teeth profiles being ground after hardening. The gearwheel rims are of 65/72-ton chromium molybdenum steel with the teeth finished by the shaving process. The teeth, of five diametral pitch are single helical. Each shaft is hollow and runs in two white metal sleeve bearings. The drive shafts from turbine and from generators pass through the hollow shafts to couplings at the remote ends of these shafts, thus gaining a certain flexibility in the drive with minimum length. The gears are enclosed in a fabricated steel gearbox. Gear teeth and bearings are lubricated from the main turbine lubricant pump.

THE MAIN AND AUXILIARY GENERATORS

Two of the three main generators form a tandem unit, their yokes being bolted together and both armatures being mounted on a common shaft carried in two roller bearings in the yoke endshields. The third main generator and the auxiliary generator form a similar tandem pair and the yokes of both tandem sets are bolted side by side to make up the generator group. An exciter is overhung from the auxiliary generator. Each main generator is a self-ventilated direct-current six pole, compensated interpole machine, the field being fed from the exciter.

The ratings to BS 173–1941 for Class B insulation are as follows:

Continuous	1,100 amp, 666 volts, 1,600 rpm
One hour	1,250 amp, 580 volts, 1,600 rpm
Maximum voltage	825 volts
Maximum current	2,200 amp

The auxiliary generator and exciter are also self-ventilated direct-current machines. The former has six main poles and interpoles and is shunt excited under the control of a voltage regulator to give 110 volts irrespective of its load and the turbine speed. Its BS continuous rating (Class B insulation) is 65 kW, 110V , 1,280 rpm.

The exciter has six main poles and interpoles and is excited by three windings – a separate excitation fed from the 110-volt auxiliary mains, a separate excitation regulated by the automatic output control gear and a reverse compound excitation directly proportional to the main generator total load current. Its BS continuous rating (Class B insulation) is 10.5 kW, 55 volts over a speed range of 1,280 to 1,600 rpm.

The methods of construction and insulation of these machines are those employed in traction motors to meet the arduous conditions of railway service.

THE TRACTION MOTORS

The six traction motors are separately ventilated four pole series and interpole machines. Each is carried on its axle by plain suspension bearings and has roller bearings on its armature. The nose side of the motor yoke is suspended from the adjacent bogie transom by a link with a rubber resilient bush at each end. This form of suspension gives the freedom of movement which is necessary without the wear associated with the more conventional nose suspension arrangements.

The transverse location of the motor in the bogie is by another rubber resilient bushed link between motor end and bogie main side frame, instead of the more conventional location thrust faces on the suspension bearings against the bosses of road and gear wheels. The chief object of this arrangement is to eliminate the uncontrolled lateral movement of the heavy mass of the motor along the axle, which is inimical to good riding at high speeds. A secondary but important advantage is the elimination of thrust wear on the bearing which is generally the critical factor in suspension bearing maintenance.

The ratings of the motor to BS 173–1941 for Class B insulation and ventilation air flow of 2,500 cfm are:

Continuous	550 amp, 666 volts, 706 rpm (33.5 mph)
One hour	650 amp, 565 volts, 580 rpm (27.5 mph)
Maximum current	1,100 amp
Maximum voltage	825 volts

The drive to the axle is by a single reduction spur gearing of 21/58 gear ratio 2.066 diametral pitch. The gear wheel incorporates torsional resilience, the rim being separate from the centre but mounted on it through the medium of a series of rubber resilient bushes which permit a small relative torsional movement. Such an arrangement cushions the transmission of shocks from rail to armature particularly at rail joints or other irregularities and reduces the corresponding stresses in rails, gear teeth, armature shaft and other armature parts, and contributes to better riding of the vehicle as a whole and to reduced maintenance.

The gear-wheel centre, rim and pinion are steel forgings. The teeth are cut after the blanks have been hardened by oil quenching.

THE AUXILIARY EQUIPMENT

Most of the auxiliaries are electrically operated from the 110 volt DC supply from the auxiliary generator. The battery, consisting of 48 lead-acid cells of 384 amp-hr capacity, is charged from this supply through a contactor which is closed only when the auxiliary generator is generating. Certain of the electrical auxiliaries are 'battery fed' and can be run only when the turbine is running.

Main Fuel and Lubricant Pump

Fuel and lubricant are supplied to the turbine by a pump set consisting of a 10 hp, 3,000 rpm motor 'battery fed', driving a fuel pump overhung from the motor and a lubricant pump mounted on a common bedplate with the motor. There are two of these sets, both carried on the main turbine bedplate. Only one works at a time, but it is automatically superseded by the other in the event of a failure of fuel or lubricant supply.

The fuel pump is of the swash plate type and can supply 7.5 gallons per minute at 650 psi.

The lubricant pump is of the 'Imo' type delivering 70 gallons per minute at 50 psi.

Auxiliary Fuel Pump Set

The auxiliary fuel pump is driven at 1,400 rpm by a 'battery fed' $\frac{1}{4}$ hp motor, the combined set being mounted adjacent to the main turbine bedplate. Its function is to supply fuel from the fuel tank on the locomotive underframe to the suction side of the main fuel pump. It is a gear type pump rated at 10 gallons per minute at 10 psi.

Auxiliary Lubricant Pump Set

The auxiliary lubricant pump is a similar set mounted on the turbine bedplate and its duty is the supply of lubricant to the turbine and gear bearings during the cooling period after the turbine has been shut down. The motor is rated at ¼ hp, 1,400 rpm and is 'battery fed' and the gear pump delivers 10 gallons per minute at 10 psi.

Lubricant Coolers

The heat carried away from turbine bearings and from the reduction gear in the lubricant is dissipated in cooling equipment comprising two air-blast radiators. They consist of rows of cooling tubes of the wire wound Clayton-Still pattern extending between top and bottom headers. One radiator is mounted in each side wall of the locomotive body and air ducts in sheet aluminium sweep inwards and upwards to converge at the entry to an axial-flow vertical axis $32\frac{1}{2}$ in fan mounted in the roof. The fan is driven at 1,480 rpm by a 10 hp series motor fed from the auxiliary generator and draws about 16,000 cfm of air through the cooling elements. The heat dissipation capacity is approximately 120 kW with 70 °F ambient and 180 °F lubricant entry temperature.

Air Compressor

A two-cylinder single-stage reciprocating air compressor gear driven by an 8 hp motor built-in unit supplies compressed air at 100 psi for operating the locomotive brakes, the electro-pneumatic control apparatus, sanders, warning horns and window wipers. The compressor is air cooled and has a piston displacement of 38 cfm at 243 crankshaft rpm or 1,200 motor rpm. The motor is 'auxiliary generator fed'. An automatic governor switches the motor on and off to maintain the pressure in the main reservoir between 85 and 100 psi.

Vacuum Exhauster

The vacuum brake equipment operates at 24 in and two reciprocating four-cylinder exhausters provide the brake power for the train. Each is driven by a flange mounted motor at 750 rpm for normal maintaining and application, and at 1,200 rpm for release. Both are stopped in an emergency application. The swept volume of each is 82.5 cfm at 750 rpm and power input is 4 hp. The two machines are capable of creating 25 in vacuum in a train of 80 cubic feet train pipe and cylinder capacity in 45 seconds. The motors are 'battery fed' so that the brakes will not be applied by the shutting down of the turbine in stations or when coasting.

Traction Motor Blowers

The three traction motors in each bogie are force-ventilated by a centrifugal blower directly coupled to a 11.25 hp 'auxiliary generator fed' motor. The 21 in diameter runner delivers about 8,000 cfm at 6 in water gauge total head at 1,460 rpm. The air is distributed to the motors by sheet aluminium ducts on the floor of the underframe and flexible leather bellows extending down to the motor air inlet flange.

Train Heating Boiler

Steam for train heating is supplied by a vertical fire tube oil-fired boiler continuously rated at 1,500 lb per hour, 80 psi. The operation is semi-automatic in that the fuel flow is controlled by the steam demand and the feed pump delivery is regulated by the water level and the fuel is cut off by loss of fuel and by low-water level. A special feature to ensure flame stability in spite of air pressure fluctuations due to high train speeds and effects of bridges and tunnels is the provision of a high pressure combustion air blower in conjunction with flow retarders at the inlet and outlet of the firebox.

An artist's drawing of the completed locomotive with the various components listed

168

Air Filters

The 40,000 cfm of air required for the gas turbine at full load is drawn through filters in the side walls of the turbine compartment. These filters are of the dry fabric type and they can be cleaned when necessary either after removal from the locomotive or by reverse blowing in position by compressed air nozzles on flexible pipes provided in the turbine compartment. It is not expected that this air filtration will eliminate the need for compressor blade cleaning, but it will materially reduce the rate of fouling.

Driving Cab Equipment

The auxiliary equipment of the driving cabs includes pneumatically-operated window wipers, double-note pneumatic warning horns, electric foot warmers, electric food heaters, and a plenum system of cab ventilation and heating. The ventilation air is tapped from the adjacent traction motor ventilation trunk and conducted by a dual duct to a combined mixing valve and 'Punkah louvre' set high up in the cab back wall. In one section of the dual duct a thermostatically-controlled electric element heats the air. The driver can manipulate the louvre to get the required quantity, direction and temperature of air.

Tanks

The combined fuel and boiler water tank is slung under the body underframe between the bogies. It is of eliptical cross-section and entirely constructed of welded steel plate. A transverse diversion plate separates the 995-gallon fuel section from the 620-gallon water section; both sections may be made available for fuel by removing a cover from an aperture in the division plate. Remote reading tank contents gauges are operated by tank floats and electrical potentiometers, with indicators in each driving cab and at the tank filling valves.

Location of Equipment

With the exception of the tanks all the auxiliary equipment is housed inside the body portion and is grouped mainly in the driving cabs and the adjacent ends of the turbine and generator compartments.

THE CONTROL EQUIPMENT

The main function of the control equipment is to provide a means for the driver to control the speed of the train by regulating the tractive effort developed at the wheels. At the cost of some elaboration of apparatus the control scheme has been designed to require from the driver the minimum of concern and responsibility for the functioning of the power plant and auxiliaries.

The procedure on taking over the locomotive in shed or siding is extremely simple consisting of the following operations:

1. Operate the key switch.
2. Press the turbine start button and when the green light appears one minute later (indicating that the turbine is running at idling speed) switch on the brake compressor and exhausters.

The locomotive is ready for service after about five minutes' warming period if the start has been from cold. To move the locomotive, either light or with its load, the brakes are released, the reversing lever of the master controller moved to the direction required and the power lever set to the position required. This lever has no notched positions but can be set and left at any position between no power and full power. For the sake of convenience and simplicity the same lever has been made to determine the starting tractive effort developed between the minimum for light engine manoeuvering and a maximum determined by wheel slip consideration.

The driver is not required to notch up this lever as the train speed rises; he may do so if he so wishes but may equally well put it directly in the position he expects ultimately to require.

One of the three-axle welded steel bogies shown in the Trafford Park works

THE LOCOMOTIVE STRUCTURE AND RUNNING GEAR

The body and underframe are built together as a single unit and almost entirely by welding. The principal members are the two solebars, consisting of continuous plates of deep section, reinforced by top and bottom welded flanges and tied together at each end by the welded headstock structures. The solebars are attached by fitted bolts to the main supporting structures, which are also welded assemblies, at the bogie centre locations; elsewhere they are cross-braced by a lattice of rolled steel sections and by the floor plate. At cantrail height a well-ribbed curved plate section of the roof forms a rigid boom running on each side from end to end of the body except the cabs. The body wall sheeting is welded to this boom, to the solebars and to the carlines, except where spaces are left for air filters and louvres. The roof sections between the booms are of aluminium alloy and are removable for most of the length of the body, for the removal of equipment.

At each end the driving cab walls and roof, in the form of a separate welded aluminium alloy structure, are mounted on the underframe platform.

The bogies also are welded assemblies constructed from plates, some with welded flanges. The side frames are connected by the headstocks and by two cross stays, all of welded plate.

Each complete bogie frame and each main welded sub-assembly of the body structure has been stress-relieved in an annealing furnace.

As has been already stated the body is suspended by swing links from the bogies. There are eight of these links – two on each side of each bogie and outside the bogie frames. Each link end contains a rubber universal joint without any metallic contact between the elements. The lower joint is, in each case, attached to the lower end of the body support brackets and pairs of upper joints are attached to longitudinal equalizing beams. At the middle of each beam is a rubber universal joint resting in the corresponding bogie support bracket.

The resilience of the rubber joints permits the necessary relative angular motion between body and bogies about the vertical and transverse axes and also the degree of lateral relative movement necessary for good high-speed riding. The restoring forces are mainly those due to gravity as those arising from deformation of the rubber are relatively small, although they provide a measure of damping against hunting. More effective damping is provided by hydraulic dampers located at four points on each bogie and connected between the body underframe and bogie frames by links

Underframe and body suspension arrangements, No. 18100

with universal rubber joints. These resist lateral displacement and vertical axis rotation of the bogies in relation to the body with forces which are functions of the rate of movement. Relief valves, however, prevent these resisting forces from exceeding certain pre-determined limits.

The longitudinal reactions between the body and the bogies, arising out of traction and braking forces are taken through a pivot pin on the body which carries a parallel motion linkage coupled to the bogie cross stays and equipped with rubber universal joints. This does not interfere with any of the other relative movements between body and bogies.

The use of rubber at the points of relative movement dispenses with the necessity for lubrication and rectification of wear of metallic surfaces, substituting the renewal of standard rubber joint-units at intervals which experience indicates are likely to be lengthy. Another feature of the rubber joints is the complete interruption of metallic connection between body and bogies and the consequent isolation of the body from high frequency vibrations due to track irregularities.

Another essential for good riding at high speed is the avoidance of axle transverse play relative to the bogie. The steps taken to reduce this to a minimum are the use of roller bearing axleboxes with only nominal play on the axles and in the horn guides. The boxes are of the Hoffmann type with two rows of rollers and one row of balls for end location; they are oil-lubricated. The boxes are very closely guided in the slides with initial clearances of only 0.10 in both horizontal directions, the wearing surfaces being manganese steel on the boxes and oil hardened steel on the guides, with grease lubrication. On each axle the close guiding in the transverse direction is applied, the other having ample transverse clearances; thus the axle is located from one end. At each end the horn guide is of the trunnion type to permit canting of the axle in relation to the bogie.

The high degree of flexibility of springing, which is another requirement for high speed running, is achieved by the use of two springs in series at each axlebox, one above and the other below the box. The arrangement has the additional advantage of eliminating spring hanger wear.

171

As indicated earlier the traction motor is located transversely from the bogie frame by a rubber bushed link, thereby eliminating the detrimental effect on high speed riding of the free play of such a relatively heavy mass along the axle within the suspension bearing end float limits, and also the wear of suspension bearing thrust faces, which is normally the most serious aspect of motor bearing maintenance. The torsional resilience in the gear drive between motor and axle is another contribution to good riding at high speed and to reduced maintenance on track and running gear.

The train brake equipment is the vacuum system but space considerations have led to the use of compressed air braking on the locomotive. The driver manipulates the vacuum brake valve to apply the train brake and a simple automatic valve applies a proportionate air application to the locomotive wheels, unless the driver prevents this interaction by pressing a thumb trigger on the brake handle.

When running light in sidings and hauling unbraked trains in territory not equipped with automatic train control, the exhausters need not be run, and the locomotive brakes can be applied directly from an independent air brake valve.

Each wheel is fitted with two clasp brake shoes. Four air-brake cylinders on each bogie operate three brake shoes each. In each driving cab a hand brake operates on the six shoes on the adjacent one and a half axles.

An interesting comment reported elsewhere in contemporary notes on No. 18100 was that a nominal output of 3,500 hp was available from the turbine if required by substituting the turbine blades for one of a different profile. It was added though that the existing power output, '. . . is more than required for the present application'.

Finally, it may be worth a more direct comparison between some of the more common features of both locomotives:

	18000	18100
Weight in working order	115 t 3 cwt	129 t 10 cwt
Continuous rating	2,500 hp	3,000 hp
Maximum speed	90 mph	90 mph
Fuel	Light oil to start, then switched over to burn heavy oil	Light oil
Auxillary diesel engine?	Yes	No
Height	13 ft 4 in	12 ft 10 in
Width	9 ft $2\frac{1}{2}$ in	9 ft 0 in
Length	63 ft $0\frac{1}{2}$ in	66 ft $9\frac{1}{4}$ in
Wheel diameter	4 ft $0\frac{1}{2}$ in – driving 3 ft 2 in – carrying	3 ft 8 in
Bogie wheelbase	11 ft $9\frac{3}{4}$ in	15 ft 0 in

APPENDIX A

Correspondence between the GWR and Metropolitan Vickers over the financial aspects of gas turbine engine No. 18100

11 February 1946. Letter from CME to Metropolitan Vickers

Confirmed verbal agreement between Sir James Milne and Sir George Bailey, viz; each company to bear 50% of total cost of providing the locomotive and carrying out necessary trials.

12 June 1946. Letter from Metropolitan Vickers to CME

Total cost of locomotive to equal cost of equipment supplied by MV *plus* cost of mechanical parts to be built by GWR *plus* cost of carrying out necessary trials. GWR to pay MV 50% of such total less what they have already spent.

MV suggest that when locomotive complete GWR should pay a further 25% of total cost of locomotive plus MV additional costs entailed during trials, whereupon locomotive would become property of GWR.

MV point out that during the trials it may be found necessary to carry out changes, the cost of which would be added to the total MV cost.

12 July 1946. Letter from Sir James Milne to Sir George Bailey

Confirm each Company to bear 50% of total cost of construction, exclusive of expenditure incurred on research, development and design (the responsibility of MV). Cost of construction to be actual cost, without profit, of manufacturing power unit, all necessary equipment, any parts manufactured by GWR and assembly of complete locomotive.

Suggested that provision of locomotive be regarded as one transaction, all expenditure subsequently incurred on trials and agreed modifications resulting therefrom to be treated as further transaction, cost to be borne equally by two Companies.

If locomotive a success, GWR on taking over locomotive to pay further 25% of total expenditure incurred by MV in connection with first transaction.

1 August 1946. Letter from Sir George Bailey to Sir James Milne

Reference to difference between terms of JM's letter of 12 July 1946 and what was understood by CME's letter of 11 February 1946. Suggested terms of agreement then set out as follows:

It is agreed that all research work on which the general design of gas turbine is based is the affair of my Company alone.

To produce a single prototype locomotive both Companies will incur expense under the heads:

1. Engineering and drawing office work in designing the actual machine to be built.
2. Wood patterns for all cast parts.
3. A minimum quantity of jigs, welding fixtures and templates to enable the prototype to be built with due accuracy and economy.
4. Material, labour and overhead costs.
5. Profit, we agree, to be NIL.

On our side such considerable elaboration would be required in items 1, 2 and 3 for the commercial production of subsequent machines that the costs incurred for the prototype may be regarded as peculiar to it. Hence I hope you will agree that all your costs and ours under items 1–4 should be divided equally between us in the first stage.

I would agree that we should treat as a second and separate transaction our combined costs of trials and agreed modifications, also to be equally divided.

In addition to the foregoing, MV agree to Sir James Milne's proposal that locomotive would become property of GWR on further payment of 25% of expenses originally incurred by MV on items 1–4 and on cost of testing and making agreed modifications to equipment of MV manufacture.

29 August 1946. Letter from Sir James Milne to Sir George Bailey

Agreed that in first instance costs incurred under items 1–4 [see above] to be borne in moieties, but suggested that if project is a success some portion of expenditure on items 1–3 be liquidated on any subsequent machines – this question to be settled at later date.

Agreed that combined cost of trials and agreed modifications be treated as separate transactions and divided equally.

Agreed that if locomotive a success GWR in taking it over to pay further 25% of cost of testing and making agreed modifications to equipment provided by MV.

In event of locomotive not being success, suggested that recovery value of parts used in complete locomotive be shared equally between GWR and MV.

11 September 1946. Letter from Sir George Bailey to Sir James Milne

Agreed liquidation of costs of items 1–3 on any subsequent machines be left to later date. Agreement then summarised under 5 points as under:
1. We will divide equally the total cost of producing this first prototype locomotive, our costs for same being as per items 1–4 of my letter of 1st August.
2. We will divide equally the total cost of making the trials and such modifications as may be found, as a result of these trials, to be necessary.
3. Should the locomotive prove a success and be taken over by you, you will pay us a further 25% of our costs under item 4 of my letter of 1st August and also a further 25% of our costs in making the trials and any modifications found necessary as a result of such trials.
4. Both your and our costs under all headings shall be subject to the examination by our respective accountants and settlement shall be made on their joint certificate.
5. Should the locomotive not prove a success the recovery value of the parts used by both you and us in the complete locomotive shall be shared equally by our two Companies.

17 September 1946. Letter from Sir James Milne to Sir George Bailey

Acknowledging letter of 11 September 1946 and setting out agreed arrangements.

12 November 1946. Memorandum of meeting held at Swindon

GWR now not able to design mechanical parts. MV to seek sub-contractor. Agreed that such arrangement would not assail essential features of the agreement as set out in Sir George Bailey's letter of 11 September 1946.

25 March 1947. Letter from Sir James Milne to Sir George Bailey

Asking for agreement that the new terms of construction (i.e. MV to find sub-contractor) would not affect the financial arrangements, and in particular that the additional 25% payment to be paid on acquisition should be related only to the costs MV would have incurred under the original arrangement and not the costs under the sub-contract for construction of mechanical parts.

3 April 1947. Letter from Sir George Bailey to Sir James Milne

Sir James Milne's letter of 25 March 1947 agreed.

Note: this is the only correspondence located pertaining to the financial terms of the construction of what was to become No. 18100 and was located among a file of papers on the locomotive at the National Railway Museum under the reference 'Box CORR/GT'. How far the agreement may have been subsequently varied upon the take-over of the GWR by British Railways and the locomotive's non-delivery until well into the BR era is not clear.

APPENDIX B

The Great Western oil-burning experiment

Consideration of the conversion of a number of locomotives to burn oil came about from late 1945. At this time the government was attempting to divert prime coal supplies away from the railways to industry. In consequence the quality of coal available to the railways rapidly deteriorated and the GWR was quick to identify the need to locate alternative types of fuel source.

The use of heavy fuel oil of the Bunker C type came about in consultation with the Anglo-American Oil Company. There were apparently copious quantities of this type of fuel available although its naturally low viscosity meant that special arrangements had to be made in relation to both storage and delivery.

No.			Converted to oil firing		Returned to coal burning		
100A1	*Lloyds*		January	1947	September	1948	
5039	*Rhuddlan Castle*		December	1946	September	1948	
5079	*Lysander*		January	1947	October	1948	
5083	*Bath Abbey*		December	1946	November	1948	
5091	*Cleeve Abbey*		October	1946	November	1948	
Old No.	New No.						
4968	3900	*Shotton Hall*	May	1947	March	1949	
4971	3901	*Stanway Hall*	May	1947	April	1949	
4948	3902	*Northwick Hall*	May	1947	September	1948	
4907	3903	*Broughton Hall*	May	1947	April	1950	
4972	3904	*Saint Brides Hall*	May	1947	October	1948	
5955	3950	*Garth Hall*	June	1946	October	1948	
5976	3951	*Ashwicke Hall*	April	1947	November	1948	
6957	3952	*Norcliffe Hall*	April	1947	March	1950	
6953	3953	*Leighton Hall*	April	1947	September	1948	
5986	3954	*Arbury Hall*	May	1947	April	1950	
6949	3955	*Harberfield Hall*	May	1947	April	1949	
2872	4800		October	1945	September	1948	*
2854	4801		November	1945	February	1949	
2862	4802		February	1946	September	1948	
2849	4803		May	1946	April	1949	
2839	4804		May	1946	October	1948	
2863	4805		May	1946	May	1949	
2832	4806		May	1946	April	1949	
2848	4807		June	1947	July	1949	
2834	4808		July	1947	January	1950	
2845	4809		August	1947	December	1949	

Old No.	New No.		Converted to oil firing		Returned to coal burning	
2853	4810		August	1947	June	1949
2847	4811		September	1947	June	1949
2888	4850		November	1945	September	1948
3865	4851		December	1945	April	1949
3818	4852		January	1946	September	1948
3839	4853		May	1947	November	1949
3837	4854		June	1947	August	1949
3813	4855		July	1947	June	1949
3820	4856		July	1947	June	1949
3831	4857		August	1947	May	1949

As late as 1959 proposals were once again rife as to the conversion of steam engines to burn oil following the successful fitting of a burner to a pannier tank, No. 3711. No doubt due to the impending demise of steam traction the matter was not proceeded with.

Although as referred to in Chapter 1 sixteen depots were originally scheduled to be equipped for dealing with the oil fuel, in practice work at only three was actually completed; Old Oak, Swindon and Laira. Work was commenced and left unfinished at a number of other sites including Reading. Besides their later use for No. 18000, what facilities that did exist were maintained in working order almost to the end of steam in case a large-scale conversion plan was again contemplated in the future.

Initially re-fuelling was accomplished by means of a flexible pipe at solebar level, this same pipe being used to discharge oil from rail tanks arriving at a locomotive depot. Such an arrangement worked satisfactorily while the number of oil-fired locomotives was small although as the number increased so the GWR sought to develop a more rapid means of replenishing a tender.

An arrangement was therefore arrived at whereby a column similar to the existing water columns was used but with all flanged joints removed, and instead a 4 in diameter hose was used. The design was also carefully arranged to avoid spillage, for it was recognized that small quantities of dropped oil could make the fuelling point dangerous. A 200 lb counter-balance weight allowed the swinging arm to rise when not in use, so allowing any oil in the pipe to fall back rather than onto ground level. A light on the end of the actual arm was also provided for night-time use. This type of standpipe was equally suitable for both the converted 4,000 gallon and 3,500 gallon tenders.

It is not certain if this type of standpipe was in fact provided at all the depots referred to above and it may have been that a number retained solebar re-fuelling techniques. At the Old Oak Common depot there were three vertical stand points together with ten discharge points for the tank cars. The total oil storage capacity was 352,000 gallons.

(Further information on the re-fuelling points can be found in the *Railway Gazette* for 26 September 1947 and also 14 November 1947.)

* Former Locomotive Inspector Tony Tyler was personally involved with the early trials involving the oil-burning engines and recollects as follows:

> I was stationed at Swindon when 2872 was 'towed' across from the factory to the running sheds and saw it placed below the extreme end of the coal stage. A rail tank of Bunker C fuel oil was placed on the stage above it and the discharge pipe was connected to the top filling point on the locomotive's

tender and there it stood for *two* days while the cold, semi-solid fuel positively dripped into the fuel bunker on 2872. The locomotive was then towed to the roundhouse and the steam coils in the fuel tank were connected to an adjacent engine. (I was given the job of keeping this engine in steam for several hours.) When the oil's viscosity permitted, the fireman Tom Robinson lit up and put 2872 in steam for the first time in traffic.

I was moved back to Tondu when the pilot scheme was introduced and Severn Tunnel and Llanelly were brought into use. My information at that time was that the fuel supply was arranged from the National Oil Refinery at Llandarcy and the price was alleged to be as little as ½d. per gallon. This local supply was the reason for keeping the pilot scheme in South Wales. My memory also suggests that in addition to the 28/38xx class locos, a number of 42/52xx class 2–8–0T and 72xx class 2–8–2T engines were to be converted. No other tender engines were contemplated at that time . . .

There were also two other conversions in connection with the burning of Bunker C fuel. A Bristol-based locomotive, 6320 I believe it was, was converted and proved very successful, so successful indeed that it was rumoured that the entire 63xx series of 100 engines were to be altered.

The locomotive was the first to be fitted with a Swirlyflow burner jet mounted in the centre of the firebox instead of the fixed one at the front of the firebox as was previously the method. [No. 6320 was returned to coal-burning by August 1949.]

The final conversion that I can remember was a bit of an anti-climax. No. 3711 an 0–6–0 pannier tank was used as an oil-burner at Swindon for some years, ostensibly to use up the residue of heavy oil stocks there! After the demise of No. 18000 it was sent to Old Oak Common for the same reason and spent many months on the coach-working pilots. It was not as successful as the larger engines and I believe it used to 'flame-out' quite frequently, possibly in part due to the residue fuel being contaminated.

APPENDIX C

Snow clearance on the GWR using jet engines

Extract from the *Great Western Railway Magazine* for March and April 1947, Vol. 59, No. 3.

In conjunction with the National Gas Turbine Establishment, Ministry of Supply experiments have been concluded with gas turbine aero engines for snow clearance.

On the Great Western Railway, preliminary tests were carried out at Dowlais Top, on the single-line branch from Bargoed to Brecon, where six weeks' intermittent snowfall had caused heavy drifts in the cuttings, and daytime thaws followed by night frost had partly turned the compacted mass

The snow clearance train at Dowlais Top in 1947 with the two jets prominent at the front of the train. Other than the extract reproduced above little is written of the experiment in official reports and it is therefore not possible to ascertain if similar trials were carried out elsewhere on the Great Western system. Certainly the severe winter encountered that year was one of those fortunately only seen at long intervals in this country and hence the need to develop alternative methods of snow clearance did not have the urgency witnessed in other countries. Not mentioned in the report is that the opposite reaction from the force expelled at the nozzles attempted to propel the train backwards! In the background the train engine would appear to be a 56xx 0–6–2T, while the two carriage-type vehicles were no doubt workshop and messing facilities for the crew

GWR

After the passage of the jet engines, with areas clearly marked where blocks of impacted snow and ice have been dislodged. It was also found that where the covering of snow was not so compacted the force of the blast would send ballast flying in all directions. Apart from this, had the experiments continued special care arrangements would have been necessary in the vicinity of stations and wooden structures to protect both from the heat and flying debris. In the photograph, however, the absolute bleakness of the surrouding terrain is apparent. Worth mentioning is that the LMS attempted a similar method of snow clearance around the same time on the High Peak line between Ashbourne and Buxton which was blocked by drifts for several miles. The results though, were identical. Evidently the original intention had been to try the first GWR experiments on the Abergwynfi Branch but this was not proceeded with. The LNER also conducted similar tests around this time

GWR

of snow into ice. Two Rolls Royce Derwent Mark 1-type jet engines were used, mounted on welded steel test frames bolted to the floor of a GW 'Conflat', and secured with their axes parallel to the track and 4 ft 6 in apart. Attached to the outlet of each engine, which was flush with the headstock of the wagon, was a discharge tube 8 ft 3 in long, supported by wire cables attached to the stanchions of the test frames. The engines were depressed to about 15 degrees below the horizontal, so that the centre of the jet would strike the rail 13 ft ahead of the end of the tube.

At the rear of the Conflat a 325-gallon aircraft fuel tank with filters was mounted. Between this and the engines stood a control and instrument panel, with 24-volt coach lighting batteries underneath for starting purposes. Behind the Conflat was a Loriot 'B' carrying an 850-gallon road motor fuel tank equipped with mechanically operated pump, to serve as a fuel storage tank in which the lubricating oil for the engine pumps could be mixed with the fuel oil.

In the tests, soft snow in sidings was almost completely removed for the whole of the length of the sleepers, with the engines at less than full throttle. Where night frost had formed ice around the rails the blast was used twice at full throttle to clear it. At times the blast worked underneath the ice and flung off lumps up to 4 ft × 2 ft 6 in. Sometimes snow was blown onto the rollers of the switch rodding, which required careful cleaning and signal wires were shaken violently, but not broken.

In general, the tests distinctly indicated the possibility of developing the gas turbine method of snow clearance. Moveable mountings would increase mobility, enabling the jet to be traversed horizontally and vertically, with the engines themselves carried at the lowest possible level. A 'fish-tail' or other specially shaped blast tube might prove an improvement on the present circular pattern. Alternatively smaller engines might be used, and three of these mounted side by side, to give a more even distribution of blast across the breadth of track.

The erection and working of the jet aero engines was in the hands of representatives of the Royal Air Force, the National Gas Turbine Establishment, and the Rolls Royce Servicing Department. Their co-operation with the local officers of the Great Western Railway was of the greatest help, and the expert advice given to the Company added largely to the success of the experiments at Dowlais Top.

Rumour suggests there were also some difficulties in anchoring down the equipment for fear it might take off. After all, the GWR was flying from Cardiff to the Channel Islands in 1937 and could have gone from Dowlais Top to eternity in 1947!

APPENDIX D

The Swiss Railway's gas turbine engine

At the beginning of 1939, the Swiss Federal Railways placed an order with Brown-Boveri for a 2,200 hp gas turbine-propelled locomotive. This was intended for service on branch lines where traffic density did not justify full-scale electrification. As with the later British engines, Nos. 18000 and 18100, the gas turbine itself was used to drive a generator from which electrical power was fed to traction motors.

Although correctly described as the first true gas turbine railway engine in the world, it should be mentioned that as far back as 1896 the firm of Brown-Boveri had co-operated with a Frenchman by the name of Heilmann in the building of a steam engine having a final electric transmission.

The 1939 engine incorporated the unusual wheel arrangement of 1A–Bo–A1, with a maximum tractive effort measured at the wheel rim of 29,000 lb. Speed range was up to 70 mph and with an overall weight of 93.5 tons spread over a maximum axle loading of eighteen tons. Four of the six axles were driven.

The gas turbine unit itself was assembled and satisfactorily tested at the Baden works of Brown-Boveri, after which it was transported to Basle for fitting to the actual locomotive.

Several innovative characteristics were incorporated in the design to prevent damage to the turbine including an automatic shut-down if the driver accidentally allowed too much fuel at the intake which in turn would permit the turbine temperature to rise excessively. A similar cut-out existed in the event of generator or traction motor failure where the loading could be suddenly reduced. Regenerative braking was also provided.

Unfortunately the actual date the locomotive entered service is not recorded although it is thought to have been some time in 1941. By March 1942 a number of test runs had been carried out including one over the Baden–Olten–Solothurn–Lausanne–Fribourg–Berne–Olten–Sissach route, on which the locomotive behaved exactly as per the manufacturer's specifications. Later in the same year additional fuelling points were provided on the Basle–Zurich–Chur route and dynamometer car tests undertaken with loads of up to 500 tons. The final tests involved starting a 200-ton train on a rising gradient of between 1 in 47 and 1 in 48, where a speed of 25 mph was attained fifty-six seconds after starting.

A small auxiliary diesel engine, started by battery power, was fitted to start the gas turbine running, which could also be switched over to provide power direct to the traction motors for shunting the engine at speeds of up to 12 mph. Riding qualities were reported as excellent.

According to the manufacturers the driver's first duty was to start the auxiliary diesel engine which was then allowed to run for approximately four minutes, after which the gas turbine burner could be lit. A time-gap ensued, '. . . which the driver can use to put on his overalls . . .'![1]

Regrettably, supplies of the heavy oil required for the engine were then exhausted and testing was curtailed.

Fuel supplies were re-established in the spring of 1943 and from 25 May the engine began operating a regular daily service involving a round trip of just under 100 miles.

1. Quote from the *Brown-Boveri Review*, May 1942.

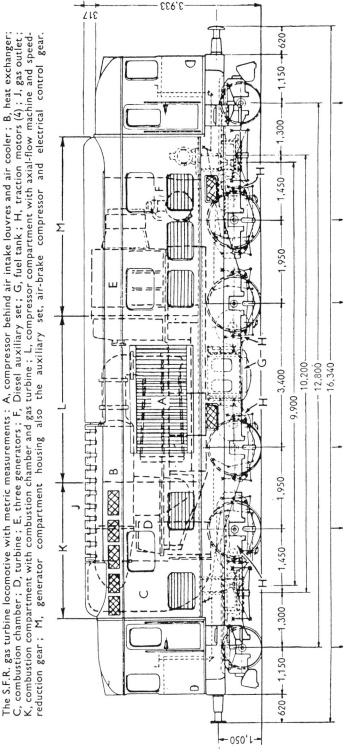

The S.F.R. gas turbine locomotive with metric measurements : A, compressor behind air intake louvres and air cooler ; B, heat exchanger; C, combustion chamber ; D, turbine ; E, three generators ; F, Diesel auxiliary set ; G, fuel tank ; H, traction motors (4) ; J, gas outlet ; K, combustion compartment with combustion chamber and gas turbine ; L, compressor compartment with axial-flow machine and speed-reduction gear ; M, generator compartment housing also the auxiliary set, air-brake compressor and electrical control gear.

183

This was either on mixed passenger or freight workings which, by their very nature, involved frequent stops and shunting. During these halts the turbine was allowed to idle but, should the halt exceed 10 minutes, it was shut down. Re-starting times varied from $2\frac{3}{4}$ to $3\frac{1}{2}$ minutes depending on the turbine temperature.

Contemporary reports suggest faults were few and the machine was quickly adapted to and popular with its drivers.

After nearly 300 days' uninterrupted daily service a further curtailing of fuel supplies occurred in the summer of 1944, by which time the total mileage run exceeded 31,000 miles. The engine was finally taken over by the Swiss Federal Railways (SBB or Schweizerische Bundes Bahner) on 1 October 1944.

Between that time in 1944 and early 1946 little is known of its movements, although between March and July 1946 the engine was on loan to the French Railways working trains between Basle and Chaumont. A full overhaul was then undertaken in August 1946 at which point the total miles run were 68,000, corresponding to 3,200 turbine hours.

The only known serious failure occurred in 1947 when a problem with the fuel oil resulted in damage to the turbine blades. This was repaired and the engine re-entered service. Modifications though, were undertaken from time to time and included replacement of the original refractory lining to the combustion chamber with an all-metal liner.

Apart from the reference to the visit made by Hawksworth and Dymond in September 1948, when the locomotive was known to have worked between Basle and Lucerne, information from then to 1949 is vague. It is reasonably clear though that the engine was in fairly regular use as the cumulative mileage had now reached 135,000. During 1950 the engine was used on demonstration runs between Switzerland and Germany and, following an agreement between the two countries' railways, operated regular express services between Basle and Munich from 16 July to 15 August 1950.

By 1951 the mileage had risen to 174,000, while by the autumn of 1951 the cumulative total was 197,000 and a second complete overhaul was undertaken. The final figures available are to mid-August 1952 and record 205,000 miles in 8,000 turbine hours.

Originally designated class Am4/6 and carrying the number 1101, the gas turbine engine was eventually converted to a straight electric unit as Class Ae4/6 No. 10851.

APPENDIX E

Report of visit to Switzerland by Chief Mechanical Engineer
– November 1949

I visited Switzerland last month, accompanied by my Electrical Assistant, Mr W.A.L. Creighton, and my assistant Mr A.W.J. Dymond, to witness rail trials of the completed locomotive which has been constructed by Messrs Brown-Boveri and the Swiss Locomotive Company. The visit lasted just over two weeks, being somewhat protracted owing to the firm changing the programme of tests from time to time during the visit.

Reports on the rail trials, and on various discussions which took place with Brown-Boveri representatives follow:

I. RAIL TRIALS

In all six trials took place, the first between Zurich and Basle, hauling a heavy freight train up the 1 in 85 bank from Brugg to Effingen, a distance of approximately 16 kilometres. At the conclusion of this trip the engine then ran light from Effingen to Basle, reaching for a period speeds in excess of 80 mph and on one stretch 90 mph. Later on this day the engine returned from Basle to Zurich hauling a passenger train. On the second trial a train was hauled between Zurich and Basle consisting of one wagon and an electric locomotive providing a load by means of its regenerative braking equipment, and on the concluding three trials passenger trains were hauled between Basle and Zurich and back, and Basle and Lucerne and back.

On each of the trials a Swiss locomotive was also attached to the train, primarily because the Swiss rolling stock is equipped with Westinghouse brake, for which our locomotive is not suitable. On the first two trials the British locomotive was at the head of the train, but on the concluding three trials the Swiss engine was in the lead. Besides providing braking, the Swiss engine also provided heat for passenger trains, couplings being provided by means of a suitable lead temporarily fitted to our engine. The trains were operated throughout practically the whole of the trips by our locomotive, except on one or two occasions when power was also exerted by the Swiss locomotive. On the last two trials, run between Basle and Lucerne and between Basle and Zurich, the Swiss Federal gas turbine locomotive took the place of the electric locomotive previously used in conjunction with our own engine.

Brief particulars of each trial run follow:

Test No. 1(a)

Goods train from Brugg to Effingen assisted by electric locomotive. Weight of train, excluding electric locomotive, stated to be 450 tons.

The intention of the test was to put the electrical transmission equipment through a maximum sustained current test on the road. Speeds to 28 mph on the gradient of 1 in 85 were achieved.

Test No. 1(b)

Light engine Effingen to Basle. Maximum speed 90 mph.

185

Test No. 2

Main-line express passenger trip Basle to Zurich with electric locomotive between British locomotive and the train. Total load including electric locomotive about 500 tons.

The gas turbine locomotive handled this train without assistance from the electric locomotive except at starting from Basle and once or twice on the rising gradient of 1 in 85.

Test No. 3

Zurich goods station to Basle with goods train, with electric locomotive at the head of the train. On this occasion the traffic offering for this train was only one wagon and accordingly the regenerative braking equipment on the electric locomotive was used to provide a constant load of approximately 2,000 hp for the gas turbine to haul.

Test No. 4

Basle to Zurich and back with passenger trains, with Swiss electric locomotive in front. Weight of train to Zurich 510 tons including electric locomotive. Weight of train from Zurich 492 tons including electric locomotive.

Test No. 5

Basle to Lucerne and back with passenger trains, with Swiss gas turbine locomotive in front. Weight of train to Lucerne 318 tons, including Swiss gas turbine locomotive. Weight of train from Lucerne 359 tons, including Swiss gas turbine locomotive.

Test No. 6

Basle to Zurich and back with passenger trains, with Swiss Federal gas turbine locomotive in front. Readings were taken on the trip from Basle to Zurich only, the weight of the train on this occasion being only 364 tons.

It became apparent as the trials proceeded that Messrs Brown-Boveri had still to make adjustments to the power unit and electrical equipment, and it was also made clear that it was not their intention to conduct in Switzerland any dynamometer car trials. In consequence it became a matter of some difficulty to obtain any accurate figures of performance, especially as it had been stated by the Brown-Boveri engineers that the trials were from their point of view preliminary only and were being undertaken essentially to give them data upon which they could effect adjustment to give the optimum performance when the engine was in service in this country. Readings of output at the terminals of the main generator were frequently taken from the volt-ammeter in the driver's cab and figures ranging from 1,900 to 2,100 hp were obtained. On one occasion 2,200 hp at the generator terminals was noted. On representation being made to Brown-Boveri concerning the absence of any reading approximate to the 2,500 hp for which the locomotive is intended, they stated that the adjustments which they had in mind would result in such performance being achieved.

The sequence of operations for starting the gas turbine locomotive and the control of the locomotive in traffic were, of course, constantly under review throughout the series of tests and gave every satisfaction. On one occasion only did the flame fail to ignite, owing to the power operated mechanism for inserting the ignition tube failing to function. The tube was, however, inserted manually and the flame ignited immediately. The failure was subsequently traced to a disconnected lead which had been removed for testing purposes and had not been replaced. The disposition of the controls on the driver's desk render his manipulation quite easy and the locomotive appeared to be extremely manoeuverable when working on the gas turbine at the lower speeds.

At the highest speeds achieved (80–90 mph), light engine, the riding qualities were exceptionally good and, in particular, at 75 mph on the undulating track between Rheinfolden and Basle, where curvatures are very slight, the speed appeared to be much less than the actual.

After each of the runs involving fairly lengthy periods of heavy working, cursory inspection was made of the electrical equipment, including the traction motors. On no occasion was there any evidence of overheating or arcing. Commutation appeared to be exceptionally good and the machine generally seems to have been rated with ample margins.

Some adverse comment was made to the Brown-Boveri engineers by myself and my Assistants concerning the excessive noise when standing in a station, caused particularly by the diesel engine, although the high pitched whining of the compressor itself also seemed to be excessive. I formed the impression that Brown-Boveri themselves were not wholly satisfied with this aspect of the locomotive, and they are actively engaged both in their own turbine department and through the agency of Messrs Saurer who built the diesel engine, to reduce the noise as much as possible. Except when starting up from cold, when a slight amount of smoke was emitted for about a minute or so, from the louvres, the exhaust when idling is practically colourless and when working at high horsepowers quite invisible.

The auxiliary equipment on the locomotive behaved in a satisfactory manner but, in addition to the occasion when the relay operating the ignition rod failed to function, an incident took place on another occasion whereby the multiple belt driving the mechanical exhauster compressor set became overheated and had to be cut away before the locomotive could proceed, the brakes in the meantime being operated by means of the electrically driven exhauster compressor set. This mishap was stated by the Brown-Boveri engineers to be due to a misalignment of the belting pulleys which had been noticed by one of their staff who had, however, not corrected the inaccuracy. During the runs the warning light indicating maximum temperature before turbine frequently lit up, but although some notice was taken of it exhibiting a warning signal, the Brown-Boveri engineers stated that the relay had been set rather on the low side and that, in fact, the maximum temperature, viz 1,112 °F, at which the turbine should normally operate was above that exhibited by the pyrometer. On two occasions the protective device dependent upon the temperature after the turbine, operated and shut down the machine but here again the explanation offered was that the relay was set on the low side.

At the conclusion of the rail trials I had formed the opinion that when the further adjustments have been carried out by the Brown-Boveri engineers the machine will achieve its specified performance. The workmanship throughout is of good quality and its appearance quite pleasing.

As it may be anticipated that dynamometer car trials of the locomotive will take place in this country, I suggested to the Brown-Boveri engineers that any views they might have about the nature of the trials would be welcomed, and they have promised to let me have their observations on this point.

II. DISCUSSIONS WITH BROWN-BOVERI ENGINEERS

During discussions which took place either at Baden or at intervals during the progress of the rail trials, the following points emerged:

(a) Earth leakage relay

As intimated in my report dated June last following my visit to Switzerland in May to witness the bench tests of the power unit, I had proposed that, as both poles of the generator are insulated, some form of earth leakage relay or indicator should be installed. Since my return in June last, some correspondence has taken place with the London office of Brown-Boveri on this point and further discussion on the matter followed during my recent visit.

Various proposals for proving such a device were considered but, after considerable investigation, I finally agreed with Messrs Brown-Boveri that no such device should be fitted. The primary reason for this decision is that Brown-Boveri have had experience in building diesel-electric locomotives in fair numbers as well as the Swiss Federal gas turbine locomotive, on all of which both poles of the electrical equipment are insulated and on none of which has an earth leakage relay or indicator been found to be necessary. Moreover it was pointed out by the Brown-Boveri electrical engineers that while such a device in certain circumstances might have been of value in detecting an incipient breakdown of insulation, there were possibilities also of the device being a source of danger, and as their experience has been conclusively against the necessity for such a device, I have, as stated above, agreed finally that it should not be fitted.

(b) Spare parts for locomotive

In October last, Messrs British Brown-Boveri submitted to me a list of further spare parts which the firm thought we should purchase in order to be able to meet any reasonable possibility of necessity for replacement. In view, however, of the fact that some considerable expenditure has already been incurred on spares, I withheld my decision on the necessity for this further list pending discussion in Baden. The list fell into three main portions, the first dealing with spare parts for the turbine and thermal equipment, which I have now established consists of many items quite readily obtainable in this country, and Brown-Boveri have now agreed to review the whole of these items and submit a revised list of those which could not reasonably be provided in this country. The second portion of the list consisted of spares for the Saurer diesel engine, and it has now been agreed that enquiries should be made with a view to ascertaining whether spares for the particular type of Saurer engine (BXD) which is fitted to the locomotive can be supplied through any firm in this country. The third portion of the list related to further electrical spares, principally spares for certain relays, spare parts for thermostats, photo-electric cells, thermionic valves, etc. As all these electrical items are of Swiss origin, there would appear to be no alternative but to purchase them from Switzerland; and a tender revised in the light of the foregoing points will be submitted by the firm in due course.

(c) Lining of combustion chamber

I was interested to hear from Brown-Boveri that they had decided not to proceed further with the segmental 'steel brick' lining units originally proposed for the combustion chamber, and a plain sheet lining of special alloy steel had been fitted.

(d) Light engine running on diesel engine

In the original proposal for the design of the locomotive, it had been suggested that when the diesel engine was supplying current for traction purposes when moving light engine at low speeds, two motors should be coupled together in parallel. The initial tests of the locomotive immediately after completion, however, revealed that the tractive effort under these circumstances was insufficient to give satisfactory manoeuverability, particularly over points and crossings, etc. One trip was run with one motor only in operation, but subsequently the firm decided to connect two motors in series giving a reasonable tractive effort and a maximum speed of about 15 mph.

(e) Diagrams, instruction manuals, etc.

I have requested and the firm have agreed that as soon after the delivery as possible ample supplies of the necessary diagrams, instruction manuals, characteristic curves, etc. will be furnished. The necessary short instructions will, of course, be provided before the locomotive is delivered.

(f) Delivery date

The firm expect to complete the whole of the outstanding adjustments in time for the locomotive to be despatched from Baden on the 28th instant. I am in communication with the Commercial Department to determine the actual date of shipment at Zeebrugge, to coincide with the sailings of the train ferry *Suffolk*, which is covered over the rail deck, as distinct from the train ferry *Essex* on which the rail deck is open to the weather.

III. GENERAL

During the course of my visit, I met the following personnel from Brown-Boveri, Baden:

Mr Vodoz – Sales Director for English-speaking countries
Dr Th.Boveri – Director of the company
Mr Neihus – ditto
Mr Seipel – Technical Director
Mr Muller – Chief of Traction Department
Mr Whitwell – Assistant Chief of Traction Department

On one trip Dr Meyer, presumably Motive Power Superintendent of Swiss Federal Railways, was on the footplate, and on another occasion Dr Steiner of the Swiss Ministry of Transport was present.

During the trips between Basle and Zurich and Basle and Lucerne, considerable interest in the locomotive was exhibited by the Swiss public, and a number of photographs were taken by the Swiss press photographers, some of which I saw in the Swiss newspapers before I left.

Signed by F.W. Hawksworth.

APPENDIX F

Brown-Boveri gas turbine locomotive – working expenditure comparisons

Comparison of Working Expenditure with Express Passenger Steam Locomotives Year Ending May 1951

ITEM	GAS TURBINE			'STAR' LOCOMOTIVE			'CASTLE' LOCOMOTIVE			'KING' LOCOMOTIVE		
	Qty	Cost £	Cost per mile s. d.	Qty	Cost £	Cost per mile s. d.	Qty	Cost £	Cost per mile s. d.	Qty	Cost £	Cost per mile s. d.
Weekdays out of service	130			79			83			121		
Miles run	33,725			40,088			47,768			51,500		
Running shed maintenance		516	$3\frac{1}{2}$		680	4		726	$3\frac{1}{2}$		849	4
Main shed maintenance		981	7		942	$5\frac{1}{2}$		1,007	5		1,177	$5\frac{1}{2}$
Cost of fuel:												
Heavy oil (gall.)	86,612	2,955	1. 9									
Gas oil (gall.)	16,028	779	5									
Fuelling, etc.		129	1									
Coal (tons) including fuelling and carriage				981	3,621	1. 9$\frac{1}{2}$	1,103	4,072	1. 8$\frac{1}{2}$	1,156	4,269	1. 8

ITEM	GAS TURBINE			'STAR' LOCOMOTIVE			'CASTLE' LOCOMOTIVE			'KING' LOCOMOTIVE		
	Qty	Cost £	per mile s. d.	Qty	Cost £	per mile s. d.	Qty	Cost £	per mile s. d.	Qty	Cost £	per mile s. d.
Water		92			79	½		89	½		93	½
Lubricants (gall.)		20		416	48	½	418	48	½	528	61	½
Total running costs		5,380	3. 2		5,370	2. 8		5,942	2. 6		6,449	2. 6½

1950 replacement costs – 'Star' class locomotive £13,025
                – 'Castle' class locomotive £13,920; 30-year life.
                – 'King' class locomotive £16,270; 30-year life.

Comparison of Working Expenditure with Express Passenger Steam Locomotives Year Ending September 1952

ITEM	GAS TURBINE			'STAR' LOCOMOTIVE			'CASTLE' LOCOMOTIVE			'KING' LOCOMOTIVE		
	Qty	Cost £	Cost per mile s. d.	Qty	Cost £	Cost per mile s. d.	Qty	Cost £	Cost per mile s. d.	Qty	Cost £	Cost per mile s. d.
Weekdays out of service	104			60			85			131		
Miles run	71,217			31,566			48,413			49,676		
Running shed maintenance		1,345	4½		881	6½		942	4½		1,101	5½
Main shed maintenance		1,709	5½		1,107	8½		1,182	6		1,382	6½
Cost of fuel: Heavy oil (gall.)	181,806	6,912	1. 11									

ITEM	GAS TURBINE			'STAR' LOCOMOTIVE			'CASTLE' LOCOMOTIVE			'KING' LOCOMOTIVE		
	Qty	Cost £	Cost per mile s. d.	Qty	Cost £	Cost per mile s. d.	Qty	Cost £	Cost per mile s. d.	Qty	Cost £	Cost per mile s. d.
Gas oil (gall.)	32,435	1,808	6									
Fuelling, etc.		70	½									
Coal (tons) including fuelling and carriage				803	3,888	2. 5½	1,130	5,471	2. 3	1,118	5,413	2. 2
Water					92	½		130	½		128	½
Lubricants (gall.)	348	46	½	339	45	½	436	58	½	534	71	½
Total running costs		11,890	3. 4		6,013	3. 9½		7,783	3. 2½		8,095	3. 3

Gas turbine: Fuel oil, heavy 9½d. per gall.
               Gas oil 1s. 1⅜d. per gall.
               Lubricants 2s. 8d. per gall.

Steam: Coal 71s. 7d. per ton.
          Carriage 25s. 3d. per ton.
          Lubricants 2s. 8d. per gall.

APPENDIX G

Gas turbine locomotive No. 18000 – daily inspection

DAILY INSPECTION. MECHANICAL AND ELECTRICAL. SWINDON, 9 APRIL 1952.

The daily inspection is to ensure reliable operation of all parts of the locomotive. It consists mainly of a superficial visual examination of all fitments together with a more detailed examination of certain equipment as set out in the schedule. Special attention is to be paid to checking levels and replenishment of lubricants and coolants.

The inspection is to be carried out by qualified mechanical and electrical fitters who will sign the daily inspection certificate for their respective items. The time of completion is to be entered in the appropriate column.

The time for the daily inspection should be approximately $1\frac{1}{2}$ hours for a mechanical fitter and mate and a half an hour for the electrical fitter and mate. However the actual time will depend upon the amount of repair work or adjustments to be carried out.

The driver will be responsible for filling in the running times of gas turbine and boiler and total mileage, and will check that the fuel oils and water are sufficient for the schedule journey.

Mechanical

It is not intended that the fitter should carry out this daily examination of each item exactly in the order set out below, it will be found more convenient to begin say at Cab 1 and to work systematically through the locomotive to Cab 2 and thence to the underframe and externally mounted auxiliaries. Where oil levels are to be checked the fitter will top up according to the requirements of each auxiliary.

M1. Inspection of equipment in cabs and engine compartments for mechanical soundness. This will include all fitments such as brake valves, window wipers, fuel valves, oil coolers, air inlet guards, barring gear, etc. Engine compartments to be cleaned through. Inspect for oil or water leaks from pipes, valves and tanks.

M2. Inspect exhauster – compressor sets for belt tension and crankcase oil level (Talpa 30).

M3. Give a half turn to Auto Klean filter for control oil.

M4. Insert one funnel full of oil (Vitrea 71) in turbine power unit frame support bearing.

M5. Diesel Unit
   a. Check sump oil level (Rotella 30).
   b. Check oil level in injection pump camshaft drive sump (Talpa 30).
   c. Check oil level in injection pump governor (Talpa 30).
   d. Give a half turn to grease stauffer (Retinax P), of coolant pump gland.
   e. Check fan belt tension.
   f. Check coolant level in tank – keep topped up to $\frac{7}{8}$ level in sight glass.
      Antifreeze in winter.
      Distilled water in summer.
   g. Inspect for oil and coolant leaks.
   h. Clean surface oil from unit and drain trays.

M6. External examination. Make a visual examination of all external fittings and auxiliaries. These will include:
   a. Buffers and draw-gear.

b. Vacuum, steam hoses and pipe lines.

c. Compressed air system and brake gear.

d. Sand gear.

e. Body and bogie supports and pivots.

f. ATC gear.

g. Heavy oil, control and cooling oil pumps and housings. Clean out surface oil.

h. Oil and water tanks and pipes.
    Particular attention should be paid to locking plates, cotters, taper pins and safety straps.

M7. Open drain cocks of compressed air system to clear away residual matter.

M8. Operational test of turbine and auxiliaries.

Should it be necessary to check certain faults reported by the driver or repairs carried out by the fitter or should the fitter consider it necessary, the turbine should be run under power and all auxiliaries should be checked.

a. diesel unit.

b. turbine power unit.

c. exhauster compressor sets.

d. fuel pumps.

e. control and lubricating oil and flow through sight glasses.

f. barring gear and cooling oil pump.

g. check level of oil in main lubricating tank.

M9. Boiler. General inspection of unit (during heating season).

Check for:

a. Water and steam leakages.

b. Clean burner and filter in burner feed line every two days.

c. Fuel oil leakage.

d. Inspect conflux feed water pump, ensure that sump is kept topped up with oil (Talpa 30).

e. Give a half turn to grease stauffer on driver pulley (Unedo 3).

Electrical

E1. Check all fuses for soundness and tightness and see that all spares are in place.

E2. Check operation of ignition rod and see that spare rod is sound.

E3. Check battery voltage under discharge (about 30–40 amps).

E4. Make superficial visual examination of contactor panels, resistances, etc. lighting and overloads.

E5. As in M8, the turbine should be started if necessary to check the soundness in operation of electrical machinery and circuits. Note the voltage of the auxiliary generator battery and voltage converter set.

The Weekly Examination

This examination can be carried out weekly or progressively in conjunction with the daily examination should it be necessary for a whole day for repair work. The date on which each item is dealt with must be recorded in the appropriate column and the artisan's signature appended.

Repairs

Any known defects must be reported by the driver on the REPAIR CARD which is to be put in the repairs card box as for normal steam locomotive practice.

The person responsible for locomotive No. 18000 maintenance must examine the card and submit it to the appropriate artisan.

Upon completion of the repairs, the artisan must sign the card and state work carried out together with total working time for himself and his mate.

Further details as to repair card practice will be carried out in accordance with the standard repair card system for steam locomotives.

Mechanical

M10. Carry out any outstanding deferred repairs booked during the week.

M11. Check brake adjustment, 7 to 11 turns of handwheel, adjust brakes as required. Lubricate hand brake spindle and bearing of hand brake wheel (Talpa 30).

M12. Exhauster Compressor Sets.

Give a full turn to grease stauffer (Unedo 3) of tension pulley of belt driven set.

Remove filters from compressor, clean and replace.

Remove filters from exhauster, clean and replace.

Drain oil from silencers of exhausters.

M13. Examine the condition of the first fixed row of blading of compressor for damage or deposit. Check the lagging around the thermal unit. Clean the 5 optics of the thermal unit.

M14. Empty drain trays beneath change-over valves.

M15. Diesel engine.

a. Grease injection pump drive and coolant pump bearing (Unedo 3).

b. Top up fan bearing (Talpa 30).

c. Clean air filters.

d. Clean lift pump filter.

M16. Boiler. (During heating season).

Clean main filter to boiler burner.

M17. Check contents of main lubricating oil tank – level of oil should be the centre line of top optic. (Turbo 29).

M18. Check condition of heat exchanger through flaps on roof.

M19. Carry out lubrication of points 9, 10, 11, 13, 14 and 21 as indicated on lubrication chart Shell Mex drawing No. 618 in maintenance manual.

To grease point 9 the weight of the locomotive must be taken on two jacks – one each side of the locomotive.

M20. Check contents of fire extinguisher (Wt. of No. $5 = 10\frac{3}{4}$ lb)

Electrical

E6. Carry out any outstanding deferred repairs booked during week.

E7. Lubricate bearings of:

a. Traction motors armature bearings and gears.

b. Barring gear motor.

E8. Check operation of indicator lamps for maximum turbine temperatures. See that lamps light when relays 765 and 766 are closed.

E9. Inspect battery, top up cells as necessary and check voltage.

E10. See that photo-electric cell window is clean and that relays 730, 731 and 732 close when a light is directed onto the photo electric cell.

APPENDIX H

Summary of four-weekly reports on No. 18000 – 20 May 1950 to 28 November 1953

Period 4-weeks ended	Total mileage	Fuel oil consumed (gall.)	Light oil (gall.)		Weekdays out of service, under or awaiting repair, including examination	Not required
20. 5.1950	Figures not given				12	
17. 6.1950	3,855	8,960	2,052	(26)	8	
15. 7.1950	1,455	5,512	1,290	(58)	13	
12. 8.1950	436	1,500	470		19	
9. 9.1950	4,391	8,035	2,289	(20)		2
7.10.1950	5,256	12,020	1,761	(88)	2	
4.11.1950	3,363	8,461	1,430	(84)	9	
2.12.1950	1,239	2,459	430	(19)	17	
30.12.1950	–	–	–		24	

Percentage availability from 7.5.1950: 55.17%

Period 4-weeks ended	Total mileage	Fuel oil consumed (gall.)	Light oil (gall.)		Weekdays out of service	Not required
27. 1.1951	–	–	–		24	
24. 2.1951	3,235	9,542	1,825	(86)		1
24. 3.1951	2,550	7,247	1,175	(162)	5	
21. 4.1951	3,154	9,343	1,745	(117)	3	
19. 5.1951	4,801	12,124	2,250	(71)	3	
16. 6.1951	2,576	4,717	675		16	
14. 7.1951	–	–	–		24	
11. 8.1951	Figures not available					
8.9.1951	5,878	15,209	2,080		7	
6.10.1951	7,207	16,632	2,887		1	
3.11.1951	129	–	–		21	
1.12.1951	4,853	12,717	2,555		8	
29.12.1951	6,020	16,621	3,230		1	

Percentage availability for year: 55.66%

Period 4-weeks ended	Total mileage	Fuel oil consumed (gall.)	Light oil (gall.)	Weekdays out of service	Not required
26. 1.1952	6,599	17,898	4,888	4	
23. 2.1952	6,991	18,425	3,720	2	
22. 3.1952	5,575	14,700	3,420	7	
19. 4.1952	5,006	12,807	2,725	7 (see note)	
17. 5.1952	7,861	18,649	2,460	–	
14. 6.1952	6,111	14,840	2,225	6	
12. 7.1952	3,350	8,609	992	13	
9. 8.1952	8,237	20,284	2,760	–	
6. 9.1952	8,261	20,171	2,665	1	

Period 4-weeks ended	Total mileage	Fuel oil consumed (gall.)	Light oil (gall.)	Weekdays out of service, under or awaiting repair, including examination
4.10.1952	2,224	6,085	795	18
1.11.1952	–	–	–	24
29.11.1952	–	–	–	24
27.12.1952	–	–	–	24
24. 1.1953	–	–	–	24
21.2.1953	363	1,720	465	19
21. 3.1953	70	–	–	23
18. 4.1953	–	–	–	23
16. 5.1953	–	–	–	24
13. 6.1953	68	1,117	275	23
11. 7.1953	105	354	370	22
8. 8.1953	487	1,240	925	19
5. 9.1953	2,804	6,948	1,235	11
3.10.1953	2,057	5,472	975	15
31.10.1953	7,483	20,387	3,405	2
28.11.1953	8,402	23,109	3,860	1
26.12.1953	Figures not available			

(Lubricating oil consumption where known in brackets, in pints.)

No figures are available for the period 1954–60.

Note: the four-weekly period was calculated on the basis of twenty-four days covering Mondays to Saturdays; Sundays were not included. On the basis of 1952 up to 19.4.1952 the availability was 80 per cent. Taken as a whole the figures from the start of the engine's career up to 19.4.1952 may be read as 58.04 per cent.

APPENDIX I

Speed and load tables. Passenger trains, Summer 1952

Dep.	From	To	Distance (miles)	Time (mins)	Speed (mph)	No. of coaches	Coaches (number) slipped	(at)	No. of coaches + or − 1952 over 1939
4.37 p.m.	Bath	Paddington	106.9	116	55.2	12	One	Reading	+5
10.17 a.m.	Oxford	Paddingon	63.5	72	52.9	12			+3
5.19 p.m.	Swindon	Reading	41.3	47	52.7	9			+5
8.28 a.m.	Chippenham	Paddington	94.0	100	56.4	12	One	Didcot	+5
9.05 a.m.	Kemble	Paddington	91.0	99	55.1	9			−
11.15 a.m.	Paddington	Bath	106.9	111	57.8	11			+3
1.15 p.m.	Paddington	Bath	106.9	111	57.8	11			+3
5.05 p.m.	Paddington	Bath	106.9	112	57.3	12			+3
10.30 a.m.	Westbury	Paddington	95.6	100	57.3	9			+1
12.00 p.m.	Paddington	Exeter	173.5	182	57.2	10			+2
1.13 p.m.	Swindon	Paddington	77.3	83	55.8	9			−3
9.37 a.m.	H. Wycombe	Paddington	84.1	91	55.4	8			+3
4.55 p.m.	Paddington	Kemble	91.0	$100\frac{1}{2}$	54.3	9			+2
9.39 a.m.	M. in Marsh	Oxford	28.3	31	54.7	10			+3
3.38 p.m.	Oxford	Reading	27.5	34	48.5	10			+3
3.30 p.m.	Paddington	Taunton	142.7	148	57.8	12	One	Westbury	−2
12.15 a.m.	Paddington	Taunton	142.7	152	56.3	8a			−1
10.30 a.m.	Paddington	N. Abbot	193.7	207	56.1	14c			−
9.30 a.m.	Didcot	Paddington	53.1	58	54.9	9			+2
12.42 p.m.	Exeter	Paddington	173.5	184	56.5	10			+2

2.30 a.m.	Paddington	Swindon	77.3	82	56.5	7a			−1
9.21 a.m.	Bath	Paddington	106.9	115	55.7	11			−2
9.30 a.m.	Reading	Westbury	59.6	65	55.0	11			+2
3.58 a.m.	Swindon	Bath	29.6	33	53.8	4a			−
11.47 a.m.	Reading	Taunton	106.7	119	53.8	9			−1
11.50 a.m.	Westbury	Paddington	95.6	109	52.6	13	One	Reading	+1
6.25 p.m.	Taunton	Paddington	142.7	153	55.9	13			+4
3.31 a.m.	Westbury	Taunton	47.1	51	55.4	13			+4
9.36 a.m.	Taunton	Westbury	47.1	51	55.4	9			+1
11.45 a.m.	Bristol	Paddington	117.6	130	54.2	10b			+1
9.37 a.m.	H. Wycombe	Birmingham	84.1	91	55.4	11	One	Leam'ton	−
2.20 p.m.	Reading	Westbury	59.6	66	54.1	13			+2
5.20 p.m.	Westbury	Reading	59.6	65	35.0	13			+1
8.40 a.m.	Paddington	Newport	133.4	144	55.5	10			+1
6.10 p.m.	Reading	Paddington	36.0	42	51.4	10			+6
1.14 p.m.	N. Abbot	Paddington	193.7	213	54.5	10d			−2
12.42 p.m.	Exeter	Paddington	173.5	184	56.5	10			−3
5.10 p.m.	Paddington	Leamington	87.4	$100\frac{1}{2}$	52.1	13	One	Bicester	−

a – Newspaper train
b – Via Badminton
c – Saturdays only
d – Stop for bank engine

APPENDIX J

Fuel and other costs, Metropolitan Vickers engine No. 18100, for 1952–3

Four weeks ended	Motive Power Depots £ s. d.			Main Works £ s. d.			Fuel oil consumed (per gall.)	Engine miles	In use (Days)	Under repair/ examination (Days)	Spare (Days)
19. 4.1952[1]	2	15	7	10	1	10	–	487	–	–	–
17. 5.1952	76	4	0	49	19	2	–	5,868	–	–	10[8]
14. 6.1952	6	19	1	16	12	9	12,510[2]	3,496	–	–	4
12. 7.1952	22	15	8	8	2	10	8,850[2]	4,288	24	–	–
9. 8.1952	29	1	1	19	2	0	22,175[2]	10,397	17	7	4
6. 9.1952	146	19	4	37	1	8	35,178[9]	9,749	24	–	–
4.10.1952[10]	20	8	11				2,369[2]	806	3	22	3
1.11.1952[11]	14	3	2				6,254[2]	1,607	8	16	–
29.11.1952[12]	74	12	8				29,215[3]	6,012	25	–	–
27.12.1952	213	11	0				48,284[3]	12,350	24[13]	–	–
24. 1.1953	384	9	3				38,780[3]	10,467	18	4	–
21. 2.1953	129	7	8				11,142[3]	3,169	6	18	–
21. 3.1953	8	14	11				–	–	–	24	–
18. 4.1953	2	5	1				–	–	–	24	–
16. 5.1953	6	6	3	3	3	9	8,356[4]	–	–	24	–
13. 6.1953	25	13	4	1	1	3	23,185[4]	3,771	14	10	–
11. 7.1953	125	5	3				38,734[5]	6,566	16	10	–
8. 8.1953	193	16	11				39,286[6]	11,335	24	–	–
5. 9.1953	179	6	5				2,691[6]	11,335	24	–	–
3.10.1953	88	11	5	15	0	4	–	725	2	22	–
31.10.1953	29	0	2	16	5	6	700[7]	–	–	24	–
28.11.1953	6	1	0	22	11	0	214	214	3	–	21

NOTES

1. Figures cover two weeks ended 19.4.1952.
2. Cost of fuel = 1s. 2⅝d. per gallon.
3. Cost of fuel = 1s. 1½d. per gallon.
4. Cost of fuel = 1s. 0⅝d. per gallon.
5. Cost of fuel = 1s. 1¼d. per gallon.
6. Cost of fuel = 1s. 0⅞d. per gallon.
7. Cost of fuel = 1s. 0¾d. per gallon.
8. Out of use for 10 days, unconfirmed.
9. Cost of fuel = 1s. 2⅛d. per gallon. Figure includes 4,840 gallons understated in return for 9.8.1952.
10. Additional £1,398 7s. 1d. expenditure incurred during this period.
11. Additional £1,137 4s. 5d. expenditure incurred during this period.
12. Additional £29 2s. 4d. expenditure incurred during this period.
13. Four days unaccounted for.

APPENDIX K

The proposed coal-fired gas turbine locomotive

An article in the *Railway Gazette* for 1949 dealing with future locomotive development stated that, '. . . the coal-burning gas turbine was not yet a feasible proposition'. Three years later however, the government had been convinced that the technical difficulties could be overcome, with the result that on 23 December 1952 an order was placed by the Ministry of Fuel and Power for a coal-fired gas turbine engine for use on British Railways.

Such a move was indeed a courageous effort although it would be interesting to learn how the decision to proceed was arrived at. Two firms were to be involved in construction, the North British locomotive works which would build the mechanical parts and Messrs C.A. Parsons of Glasgow which would be responsible for the turbine.

Sources within the National Railway Museum reveal that this was not in fact the first time a coal-burning gas turbine had been proposed.[1] In 1946 there is a reference to the 'Third Report on the Proposed Coal Fired Gas Turbine' although this fails to reveal much useful information. Neither was this the first time pulverized coal had been suggested as a locomotive fuel, for a number of experiments had been made by the various railway companies in earlier years using this type of combustion. On the whole they had ended in disappointment and with no significant advantage over conventional firing.

Initial proposals for the new engine showed it to be of the C–C type, developing 1,800 hp allied to a weight in working order of 117 tons. (The nominal output was later reduced to 1,500 hp as a result of an alteration to the turbine blading in an attempt to resolve difficulties with ash deposits.) The turbine was to be operated on the exhaust-heating principle while a mechanical drive incorporating a two-speed gearbox together with other gearboxes and cardan shafts divided the load equally between the driven axles. Two forward speed ranges were specified, one suitable for passenger working and the other for freight.

The technical specification was as follows, from which it can be gleaned that this was envisaged as a medium-power, rather than a high-powered, machine:

> At 72 mph, 30,000 lb tractive effort
> At 50 mph, 45,000 lb tractive effort
> Anticipated efficiency of 10% at 1/10th load
> Anticipated efficiency of 16% at half load
> Anticipated efficiency of 19% at full load

By 1954 development had reached the stage where bench tests were being carried out with the gas turbine power unit although difficulties were encountered with blade erosion caused by minute particles of ash. Despite such problems every effort was made to overcome them, with the result that in the September 1955 issue of *Railway Magazine* it was confidently reported that the actual power unit would be ready for full bench tests at the end of the year and, it was hoped, full road trials in the summer of 1958. In the meantime the mechanical parts of the engine had been completed and stood idle awaiting the power plant.

---

1. Reference within the E.S. Cox papers as revealed by C.P. Atkins.

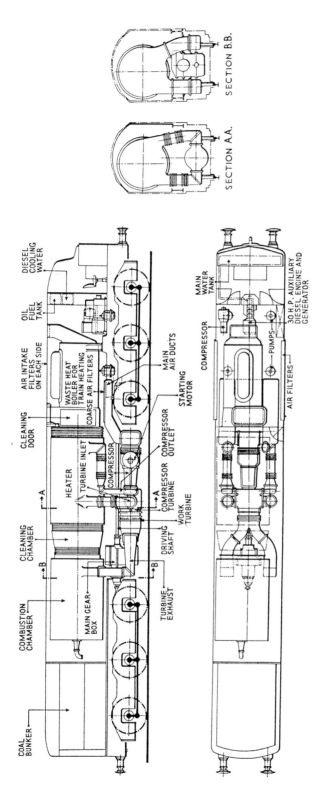

SECTION B.B.

SECTION A.A.

COAL BUNKER

COMBUSTION CHAMBER

MAIN GEAR BOX

CLEANING CHAMBER

TURBINE EXHAUST

DRIVING SHAFT

HEATER

CLEANING DOOR

TURBINE INLET

COMPRESSOR

WORK TURBINE

COMPRESSOR TURBINE

COMPRESSOR OUTLET

STARTING MOTOR

COARSE AIR FILTERS

WASTE HEAT BOILER FOR TRAIN HEATING

MAIN AIR DUCTS

AIR INTAKE FILTERS ON EACH SIDE

OIL FUEL TANK

DIESEL COOLING WATER

COMPRESSOR

PUMPS

AIR FILTERS

30 H.P. AUXILIARY DIESEL ENGINE AND GENERATOR

MAIN WATER TANK

Side elevation and section of the first proposals for the NBL/Parsons coal-burning gas turbine. Six tons of fuel would be carried at one end which was sufficient for 500 miles' running. Starting would be by light oil and with a change-over to coal after a twenty-five-minute warm-up period. Note in particular the single cab at one end and offset turbine so as to afford a passageway along one side – shades of 'Leader' perhaps? By 1956 the design had been modified to a 1A1A–A1A1 type, the result of an increase in weight to 150 tons while the nominal output was stated to be 1,750 hp

203

Unfortunately it was found impossible to resolve the difficulties caused by ash deposits and accordingly the project was finally abandoned in 1960. Similar difficulties had also been responsible for the curtailment of an American project in 1946 which proposed two coal-burning gas turbines, one of 4,200 hp and the other slightly smaller at 3,750 hp. Interestingly a copy of the US experience on these engines was passed to the LMS Advisory Committee on scientific research.

A model of the proposed engine has survived, in the Kelvin Hall of Glasgow Transport Museum, while a very fair artist's impression appears in Robin Barnes' book, *Locomotives that Never Were*.

APPENDIX L

'GT3'

This was the last conventional gas turbine locomotive to be built in Britain (APT involved a multi-engined vehicle) and was constructed as a private venture by the English Electric Company at its Vulcan Foundry. Not appearing until 1959, the design had been commenced as early as 1946, although the generally austere conditions prevailing at the time meant that design work alone was to occupy some eight years.

In 1946 it was thought the best means of success could be achieved by utilizing a gas turbine power plant on a conventional steam chassis with the design then centred around this basic criteria. (E.N. Bellass in his article on GT3 in *Rail Enthusiast*, 1981, comments that the use of a GWR 'Castle' chassis was rumoured while another source suggests the use of a 73xxx chassis.) It was indeed unfortunate that by the time GT3 eventually appeared the design was somewhat dated.

In outline the locomotive resembled a steam engine more than a product of the latest technology and was carried on a 4–6–0 chassis, having a driving cab at one end behind

GT3 nearing completion at the Whetstone works of English Electric. Nick-named 'The Chocolate Zephyr' because of its light brown livery with dark green frames, the engine was a bold attempt to prove the gas turbine principle was worthy of further consideration. The steam ancestry in the form of the 4–6–0 wheel arrangement and tender is clearly visible

Collection Colin Marsden

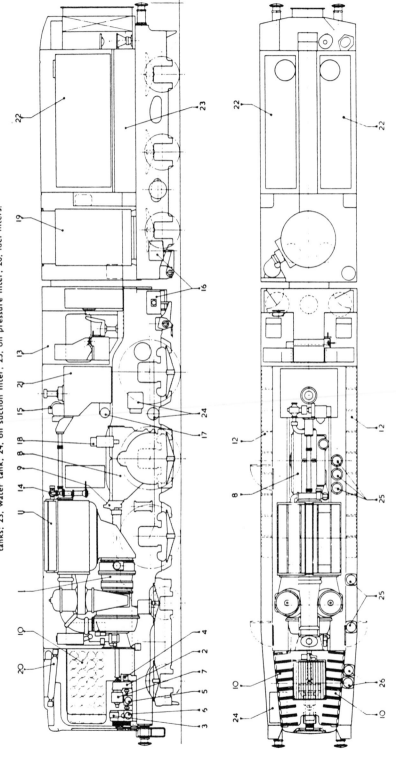

1, engine—EM27L recuperative gas turbine; 2, engine-driven auxiliaries gearbox; 3, alternator; 4, fuel pump; 5, lubricating oil pressure pump; 6, lubricating oil scavenge pump; 7, starter motor; 8, transmission gearbox; 9, power turbine balance gear; 10, air intake filter; 11, exhaust chimney; 12, batteries; 13, driving cab; 14, vacuum brake ejector; 15, air-motor-driven exhauster; 16, brake cylinders; 17, electric-driven cooling pump set; 18, electric-driven cooling pump set; 19, train-heating boiler; 20, oil cooler; 21, oil tank; 22, fuel tanks; 23, water tank; 24, oil suction filter; 25, oil pressure filter; 26, fuel filters.

General arrangement drawing of GT3. Prior to completion an early drawing depicts the engine carrying the number 19000, with the name 'Lord of the Isles'. Starting was via a battery, a process which took 100 seconds, similar to the time taken to start the engine of an aircraft

The Oil Engine and Gas Turbine

which was a six-wheeled tender. The design was not dissimilar to the Vulcan Foundry-built Type 1 diesel class – later class 20.

The chassis housed the actual power plant of the locomotive, a version of the 9,000 rpm, 2,750 hp English Electric EM27 gas turbine which was designed and built at the company's Whetstone works and specially developed for direct mechanical drive. Transmitting this movement to the wheels was via a specially developed neutral, fixed reduction and reverse gearbox which drove the centre coupled axle through flexible gearing and so compensated for vertical movement of the axleboxes, misalignment of axle and gear caused by the rolling of the locomotive on its springs and small relative axial movements of the gear and axle.

Trials began at the Rugby testing house in early 1959, with the engine destined to remain at this location for eleven months. At this stage the superstructure had still to be added and the tender was not completed. At Rugby No. GT3 became the first non-steam engine to use the plant and achieved an equivalent of 97 mph on rollers. Following the tests the engine was submitted to initial track trials on a roughly laid 1 in 44 gradient with $5\frac{1}{2}$ chain curve and two LMS Stanier 2–8–0s acting as the test load. Interestingly, an oil tank wagon was used as the fuel reservoir at this time due to the non-availability of the tender.

Following the trials the engine was returned to English Electric for completion and then placed on exhibition at Marylebone for the Institution of Locomotive Engineers.

Main-line trials began on the Shropshire lines from Crewe on 9 January 1961, and to Whitchurch and Chester, mainly via the little-used Malpas route. It was intended that a series of high-speed runs along the coast route to Llandudno Junction would follow though this was never implemented and instead the engine was sent to Leicester where it was used to haul empty stock between there and Marylebone. Certainly No. GT3 created quite a stir of interest in its overall light brown livery lined with dark green and orange bands and with dark green frames and wheels. A series of problems with the reversing gear during terminal manoeuvres led to further test runs between Leicester and Woodford Halse.

Between June and September 1961 the engine was again tested on the former GC main line, this time with a dynamometer car and set of former LMS coaches. From October 1961 trials recommenced from Crewe northwards towards Carlisle where GT3 was to achieve its finest performance, taking twelve coaches from a standing start at Tebay to Shap with a minimum of 44 mph recorded at the summit. Other trials on the same line involved trains of up to sixteen vehicles. There is no evidence that revenue-earning turns were ever undertaken.

Unfortunately the clean external lines were marred slightly by the necessity to provide an access door at the front end of the locomotive, although the air intake louvres either side of the 'smokebox' could almost be described as resembling a tapestry.

The tender carried 2,000 gallons of fuel oil, the 'Spanner' train heating boiler and 1,765 gallons of water. (It has been suggested that the engine burnt a low grade fuel oil although it is not confirmed exactly what this was.) In addition crew comforts were not forgotten as there were lockers, a toilet and wash basin for the crew, though whether there was any real necessity to carpet the driving cab must be left open to comment! (Some years later the 'Yeoman' Class 59 engines running on BR would also have a carpeted driving compartment.)

Total weight 123.4 tons (79.4 tons locomotive and 44 tons tender)
Adhesive weight 59.25 tons

Driving wheels 6 ft 9 in
Bogie wheels 3 ft 0 in
Tender wheels 3 ft 3½ in

Starting TE 38,000 lb	Starting hp 2,750
at 20 mph 28,800 lb	at 20 mph 1,540 hp
at 60 mph 16,100 lb	at 60 mph 2,570 hp
at 90 mph 9,400 lb	at 90 mph 2,260 hp

English Electric hoped that following two to three years of successful trial running orders would be achieved at the rate of five to six engines per annum. This, however, was not to be and in late 1962 the engine was returned to its maker.

Here it was to languish for some four years under a tarpaulin, until at an English Electric press day an inquisitive journalist happened to take a peep underneath. The next day the national newspapers took up the story under the banner headlines, 'Secret Jet Loco Rusts in Lancs Works Yard' and 'BR Dump Jet Loco'. It was all too much for English Electric and GT3 was taken back into the works for the removal of its power equipment. The chassis was then sold for scrap to Wards of Stafford for just £600. No. 75032 being utilized to tow away the remains in February 1966.

Although full details of the trials and failures of GT3 are not available it would appear to have offered potentially the best hope for a prime mover gas turbine. Its downfall was that it no doubt came too late, allied to the fact that the single, centrally-mounted cab failed to afford the vision the conventional diesel and electric locomotive could offer. To retain and develop the class would either have meant a fundamental re-design or retention of turntables. Ten years earlier and it may have been a different story as an amount of saving could have been involved by utilizing redundant steam chassis. If GT3 came too late, it is a wonder that it was ever built at all.

BIBLIOGRAPHY

Books

APT – A Promise Unfulfilled, Ian Allan.
Allen, G. Freeman, *The Western Since 1948*.
Barnes, Robin, *Locomotives that Never Were*.
British Railways, *The First British-built Gas Turbine Locomotive*.
Gibson, Revd John C., *Great Western Locomotive Design – A Critical Appreciation*, David & Charles.
Marsden, K. *BR Motive Power*.
McKillop, N., *Top Link Locomotives*.
Nock, O.S., *60 Years of Western Express Running*.
Nock, O.S., *The GWR Stars, Castles and Kings (Part 2)*.
RCTS, *Locomotives of the GWR*.
Stoffles, Wolfgang, *30 Years of Gas Turbine Locomotives*, (German edition, 1964).
The Railway Executive, *Britain's First Gas Turbine Locomotive*, (Undated).
Webb, Brian, 'Three more Gas Turbine Locomotives for British Railways', article in unknown magazine.

Periodicals

BR Western Region Magazine
Diesel Railway Traction
Proceedings of the BR(W) London Lecture and Debating Society
Rail Enthusiast Magazine (1981 articles by E.N. Bellass on GT3 and by Roger Bradley on Jet-Propelled Locomotives)
Steam Days (articles by Chris Leigh, July–Dec. 1986)
The Brown-Boveri Review
The Engineer
The Great Western Echo
The Great Western Magazine
The Journal of the Institution of Locomotive Engineers
The Journal of the Stephenson Locomotive Society
The Locomotive
The Metropolitan Vickers Gazette
The Oil Engine and Gas Turbine
The Railway Gazette
The Railway Magazine
Trains Illustrated

During the early spring of 1952 No. 18000 failed at St Anne's Park just east of Bristol while at the head of the 9.15 a.m. from Paddington. A pannier tank shunting nearby was hastily commandeered and attached to the recalcitrant gas turbine, pulling it and its train the two miles to Bristol Temple Meads. The occasions of an 0–6–0 tank engine sporting a Class A express headcode must be rare indeed

A.C. Sterndale

INDEX